A WRITER'S COMPANION

A WRITER'S COMPANION

Richard Marius
Harvard University

Alfred A. Knopf   New York

THIS IS A BORZOI BOOK
PUBLISHED BY ALFRED A. KNOPF, INC.

First Edition

98765432

Copyright © 1985 by Alfred A. Knopf, Inc.

Library of Congress Cataloging in Publication Data

Marius, Richard.
  A writer's companion.

  Includes index.
  1. English language — Rhetoric. 2. Exposition (Rhetoric) I. Title.
PE1429.M27   1984   808'.042   84-21774
ISBN 0-394-32745-4

Manufactured in the United States of America

For Willis C. Tucker
and
John Lain
The School of Journalism
of
The University of Tennessee

Preface

I owe major debts for this book. Richard Garretson commissioned it one evening while we sat at dinner together in Cambridge. Later on Steven Pensinger shepherded the manuscript through two major revisions, acting always as a good friend to both me and it. Elisa Turner was always ready to talk on the telephone to offer encouragement and advice. I am grateful also to the reviewers whose commentary on earlier versions of the manuscript was sometimes harsh but always helpful — Linda Peterson, Yale College; Tori Haring-Smith, Brown University; William S. Robinson, San Francisco State University; Richard Larson, Herbert H. Lehman College; John R. Wilson, University of Maine; Stephen J. Spector, University of Bridgeport; John Auchard, University of Maryland; John Milton, University of South Dakota; and John Trimble, University of Texas. Writing the book was difficult — as writing always is — but it has also been a lot of fun. And I hope that teachers and students and others who love to write may learn from it, perhaps argue with it, but also enjoy it.

All books come out of experience, and so it is with this one. My late mother was a newspaper woman at a time when women seldom kept such bad company as the men who hung out in the typical newsroom. She survived labors on the Montgomery (Alabama) *Advertiser*, the Beaumont (Texas) *Journal*, the Kansas City *Star*, and the Knoxville *News-Sentinel* and taught her children to love language and to understand how difficult it is to write well. She herself was dauntless; when she and her brother Fred, also a reporter, decided to leave their jobs in Beaumont about 1915 to do a stint in Kansas City, they made the journey by motorcycle, and Mother always recalled that the motorcycle was so weak that it would not carry them both up hill. Since she couldn't drive the motorcycle, she had to dismount at the hills and walk up while my uncle Fred rode to the top and waited — and sometimes yelled at her to hurry up. And so they made a hot summer journey of several hundred miles and got to where they were going.

She once mused that good writing was a lot like that journey; sometimes you could ride, and sometimes you walked up hill in the sun, but if you were a writer you had to keep at it because there was nothing else you *could* do.

I am grateful also to the memory of the late Lloyd Hickman, garrulous autocrat of the *Lenoir City* (Tennessee) *News* who let me write about our high school for him and in 1948 sent me out to interview our new Senator, Estes Kefauver, and when I returned with the story, sat reading it at his astonishingly cluttered and ancient desk and then, muttering some profane assault on my prose, wrote out a check for ten dollars, threw it down in front of me, and stalked back into the pressroom with my pages. That day, at age fifteen with my byline on a front-page story and ten dollars in my pocket, I decided I really did want to be a writer.

After Lloyd drowned trying to save another life, Bill Bayne eventually took over the little paper and made me news editor (I was eighteen). We worked for three happy years together, while I attended college classes in the mornings and wrote for him in the afternoons, and I am glad he is still in the trade to receive a copy of this book.

At the University of Tennessee where in 1954 I was in the first class to receive a Bachelor of Science in Journalism, Professors Willis C. Tucker and John Lain knocked me around and told me I might learn to write if I worked at it the rest of my life. They remain severe critics and dear friends. Willis Tucker offered many valuable suggestions as I was writing the three drafts of this manuscript. This book is dedicated to them.

My wife Lanier Smythe did not type a word of the manuscript, but we did talk about it a lot, and when she read it, she laughed at all the right places and said with a tone of evident surprise that she agreed with me on most points.

My gratitude to colleagues and students in the Expository Writing Program at Harvard is unbounded. On general principles, I cannot publish anything without expressing my appreciation to my primary editor at Knopf, Ann Close.

Richard Marius
Belmont, Massachusetts

Contents

A Writer's Companion

INTRODUCTION

Some Preliminary Remarks

This book is intended to be an informal and friendly guide for writers. It is directed primarily to writers of nonfiction, but fiction writers may also find it helpful.

The plan of the book follows the route most writers take from the beginning to the finished essay. I start with some general reflections about writing and proceed step by step through various stages of the writing process to the point when a final draft is stacked up beside the typewriter—or on the floor under the printer of the word processor. Each chapter considers a different part of this writing process.

In some respects the plan is deceitful. In practice the parts of the writing process cannot be neatly separated. In this book the chapter on paragraphs comes before the chapter on sentences. This is because the general order of an essay depends on the flow of orderly paragraphs from one to the next, but, obviously, we cannot write paragraphs without sentences. The chapter on diction, on how we use words, comes far along in the book, but we cannot begin to write without knowing words and how they work.

Writing draws together an astonishing number of mental and physical actions, many of them going on simultaneously as the process unfolds. It is one of the most complicated things we do, and that is why it is always difficult. But mysteriously and wonderfully, most writers who work hard at their task eventually fall into a rhythm and do it, coordinating many impulses and many motions much as we do when we dance or sing or talk or play baseball or ride a bicycle. I will consider the elements separately. You will use them simultaneously.

This book is for advanced writers, and so it abounds with rules. Beginning writers should probably stay away from books about writing. Beginning writers should write and write and write without worrying about whether what they say sounds elegant or conforms to standard usage and without thinking of anything but what they want to say.

Writing should be a habit, and most of us develop the habit by lunging into words in the way that children learn to swim by belly flopping into a pool and splashing happily around, realizing that they are not going to drown. Only after we have become accustomed to the medium do we start thinking about our strokes and our kicks and our style in the water—or on the page. Then a coach may give us some friendly advice in the form of various rules to help us to better what we are already doing.

So it is with this book. It has lots of rules: Begin most of your sentences by putting the subject first. If you don't begin with the subject, open your sentence with an adverbial word, phrase, or clause. Don't combine a complicated subject with a complicated predicate. If your subject must be complicated, simplify your predicate. If your predicate must be complicated, simplify your subject. Keep dependent clauses to a minimum. Avoid the passive voice. Build paragraphs on a thought you express in the first sentence. Don't digress in the middle of a paragraph unless you let your readers know you are disgressing. (Usually set off such digressions in parentheses.) Use the traditional and commonly accepted meanings of words. Use words that call up the memory of sensory experience—words about color, taste, textures, smells, sounds, shapes, weight, size. Learn the names of ordinary things, and use those names when you write. Tell stories, or give other concrete examples to illustrate generalizations. Let your readers use their memories to help them experience what you want to tell them.

These rules are hardly as strict as the Ten Commandments or the rules for registering motor vehicles. You can break most of the rules for writing now and then and not be thought illiterate. This book will tell you what most professional writers do most of the time. No book can tell you what all good writers do all the time. Sometimes you must take a risk and break the rules; if your audience likes what you do and respects you for it, your risk has paid off. You are much safer if you follow the conventions and do the things that have been successful for others. And this book will describe those conventions.

Describe is an important word in this book, because it aims to be descriptive. It explains how professional writers do their jobs and create their effects. I have drawn many examples from magazines you can buy at any good newsstand. I have also taken examples from well-written books, books we read for both information and pleasure. My theory in these pages is that we can learn how professional writers accomplish the marvelous art of giving both information and pleasure if we closely observe the way they use words.

Professional writers begin by trying to interest readers. They never start by saying, "How can I avoid making mistakes?" They ask themselves this question instead: "How can I make people pay attention to what I am saying and take my writing seriously?" Good writers want to be correct. They know that if they use incorrect spelling, sloppy punctuation, erratic grammar, and rough syntax they will destroy the effect of their writing—just as a pianist who hits a few wrong notes will destroy the effect of a Beethoven concerto. But professional writers never assume that correctness is enough in itself. They want to engage readers and keep them engaged.

Professional writers are efficient. They use as few words as possible to say what they want to say. They write direct sentences that quickly convey meaning. When they revise their early drafts, they prune away the nonessential. E. D. Hirsch, Jr., in his fine little book *The Philosophy of Composition*, gives several translations of the same text from Giovanni Boccaccio, the greatest of the fourteenth-century storytellers. Hirsch shows that as the English translations come forward in time, they use fewer and fewer words, and they use sentences that are more and more direct. Here is a version Hirsch gives from the sixteenth century:

> Saladin, whose valliance was so great that not only the same from base estate advanced him to be Sultan of Babylon, but also thereby he won diverse victories over the Saracen kings and Christians; who through his manifold wars and magnificent triumphs, having expended all his treasure, and for the execution of one exploit lacking a great sum of money, knew not where to have the same so readily as he had occasion to employ it. At length he called to remembrance a rich Jew named Melchizedech, that lent out money for interest in Alexandria.[1]

An eighteenth-century version reads like this:

> Saladin was so brave and great a man, that he had raised himself from an inconsiderable person to be Sultan of Babylon, and he had gained many victories over both the Saracen and Christian princes. This monarch having in diverse wars and by many extraordinary expenses, run through all his treasure, some urgent occasion fell out that he wanted a large sum of money. Not knowing which way he might raise enough to answer his necessities, he at last called to mind a rich Jew of Alexandria named Melchizedech, who lent out money on interest.[2]

[1] Quoted in E. D. Hirsch, Jr., *The Philosophy of Composition* (Chicago: University of Chicago Press, 1977), 60–61.

[2] Quoted ibid., 61.

Though Hirsch does not give it, an even more modern and more efficient translation of the same passage may be found in the Modern
Library edition of Boccaccio:

> Saladin, who was so powerful that he rose from an ordinary man to the
> rank of Sultan of Babylon and won countless victories over Saracen and
> Christian rulers, found that he had exhausted all his wealth, both in war
> and in the exercise of his extraordinary munificence. Now, by some
> chance, he felt the need of money, and a lot of it, too, and not knowing
> where he could get it as quickly as he wished, he thought of a rich Jew called
> Melchizedek who was a moneylender in Alexandria.[3]

We can understand the first version only if we read it aloud very
slowly — as people read in the Middle Ages and in the sixteenth century.
We can understand the second version fairly well by reading it silently,
and we can comprehend the third even more easily. Since swift, silent
reading is normal in this hurrying century, prose must be efficient to ac-
commodate the greater rapidity of reading that we now do.

Efficiency does not require writers to express only bland or simple
thoughts. If you have complicated thoughts, you must sometimes use
complicated language to express them. But however complicated your
thoughts, you should express them in language as simple and direct as
possible. The greatest writers in English have managed to express complicated ideas at great length in sentences that any educated person can
understand in one careful reading.

Yet today many writers believe they must write obscurely to be
taken seriously. So we get sentences like this one:

> Individuals with a strong home defense orientation in living areas noted
> for multiple instances of criminal behavior in urban situations are more
> likely to practice the acquisition and continuing possession of firearms.

The writer means this: "In urban neighborhoods with a lot of crime,
people may buy guns to defend their homes." The second version is efficient; the first is not.

Efficient prose does not necessarily mean brevity. Sometimes a
longer version of a thought may be more efficient than a shorter version. The shorter version may leave out something necessary, perhaps
abbreviating ideas so much that readers have a hard time following what

[3] Giovanni Boccaccio, *The Decameron*, trans. Frances Winwar (New York: Modern
Library, 1955), 16.

is being said. Here is a sentence from an article that appeared recently in a scholarly journal; the article analyzes white people's beliefs about opportunities for blacks in our society:

> The category of persons who see black opportunity as average and not greatly improved appears to contain a subtype who seem to be saying that opportunity for blacks has always been equal, denying the existence of past inequality of opportunity.

After reading the rest of the article, I think this sentence can be translated like this:

> Some people think that opportunities for blacks are about equal to those for whites and that there has been no great increase in opportunities for blacks in recent times. Some of these people seem to think that blacks have always had equal opportunity and that inequality of opportunity for them never existed.

The second version is longer, but it is more efficient because it is easier to understand. Efficient prose allows readers to move through it without having to back up and read again. It does not mean that good writers sound like a first-grade primer.

Good writers also write engagingly. They stimulate the imaginations of their readers, especially the picture-forming ability of the mind. The children of my generation listened to radio drama and made pictures in their heads of what was going on. Ages before that, bards singing the epic tales of the tribe by the fire at night summoned up pictures from the minds of every person silently listening.

These pictures are constructed from the experience of readers and listeners. A good writer describes a scene, and readers understand because some of the words the writer uses call up something they have experienced. I tell a story, and you are interested in it because it somehow stimulates a flood of your own memories.

Here is a paragraph from an article by Michael Winn in the April 1982 issue of *Smithsonian*. Winn describes a trip he took across the ancient "silk road," the route traders used in the Middle Ages to go by land from Europe to Asia. He begins his piece with an account of a Jeep ride over a dangerous, twisting road in the high mountains of Pakistan:

> Except for the whine of four-wheel drive, there was silence as our driver, palms sweating, backed up once, twice, often three times to get around the

hairpin turns. I sat helplessly over the rear bumper as it swung several feet out over the gorge, giving me a nightmare view into a 2,000 foot abyss.

Winn could have said, "We had a hard time getting the Jeep around the hairpin curves." Instead he put together words and phrases rich with sensory experiences we have had — the metallic whine of machinery, the silence of people afraid, the sweat running off our palms when we grasp the slippery steering wheel of a car in hot weather, the fear of high places. We put ourselves in Winn's position because he has given us enough details to put us in his skin. And so his prose lives.

When teachers say, "Be concrete," or, "Be specific," they mean that you should use the solid, sensory words good writers use to call up some memory, some experience, something readers have seen and heard and felt and smelled and tasted. All good writers give us details that help us make pictures in our minds from what we already know.

You do not have to make pictures in every line you write. Your audience determines many of the choices you make in writing, and if you can assume a great deal of interest for your subject in your readers, you can be less vivid. That is why many articles in specialized journals seem dull to outsiders: they are not addressed to outsiders; they are addressed to people who already have a burning interest in the subject. Researchers interested in new findings about cancer usually want to get right to the details, and they do not want to read through a long, vivid description of a dying cancer patient as an introduction to the piece.

Yet even articles in specialized journals depend on vivid examples now and then, and the usual flaw in most writing is that writers forget to keep the minds of their readers alert and responsive. A few years ago one of my students used the word *relationship* fourteen times in a three-page essay. I circled the word each time it appeared, and when we talked about the paper, I tried to explain that she might have made another choice. The word *relationship* carried no associations with sensory experience, and it summoned no sharp memories. But my student never believed that this monotonous repetition should be held against her prose. "It makes sense," she said. "It's grammatical. I don't see why you criticize me when it's right."

She had been taught that the chief aim of writing is to be correct, to obey the rules of grammar and syntax. No one had ever made her think of what goes on in her own mind when she reads something, the swift judgments she makes when she decides whether a piece of prose is worth her time or not. She did not see that writers must always court readers and convince them that a piece of prose is worth the time and the effort required to read it. Efficiency and vividness are precious gifts writers give to readers in this courtship. Her attitude was, "It's correct. Take it or leave it." Confronted with that attitude, most readers will leave it.

The aim of this book is to help you win readers to your prose and to your point of view. If you read it carefully and apply its precepts to your own prose, you should write more efficiently and more vividly, and you may win some other rewards as well.

ONE

Writing and Its Rewards

Writing is hard work for anyone, professional or amateur, who tries it, and although it may become easier with practice, it is never easy. Gene Fowler said: "Writing is easy; all you do is sit staring at a blank sheet of paper until the drops of blood form on your forehead." He speaks for most of us who face the blank sheet of paper every day.

Above all, writing takes time. Good writers do not think that they will dash off a piece and get on to more important and more enjoyable things. They do not wait until the night before a deadline to begin to write. They set aside time for the task, and during that time writing is everything. For even small writing tasks the time is sometimes enormous. So the first thing you must do if you are to become a writer is to be willing to spend time in solitude and dedication to your work. Dr. Samuel Johnson, the eighteenth-century author and lexicographer, said "What is written without effort is in general read without pleasure."

In a fast, busy world like ours, spending time on writing requires taking a risk. When we begin to write, we never know how our writing will come out. To write well you must be willing to be knocked down by failure and then to get up and try again — and again. You have to pay attention to details — to the thousands and thousands of details embodied in words and experience. You have to trust your uncertain intuitions: if something does not sound right to you, you must do it over and over again until it does sound right. Finally, you must present your work to your readers as an example of the best you can do. Once you have submitted a final draft, it is too late to make excuses for it, and you should not do so. Not everybody will like your final version even when you have done your best. You will probably be more sensitive to criticisms of your work than to occasional praise. And even when you like something you have done, you may realize in time that you have done part of it badly. Writing becomes a parable for life itself.

All good writers fail at times. All of them suffer writer's block in one form or another. All of them have trouble doing the daily task. Peter de

Vries said, "I love being a writer. What I can't stand is the paperwork." So if you have trouble putting words on paper, you are in good company. Nearly everyone does.

Yet writer's block is seldom a matter of sitting at a desk while words refuse to come. Usually writer's block is an unwillingness to commit ourselves to the desk, to the pen or typewriter and paper, and to the time it takes to write. We are impatient at our progress, which is always slow. We tell ourselves we are going to write in the evening and go to a movie afterward. And very quickly we change our plans and decide to go to the movie first and do our writing afterward. We procrastinate—procrastination is the most common form of writer's block.

Our unwillingness to sit still and write helps us deceive ourselves. Even prolific writers seldom spend more than about four to five hours a day at their task. An inefficient writer who speaks of working all night long on a paper often measures not the time spent at the desk but the time from the beginning to the end of the writing task. You should measure the time you spend at writing itself, the time you spend at the desk, your fingers on the keyboard or wrapped around your pen, putting words on paper. Years ago B. F. Skinner, the behavioral psychologist, rigged a clock to a light over his typewriter. When he sat down to write, he turned on the light, automatically starting the clock. When he got up, he turned the light off, stopping the clock. He wanted to spend four hours a day writing. The clock let him know when he had completed his task. Mechanical? Yes. But it worked. His device kept him from imagining that he spent more time writing than he actually did, and he has been an astonishingly prolific writer.

The first rule in writing is to sit down and spend time. Stay at the desk. Keep going. We all get discouraged quickly—especially when we start writing the first page of the day. We have trouble organizing our thoughts. We write a page or merely a paragraph and immediately start thinking that we ought to change it. Writers love new beginnings, clean slates, new pages. We easily imagine that our previous effort has failed but that now, with a new start, we will get it right. But if we begin and begin and begin again, we are still deceiving ourselves. We are only looking for an excuse not to get on with the task. The habit of starting again and again easily leads to the impulse to give up for the day—"I'll do it tomorrow. I've made myself so nervous by all these false starts that I can't go on today." And so the game is lost.

Your best bet in writing is always to write a draft through to the end; no matter how terrible it is, no matter how disorganized, finish it. Then you can revise.

Revision also takes time. You must read your paper over, pencil in notes to yourself, cross out some words, add others—do another draft. Too many student writers hand in their first drafts with the air of tired and hurried people shedding their dirty clothes. In the army, sergeants regularly tell recruits in basic training about the unfired rifle in combat. Many soldiers in the thick of a fight refuse to fire their weapons, seemingly afraid of attracting any hostile attention to themselves. A similar affliction curses young writers who cannot bear to look back over their work once it is done. They cannot even proofread it; all they can think of is getting rid of it as soon as they can.

It may be helpful to know that professional writers suffer similar pangs. If anything, their unhappiness is greater than that of the beginners because they make a living from the words they put on paper, and their first drafts often tempt them to believe that their children will soon go hungry.

But professional writers do not see a first draft as a final draft. They expect the first draft to be like a blob of shapeless brown mud that a skilled potter flings onto a whirling potter's wheel. Potential beauty resides in the blob; it can be brought out only by the delicate touch of the potter's hand.

You must consider your writing important enough to be worth a big chunk of your life, to be worth the sacrifice of other things. You must reconcile yourself to slow improvement rather than instantaneous perfection. In this painful slowness, writing is much like preparing to give a musical concert. A good pianist must play every day, continually accepting the challenge to try harder and to work at the piece he will perform at last before an audience. Good pianists make sacrifices for their music. Good writers must do the same.

But for splendid rewards! Writing is one of the performing arts. The pleasures writers enjoy in pleasing an audience are the same as those concert pianists, ballet dancers, baseball players, and good lecturers enjoy. These are honorable pleasures. They make us part of the human community, for our desire to please makes us value both ourselves and the audience out there we yearn to reach.

No writer should try deliberately to pander to the lowest tastes of readers, but writing of all kinds—including student writing—would be much better if writers worked hard not merely to get things right but to give pleasure as well. Perhaps much of the fault here lies with writing teachers, for they easily fall into the trap of believing that their job is only to correct papers. Too frequently they tell students only what is wrong with a piece of writing, when they should be identifying those things a student does well but can do better. Many teachers would do well to praise more and criticize less.

The rewards of writing go beyond enjoyment. They are practical because for most of us we must write well if we are to work well at our jobs. Our society has moved from the industrial revolution to the informational revolution, and about half the jobs in America nowadays involve the transfer of information, much of it by writing. The average engineer probably writes more pages each year than does the average professor of English. Many people spend their workdays doing nothing but writing letters, memos, and reports. Technical writing—writing that explains technical processes—is one of the biggest fields in American business. The explosive multiplication of copying machines and word processors shows one side of the demand for writing in our society. No wonder some people speak of a writing crisis—no society in history demanded as much writing of its citizens as ours requires.

We know that writing communicates to others; often we forget how writing helps us know things ourselves as we seek to communicate our knowledge. Nothing helps the mind and the memory more than writing things down. Everyone who has taught a discipline in the humanities—literature, history, or philosophy, for example—has had the student who protests, "I know it; I just can't write it." The reply should be that the person who cannot write intelligently about the discipline rarely knows it.

History, for example, does not come to us by divine inspiration or by the immediate intuition by which we know colors. History comes to us through words—words written down in fading ink in archives, in attics, in cellars, or in libraries, words carved in stone, words printed in books, words of teachers telling us about the past. We do not know the history of the American Revolution if we are able only to make the right identifications on a multiple-choice test. History is the story of human relations over time, and such relations are far too complicated and subtle to be captured by the common simplicities of a multiple-choice examination. To make sense of history, historians write carefully about it, and only when they are able to write about it do they consider that they know it.

When we write a narrative about a historical event, we are forced to think carefully from step to step. That process is extraordinarily difficult. I once gave a class a collection of British and American primary sources—firsthand accounts—for the battles of Lexington and Concord that began our Revolution on April 19, 1775. The assignment was simple: Write a narrative of what happened on that day. My students quickly discovered that the sources were sometimes contradictory, that they were all incomplete, that they were biased, and that they were generally confusing. These young writers realized that they had to read the material with great care, and then they had to use their own common sense and experience to put it together in a story. As they wrote through successive drafts, they kept asking themselves more questions. They found some of the answers in the sources, but they could not find some of the answers at all. They had to guess at the answers—and say they were guessing—or they had to draw up before the silence of time. Having to tell a story, to provide a narrative, made them see how complex the human story is, and the experience of writing taught them something about both the battles and the nature of history itself.

So it is for most disciplines in the liberal arts, for many of the sciences, and for much of life as well—the best measure of our knowledge is how well we can write about something. This statement is true not only about disciplines of knowledge but also about our own experience. Good letter writers reveal an understanding of their own experience often lacking in those who never bother to express their thoughts and acts with pen and paper. Good letter writers tell what has happened to them; from letters we gain understanding of what is important in the lives of our correspondents. We do not know everything, for writing cannot communicate everything; but writing reveals more than nonwriting does, and when we write about ourselves, we learn something essential about who we are.

Writing enlarges our knowledge in another way that all writers find mysterious. As we write our thoughts down, our minds give birth to new thoughts. Word pours out on word, thought on thought. Suddenly we see that we have a piece we could not have predicted when we began. Young writers often say they cannot think enough thoughts to fill a five-page assignment. But if you observe carefully and write honestly and write your first draft by setting down whatever comes into your mind when you think about a subject, you will discover that you can say much more than you imagined when you began.

The best proof of how writing stimulates the brain is to try writing about something you know fairly well—perhaps a conversation you had with a friend this morning. You will discover as you write that you remember more and more of what went on—what she said, the tone she used to express herself, what you said to her, her responses, her sincerity, how you judged her as a person while you talked. You will probably see that as you write, you think through the conversation and find more things to say to your friend at a later occasion.

At some time when you have seen a movie or heard a lecture, write about it afterward. You will forget some things, but you will get most things right. Your mind will create the moment anew, and once you have written your thoughts down, you will remember them much better. When you make the discovery of what the mind resurrects as you write, you will want to write more, and you will enjoy writing in ways you never did before.

But perhaps the greatest rewards of writing lie in the pleasures of designing and preserving. I remember reading once that writers remember details others do not notice—details like the fall of light after a storm on a summer afternoon, the smell of wet grass on a sunny spring morning, the gesture someone made on hearing news of a death in the family, the sound of a voice others have forgotten, the laughter of an aunt in the kitchen at Christmas long ago.. Writers observe in a world of relentless change. In setting their observations on paper, all writers create something—a design that makes the observations make sense, something that relates them to the rest of our thought and feeling, something that may make them memorable.

All writers create. I am always annoyed to hear fiction and poetry called "creative" writing as if writing that explains, describes, and narrates—nonfiction—should somehow be relegated to the basement of the writing enterprise to dwell with the pails and the pipes. To assume that only fiction and poetry are "creative" is to imagine that fiction writers and poets are somehow superior to scholars, journalists, and others who report, explain, and describe. A good case may be made for the proposition that the most truly original and creative writers in our society today work in nonfiction—Tom Wolfe, Gloria Emerson, Roger Rosenblatt, Carl Schorske, Joan Didion, Joe McGinniss, John McPhee, Garry Wills, Robert Caro, David McCullough, Roger Angell, Barbara Tuchman, and a host of others. Certainly nonfiction supports the publishing houses of America. Fiction has turned to fantasy and narcissism, making us suppose that if the novel is not dead, most novelists are. Readers nowadays prefer to buy books about the world they know or the world they would like to know—a world many novelists have forsaken. Except for a few blockbuster novels, fiction sells poorly because readers do not find it creative; they find it dull.

The art of the nonfiction writer is to make a design that joins disconnected observations and pieces of information, uniting them under some generalizations. How a writer puts that design together requires as much creation as any novel. A biographer takes the different relics of a life and weaves them together to reveal a plausible human design, one we can recognize as part of the human experience we know, yet one that stands out in a unique way. A historian makes connections between people and events that may not have been understood by the inhabitants of the period the historian describes, and readers take pleasure in seeing how the historical account corresponds with what they think they know of human existence—the play of rationality against irrationality, the motivations, ambitions, evil, and goodness of human beings. The design of the story somehow belongs to the writer. Charles Darwin perceived the design of natural selection in biology and developed his theory of evolution, and although his uncounted disciples have worked more than a century to refine his thought, to correct his mistakes, and to build on his foundation, the theory somehow remains *his*—a creative act of observation, thought, and writing that endures.

On occasion, students have worried that if they studied a subject carefully and wrote about it, they might duplicate the thoughts and the design of someone they had never heard of and be accused of plagiarism. It is indeed possible that two different people, studying the same material, and writing at the same time, may arrive at similar conclusions. Darwin and his fellow Englishman Alfred Russell Wallace worked independently of each other in the early nineteenth century on the theory of biological evolution by natural selection. Darwin published first—and spoke respectfully of Wallace in his preface. There are many other examples of people who came on some of the same truths almost simultaneously, but it is impossible for two people to write their conclusions in the same language if they have not read the work of one another. Minds are far more individual than snowflakes; no one else will ever quite duplicate the form you stamp on an essay or a report. Once you have created that form, it remains yours for all time.

With the design is always substance, and sometimes we surprise ourselves by finding how interesting the substance can be, by seeing a subject in a different way in the light of our design for it. One of the best books I have read in recent years is David McCullough's *Mornings on Horseback*, a biography of Theodore Roosevelt that carries Roosevelt's story only to his unsuccessful campaign to become mayor of New York City in the election of 1886. The design of the book is not to tell about Roosevelt's political career. No, the design is to tell of his development within his family, and that design makes McCullough notice the details of family life that a political biographer might have ignored—how the Roosevelts lived, the letters they wrote one another, the clothes they wore, the vacations they took, the diseases they suffered, and a huge number of other things that make for a vastly informative and entertaining narrative. McCullough told me that once he arrived at his design, he began to see things about the Roosevelts that other biographers had slighted or else passed over in silence because they did not see those things at all. Our ideas of design, of purpose, always affect how we see the world, and may lead us to a new vision.

It is a vision that gets preserved, and the role of preservation by writing is important both for our private records and formal publications and even for the papers we may do on assignment in college. Most writers take pleasure in imagining that someone may read their works long after they themselves are dead. Writers great and small, modern and ancient, come alive whenever an inquiring reader takes their work from a shelf. A colleague of mine several years ago discovered that he was dying of cancer. He sat calmly in my office one morning not long before the end, telling me with quiet pride that he knew he had written a book that would be valuable to others long after his own death. I was moved by his soft rumination — and understood him perfectly. The thought was not morbid. It was rather a gentle counterattack against time and death that writers of all kinds make with their words.

Here is reason to keep a journal. You will learn how to observe the things that happen to you, how to sort out the important from the unimportant, how to put your observations into words, and perhaps how to make sense of your life. The daily practice of writing your own autobiography will develop the habit of writing that is essential to anyone who wants to become a writer. In years to come you can rediscover your own life by seeing what you have preserved of your earlier thoughts and experiences. When you write every day about yourself and your immediate world, you will develop habits that will help you observe the greater world beyond yourself.

TWO

What Makes an Essay?

Most readers of this book will be writing essays, extended pieces of non-fiction prose, to persuade readers to do something or to believe something the writer wants them to believe.

Essays differ according to the subjects they address and the audiences they assume. You write one kind of essay to those who know a lot about your subject; you write another kind of essay to those who are less well informed. Every discipline carries with it a special terminology and a special way of getting into a subject. Historians do not write exactly like literary critics; sociologists do not write like naturalists; scientists do not write like journalists. An essay in a scholarly journal will be different from a piece appearing in *Time*.

THE DEFINITION OF AN ESSAY

Despite the differences, some qualities of the good essay remain the same no matter what the subject or the audience. What makes an essay? By defining the essay early in this book, I hope to clarify the process by which all of us struggle to reach a final draft of a good book or article. By perceiving the general form of the essay at the beginning, you will have a standard in your mind for your later thinking about your goals in writing.

The word *essay* was coined by a Frenchman, Michel de Montaigne, who invented the art in the second half of the sixteenth century. His essays resembled public letters about things he observed, read, heard, or thought about. He rambled much more than essayists do now, although his rigorous honesty and quiet wit continue to make disciples of his thought nearly four centuries after his death.

Montaigne's subjects were usually the ordinary experiences of daily life. He tried to look at everything through his own eyes, without accepting the prejudices of the crowd and without writing what he thought someone wanted him to write. He never talked down to his readers as if he thought they were ignoramuses. He never feared to be in the minority. He tried to see things as they really were, and so his observations were suprising for their freshness. He proved that an honest observer always has something new to say. He called his pieces "essays" from the French word meaning "attempts," or "trials." For him an essay was just that—an attempt to think clearly. He was far too humble to claim that he had established truth beyond all doubt; he had made only an *essay* toward truth, observing honestly, marshaling his evidence, reflecting on his experience, and interpreting all of it as fairly as he could. When he could not answer a question he posed, he admitted his ignorance.

He knew his conclusions would not satisfy everyone. Still he advanced them tolerantly, serenely, without insulting his opponents, without heating his prose with highly emotional language, except on the rare occasions when he condemned the religious wars that were burning across France in his time. He was remarkably confident. He did not believe he had to save the world with his prose. He did believe that reason, clearly and gently set down on paper, would win its own battles. He did not try to crush his foes. He remained a little detached from his topics—somewhat like a man calmly walking around a building and expertly pointing out its interesting features to someone who did not know it well.

Most essays you write should be akin to those Montaigne wrote while he was inventing the genre—civilized efforts to arrive at truth without fighting, without destroying those who disagree with you. You should appeal to the best in your readers, to their sense of fair play, to their best emotions, to their reason, to their wish to do the right thing.

Now and then you may be tempted to write passionately for a great cause. You should resist the temptation. A few writers have managed great passion for great causes, but success is rare in passionate writing because so few writers control passion well. Passion becomes bombast if it is angry. It often becomes fulsome sentiment when it tries to express love or admiration too openly. Few readers are convinced by superheated prose; they are more often embarrassed, and sometimes they are enraged.

THE QUALITIES OF AN ESSAY

The best prose is written in a tolerant and cool voice. If you are temperate and measured, and if you marshal your evidence with the attitude that your reader is a friend you want to persuade rather than a foe you want to slay, you will probably have a better chance of carrying your point.

Here are some of the qualities that make an essay. Study them carefully.

1. Most good essays are short enough to be read at a single sitting.

Some books are sometimes called essays since a serious, nonfiction book involves a sustained argument that is meant to make us believe something the writer wants us to believe. But in the more common meaning of the word, an *essay* is a short nonfiction piece.

The longer your essay, the better you may argue your point—but the less likely readers are, in a hurried age, to finish it. The shorter your essay, the less likely you are to make your point beyond any reasonable doubt—but readers may read all of it.

For young writers, long essays often seem impossible to write, but for experienced writers the short essay is far more difficult than the long piece. Experienced writers gather much knowledge on a subject before they begin to write about it. They usually make a list of points they want to cover, and when they start writing, they find it impossible to put down everything they know in the space they have for their task. Experienced writers usually write a long first draft and then cut.

2. A good essay gets to the point quickly.

You write everything for a purpose; your readers want to know what that purpose is as quickly as possible. Nothing quite so annoys a hard-pressed reader as going on and on in a piece of prose, not knowing what the writer wants to say and not seeing the point of the essay. Nearly all magazine articles and essays in scholarly journals get to the point in the first paragraph.

Titles help you get to your point. Titles are difficult, and at times they are tedious. We all love the title with a colon in the middle, a device that allows us to say something catchy and then explain it: "My Hideous Progeny: Mary Shelley and the Feminization of Romanticism"; "History, Fiction, and the Ground Between: The Uses of the Documentary Mode in Black Literature." These two titles appeared in one recent issue of the *PMLA* (the publication of the Modern Language Association). The issue contains five articles, and four of the titles have a colon in the middle. The device is not to be scorned, although it should be used less. It makes the writer compress what he is going to say in a tight phrase, and it informs the reader quickly of what to expect.

When you force yourself to give a title to your work, you give yourself a statement of purpose. Some inexperienced writers never do make themselves write a statement of purpose in an essay. Some put it off too long, perhaps not telling their audience why they are writing until they have gotten five, six, or seven pages into the work. Some students love surprise endings. They have seen movies and television programs in which the surprise ending evokes astonishment and appreciation, and they want to create a similar effect in their essays. Their object seems to be to tantalize readers and to keep them going, to suspend the point in the essay until at the last they reveal all, like some magician pulling back the curtain to reveal how he made his assistant disappear. But writing is not a magician's trick, and such essays seldom tantalize us; they annoy us because they seem to waste our time or treat us like children or make us believe that the writer feels herself so superior to us that we must follow her as a slave must follow a master. But readers are not slaves, and they can rebel easily by putting aside a piece of prose they do not understand.

Your own introductions should announce your subject and give your readers some idea of where you want to take them. You do not have to announce your conclusion right away; if you do, you may give readers no reason to go on with your piece. But you do have to say something that sets the course of your essay so that readers know whether they want to go on with it.

3. *Although a good essay announces its topic early, it seldom gives a blueprint of everything the writer is going to say in the piece itself.*

The blueprint introduction usually begins like this:

> This essay represents a study made of the personality characteristics of crop-dusting pilots in the state of Mississippi. It will survey their origins, their education, their family lives, and their ambitions. It will show that such pilots bear a remarkable resemblance to each other in their personality profiles, and it will also show that they most resemble graduates of the nation's business schools. It will conclude that crop-dusting pilots and major corporate executives share many important personality traits.

Such an announcement may attract someone already passionately interested in the subject, and it is legitimately used in some professional journals, especially in natural and social sciences, where the object is to present research findings to specialists. Writing such an introduction may also help an inexperienced writer get started, and if you cannot get started in any other way, by all means use the blueprint beginning. It does organize your thoughts and get you going.

But most such bare, flat statements fail to win the interest of those not interested to begin with. Professional writers who must interest a broad audience of educated people seldom use them. Imagine how startled you would be to read the following introduction to an article in *Sports Illustrated*:

> This essay will tell you about the Superbowl. It will announce the contesting teams, give you some background about their seasons and their victories in the playoffs, describe their coaches, their players, and the players' families, and make some remarks about their fans. It will include a summary of events in the first quarter, the second quarter, the third quarter, and the fourth quarter, and it will conclude with the final score as well as with some comments made by coaches and players after the game.

You know—almost unconsciously—that this kind of beginning is tedious and uninspiring. Writers who open their essays this way usually ignore their audience and forget that readers want to be captivated and entertained by a lively, interesting, and substantial style. A good journalist would begin an essay like this:

> Corporate executives and crop-dusting pilots share many personality traits. That is the not-so-surprising finding of a three-year study recently completed by the National Endowment for Sociology. The pilots and the executives love to take risks, love to do jobs others won't do, and love to think themselves superior to ordinary mortals who live ordinary lives. "Take the average high-powered executive out of the board room and put him in the open cockpit of a crop-duster, and he'll dive on those boll weevils like a hawk onto a chicken," says Professor I. B. Stoned, chief researcher in the project.

A good essay in a scholarly journal might begin like this:

> In a survey of 314 occupations, successful crop-dusting pilots and successful corporate executives were shown to share more personality traits than any other pair that could be made from the list. The survey, conducted by the National Endowment for Sociology, was intended to classify the attributes that contribute to success in jobs ranging from the highly responsible to the menial. The findings that showed remarkable similarities in the crop-dusters and the executives came as a surprise, al-

though researchers agreed that the results were less startling than they might first appear.

You can make your own suggestions about how to begin such an essay. But both these examples will probably win readers who might not pause to read the summary introduction that the blueprint beginning makes.

4. *A good essay seldom begins with a justification for the topic or with a long historical introduction to the topic.*

Many inexperienced writers love to begin essays with an apology in the form of a justification for deciding to treat the subject: "Why should we discuss the minor characters in Shakespeare's *Macbeth?*" "The difference between the theology of Luther's sermons and his formal theological treatises has often been treated by scholars of the Reformation." It is much better to start your essay by stating the thesis that you are going to prove about the minor characters in *Macbeth* or by saying what you think is significant about the difference between the theology of Luther's sermons and that of his theological treatises.

Once in a great while some hotly controversial topic may merit an introduction that tells why the writer decided to choose this subject and not another one, but it is almost always better to plunge right in and say something so interesting about the topic at the beginning that readers will go on. Once you have caught their attention, you may tell them what other scholars have said about the subject or why you think the subject should be studied. Readers are seldom interested in such information at the beginning, and if you must include it, you should put it later in your essay. Begin with the strongest thing you have to say. That is what will make your readers keep reading.

> In his formal theological treatises written in Latin for other theologians, Martin Luther wrote eloquently of predestination and of the God who would never let His elect fall to damnation no matter how much they had sinned. In his German sermons, preached to a congregation of not-so-educated people in Wittenberg, Luther often spoke as if what people did could save or damn their souls. But the difference is perhaps not as great as might first appear.

Avoid, too, generalizations about how important your ideas have been in history. Don't start a paper like this: "From earliest times human beings have considered the family important and have tried to understand what kind of family is best for society." And don't start like this: "Sports have always been part of the human experience." Or like this:

"Discussions of slavery have always been common in human culture
because slavery of one kind or another has always been with us."

5. A good essay does not begin by quoting a dictionary definition.

Inexperienced writers love to begin papers by making a reference
to the dictionary. The dictionary is an authority, and writers need authority. A dictionary definition may contain a kind of outline that an inexperienced writer may follow to a good end. But the ease of this opener makes it trite and boring. Every writing teacher reads that tired old
dictionary beginning hundreds of times in a lifetime. We nearly all
groan when we see it, and writers should not address their subjects in
ways that make readers groan.

The only reason for writing an essay in definition is that different
people have used the same word in different ways. What does *socialism*
mean, for example? You will hardly satisfy demanding readers if you
begin an essay on socialism by referring to a dictionary. The dictionary
definition of such a term will likely be so bland and general that it will
offer only a hint to the astonishing diversity of interpretation that has
surrounded the history of the word. If you know enough about a topic,
you can give your own definitions of the important words your topic
embraces. And your definition, derived from your own study, will make
the substance of an excellent essay.

6. A good essay can begin in one of many ways.

No book can tell you every way to begin an essay. Your best bet is to
pay attention to how professional writers begin essays or chapters in books.

An article in *Smithsonian* begins with a striking story, told in the
first person:

> Barely able to see in the dawn light, I fought my way through yet
> another tangle of vines and bamboo and shivered in the damp cold. I
> fervently hoped it was too cold for cobras to be active, and I worried about
> finding Khao Chong Pran Cave in time to photograph the spectacular
> morning return of its three million bats.[1]

The writer in this story proceeded to an account of his own research
with bats and to a general discussion of how beneficial bats are despite
their bad reputation.

[1] Merlin D. Tuttle, "Harmless, Highly Beneficial, Bats Still Get a Bum Rap," *Smithsonian*, Jan. 1984, 75.

You may imagine a typical scene that illustrates a topic you wish to explore. Here are the first two paragraphs from a recent article in *Popular Mechanics*:

> You take an elevator to the top of a skyscraper and look at the city below. Suddenly, you're overcome with terror; your heart races, and you break into a sweat.
>
> Scientists are no longer saying that such intense fears are psychological—merely states of mind. There is new evidence that irrational, paralyzing phobias are inherited biological disorders. And the way your brain is organized may predispose you to them.[2]

A recent article in *The New Yorker* begins:

> On an afternoon in late April of 1981, Carol Ann Davenport, her husband, Frank, and her friend Sandra Turner stormed into the library of the Woodland High School, in Baileyville, Maine, with a book that Frank's fifteen-year-old daughter had checked out of the library. The book had a number of four-letter words in it, one in a chapter title. The Davenports had come to the school to find John Morrison, the principal, but, as he was out, they went to the library to complain. The librarian, Grace Schillich, looked up to find them standing in front of her waving the book. She listened to them and asked for the book—which, as it happened, she had not read—but the Davenports refused to give it to her. They said that they were going to take it to the chairman of the school committee and to the superintendent of schools.[3]

We love stories, and they always make good beginnings as long as you can make something significant out of them. One caution: always be sure you have evidence to support the story you tell. Don't make things up to add dramatic effect. Don't start a paper like this:

> It was night in the palace in Greenwich, and a sleepy silence hung over the dark corridors and the rooms where royal servants lay abed. Only Henry VIII was awake, and he walked the floor aimlessly before the great fire that blazed on the hearth in his room. He could not sleep because he could not purge his mind of the greatest problem of his reign: How could he have a son?

You may imagine that Henry VIII had every reason for doing exactly what this writer has him doing here—walking the floor at night and

---

[2] "Phobias: The Battle in the Brain," *Popular Mechanics*, Jan. 1984, 162A.
[3] Frances FitzGerald, "A Reporter at Large," *The New Yorker*, Jan. 16, 1984, 47.

worrying about the succession to the throne. But no document gives
any evidence that such a scene took place. You would cast doubt on the
rest of your essay on a historical event if you started it by telling a story
you made up.

Quotations make good openings. The quotation often makes a
general statement that the writer can develop in the article. Here is a recent beginning from the *National Geographic*:

> "Papa, don't tell me the world knows anything about Catalonia and
> our struggles," shouted the shaggy-haired Barcelona teenager across the
> table from me.
> "Then the world has its head in the sand," spat his father. "People
> should know we're having the sweetest liberation in Spain."
> Strong dinner conversation, but not unusual for Catalans today.[4]

Here is a quotation that begins a chapter in a scholarly book, *Roll
Jordan Roll*, a social history of American black slavery by Eugene D.
Genovese:

> "Slaves being men," the Supreme Court of Louisiana declared
> sternly—if not without some ambiguity—in 1827, "are to be identified by
> their proper names." If any class in the United States understood the im-
> portance of names, the slaveholders did.[5]

Occasionally the rhetorical question makes a good beginning. It is
asked so that the writer may provide an answer and then proceed to the
rest of the essay. Here is a recent introduction from an editorial in the
New York Times:

> How did a 12-year-old victim of sex abuse become the only one locked
> up after the start of legal proceedings designed to protect children? That's
> the story of Amy, who spent eight days in solitary confinement at the
> order of a California court. It bears study.[6]

A splendid way of beginning an essay is by a simple, straightforward announcement of the proposition you are going to prove in your
work. Here is the opening from a chapter in Kirkpatrick Sale's book
Human Scale:

---

[4] Randall Peffer, "Spain's Country within a Country: Catalonia," *National Geographic*,
Jan. 1984, 95.

[5] Eugene D. Genovese, *Roll Jordan Roll* (New York: Random House, Vintage Books,
1976), 444.

[6] "Amy's Story," *New York Times*, Jan. 15, 1984, 22E.

These twin characteristics of big government—its enormous size and its inevitable bureaucratic shape—are the reasons for its failure. One might suppose that with such an edifice great things were being done; that it achieved, if only imperfectly, an increase in the abundance of the nation or the serenity of its streets or the livability of its environment or the happiness of its citizens. But that is not the case at all. On the contrary, it is precisely during this period of rampant governmental growth that the country has suffered its acutest problems, and is *still* suffering them, as we have seen.[7]

A chapter in Nigel Calder's *Einstein's Universe* entitled "Waves of Gravity" begins with statements about tides and then fits this information into a discussion of the configuration of gravity in the universe:

> The tides of the sea are among the most impressive of everyday phenomena. When tidal currents flow among the rocks, sailors are wary. To see a harbour emptying itself of water, leaving boats canted on the mud, and then to think of the water across millions of square miles that will have to heave itself up within a few hours to make them float again, sharpens one's sense of the power of gravity. The tides are a vivid manifestation of the curvature of space in the vicinity of the Sun and the Moon.
>
> As cosmic bodies go, the Moon is but a pebble; yet, because it is so close to the Earth, its tidal influence is more than twice as great as the Sun's. So we can simplify the story by considering only the Moon's effect. The tides are due to the *differences* in gravity at different distances from the Moon.[8]

The direct statement at the beginning of an essay challenges readers; it challenges writers, too, for it forces them to define what they are going to do and makes them quickly get on with doing it.

7. A good essay stays with its subject to the end.

Your opening sentences should win the attention of readers by promising to discuss something that will interest them. The rest of your essay should keep that promise. When you have finished writing, you should be able to tell in a single sentence what your essay is about.

A good essay makes one major point. It does not waver into long digressions. It does not parade the knowledge of the writer. It does not tell interesting stories that have little to do with the matter at hand.

Inexperienced writers often produce incoherent essays because

[7] Kirkpatrick Sale, *Human Scale* (New York: Coward, McCann & Geoghegan, 1980), 107.

[8] Nigel Calder, *Einstein's Universe* (New York, Viking, 1979), 67.

they try to stuff too much into them. Often they think of themselves not as writers but as people taking an examination or enduring some other test through their writing. So they put everything they can think of into the essay, and it becomes not an essay at all but rather a kind of stew in which none of the tastes is identifiable.

Digression may help you write a first draft, for when you are putting your first words on paper, you may wander all over the place. But by the time you write your final draft, you should have decided what you want to say, and you should stick to the point. Look at each sentence to be sure it contributes to the point you are trying to make. If it does not, cut it out.

Another word about using history in an essay: sometimes writers must provide some kind of historical background to their subject, but often they throw in a little history when they do not know how else to proceed. Historical background takes up space, and it can sound learned. Many writers get carried away with history, however, and forget what they are trying to say about their subject in the here and now. My best advice is to use historical background only when you must. If you are writing about a short story by John Cheever, it is probably not necessary to give a historical background of Cheever's life and work. If you are writing a review of a war movie, it is probably not necessary to give a long account of the war the movie is portraying. This matter is not one for binding rules, but you can often save yourself and your reader a lot of tedium if you write historical background only when it is clearly necessary to the point you are making.

> 8. *A good essay always includes concrete evidence to support the thesis it is trying to prove.*

When we tell stories in conversation, we nearly always provide concrete evidence to support the general statements we make:

> My friend John has a violent temper. I beat him at chess last night, and he threw the pieces on the floor and jumped up and down on them and then threw a beer bottle through the window and threw a potted plant at the cat and tore the chessboard into two pieces. Then he told me that if I didn't come back tonight and play again and give him a chance to get his revenge, he would never speak to me again.

By the time somebody finishes telling this little story, we agree that John has a violent temper. We know some concrete details about John that support the generalization about his temper.

Don't try to support one general statement with another general statement. "Latin should be taught in all public schools. People who learn Latin write English better than people who do not." Both these statements are opinions. The second statement appears to support the first, but it is not evidence, it is only another assertion. Has there been some sort of test of the writing ability of those who know Latin and those who do not? The results of such a test would be concrete evidence. Without evidence we have only a couple of opinions, and we do not know why we should accept them. People have said that knowing Latin helps one write better English, but no one to my knowledge has ever demonstrated that scholars of the classics are more engaging writers than are scholars of history or literature who have either never learned Latin or forgotten everything about it they ever knew.

What is concrete evidence? Observations that call up sense experience—colors, shapes, textures, tastes, smells, and sounds—are concrete. Quotations from texts are concrete. Statistical charts are concrete. Examples and illustrations are concrete. So are the stories you tell from your own experience.

Concrete evidence may not be sufficient to prove your thesis beyond a shadow of a doubt, but without evidence you cannot build even a plausible case. If you are trying to make an argument about a work of literature, you must quote from the work to show why you have reached the conclusions you present in your paper. Someone else may interpret these quotations differently, but the quotations give you some basis for argument, and without them or some other clear reference to the work your generalizations about it will be only so much mush.

Vladimir Nabokov, the late writer and teacher of literature, taught his students to begin their study of a novel or story by noting exactly what the writer said. "Exactly how does Anna Karenina die?" That was the kind of specific information Nabokov thought important in a novel, and he demanded that his students do a close reading of the literary texts they wrote about. That close reading, that intense preoccupation with exactly what can be found in a source, should guide any writer in the search for evidence. Teachers groan within when they read a paper filled with generalizations that are unsupported by any particulars that would give them reason to believe those generalizations.

9. A good essay on a controversial subject always includes evidence that may seem to contradict the point the writer is trying to make.

If you do write on a controversial subject, you must consider contrary evidence and contrary opinions. Careless or dishonest writers ignore contrary evidence. They imagine that they will weaken their case if they mention some of the points held by the other side. But somebody will always know when something that speaks against a case has been left out.

Every year thousands of writers in college courses argue important issues without considering contrary evidence and often without acknowledging that any contrary evidence exists. They will, for example, write a paper attacking proposals for a military draft, and they will make out that everyone favoring the draft is an ignoramus, an imperialist, a militarist, or a tyrant. Those favoring the draft will, in a similar spirit, argue that foes of the draft are pampered youths, kooks, or cowards who refuse to give anything of themselves to their country.

Controversial issues rarely divide the good guys and the bad guys. Papers that assume this moral division convince only the naïve; they do not change the minds of the thinking, wondering audience that looks for genuine guidance, the audience you should be trying to persuade when you argue any important issue. If you persist in writing as if every opponent is a knave or a fool, fair-minded readers will dismiss your work.

Contrary evidence may be handled in two ways. You may concede its truth and argue that it still does not damage your case. Or you may concede its truth but argue that it has been misinterpreted by your foes. If, for example, you decide to argue for a military draft, you must consider the question of such a draft discriminating against young men since young women are not drafted for combat duty. Do you concede that this discrimination will exist but that it must be accepted as a lesser evil in a society that needs a conscription army? Or do you argue that just because the draft has discriminated against young men in the past does not mean that now women should be exempt from the draft and from combat duty? You should choose your tactic on the basis of your own convictions. My point here is that you must consider as fairly as you can the opposing arguments, and you must try to deal with them.

Never be too proud or too fearful to make a concession. To concede a point in an argument gives the appearance of fair-mindedness — an appearance that is valuable in essays that try to persuade. Strategic concession has always been recognized as a major strength in writing or speaking.

> Yes, I concede that the bottle bill is going to be a pain for all of us. We can't throw the bottles away any more. We will have to pay more for

Cokes and beer. We will have to haul the bottles back to the stores to collect our deposit. I freely admit it. The bottle bill is going to cost all of us more time and money than we like to spend.

Such a concession allows us to come back with a stronger argument for our position:

But the bottle bill may save some money, too—money now spent in cleaning up the litter tossed along our streets and highways, money spent in repairing the damage done to tires and sometimes to bare feet by broken glass. For the experience of other states with bottle laws is that litter is dramatically reduced when people have some financial incentive to return bottles to the store rather than toss them away when they are empty. Once people experience a cleaner environment, they may decide that the little extra time and money they spend because of the bottle bill are well worth the cost.

Always remember that those who argue vehemently and blindly for a cause without conceding that their foes have any right on their side generally sound like fanatics. Only fanatics listen to fanatics. Your aim should be toward attracting another kind of reader.

10. A good essay is written with its audience in mind.

Always remember your audience. Don't write papers with only your teacher in mind. Think of the kind of person you would like to interest — your roommate, your parents, your best friends, someone you admire. Ask yourself this question: "How can I get this person to read my writing and take it seriously?"

Better still, share your writing with your friends. Get them to read what you have written and to tell you what they think you have said. Don't ask them, "Do you think this is clear? Do you think this is good? Do you think this is well written?" Human beings almost always want to please, and most of the time your friends will answer "Yes" to all those questions. But if you ask them to tell you in their own words what you have said, you put another kind of obligation on them, and you may learn a lot more about your prose.

Most professional writers share their work with one other person or with a small group of friends. An acquaintance of mine says that he writes for about five people he knows — all of them critical but tolerant. I write for my editor. She is a woman of taste and intelligence, and I believe that if I can get her interested in what I say, others will also be interested.

Writing for an audience does not mean dismissing your sincere thoughts in favor of a hypocritical effort to please at any price. It means that you have your own opinions, your own knowledge, your own ambitions for your piece but that you try to express them in a way that will please and persuade special people you know. What greater pleasure can you imagine than that of making someone you admire say, "You have done a good job on this. You have convinced me, and I like the piece."?

My editor is a good person who loves to read. She will not let me get away with insulting people, with making sweeping generalizations, with being cute, or with being vague. Writers writing about things they care about may make all these errors. My editor marks them, and when I write, I keep her in mind as the words go down on the paper. When I fall into overstatement or contentiousness or vagueness, I imagine how she will react, and I try to write without the flaws that irritate her. I do not always succeed. I have streaks of abysmal failure. But she is my audience, and my sense of her as a person makes my writing better than it would be without that.

You should write in a tone that is respectful of your audience. Make your audience respect you. Wayne Booth, a noted authority on writing, has said that every piece of writing has an "implied author." That is the person your audience finds standing behind the words on the page. Often the implied author is different from the conception the writer has of herself. Students are sometimes amazed and even hurt to discover that the impression of themselves they convey when they write is not what they want readers to believe about them. Your own implied author should be sincere, humane, convincing, tolerant, and interested, fair-minded and honest, showing confidence in the intelligence and fair-mindedness of your readers.

Don't be cute. But don't be excessively formal either. Write naturally. Use simple words. Don't qualify your remarks to the point that your readers will think you unwilling or unable to make a direct statement. Write as if you like your audience and people in general. Do everything you can to help your readers understand you. Don't show off. Don't condescend. Be honest and forthright, simple and direct.

11. A good essay is mechanically and grammatically correct and looks neat on a page.

Telling a writer to use correct grammar, punctuation, and spelling is like telling a pianist to learn to read music. The mechanical conventions we use in writing and reading have developed historically and sometimes without much logic. English spelling seems especially illogical to people who do not know it well. But these conventions are the symbols of communication and are now part of our language, and your observing them helps readers get through your prose. If you do not follow the common conventions of the written language, your readers will usually suppose that you are careless, illiterate, or stupid.

You should type your papers and anything else that is meant to be read. If you don't know how to type, you should learn. The new word-processing programs for personal computers offer speed, convenience, and peace of mind, and writing with a computer is far more swift and easy than writing with the best electric typewriters. But you have to know how to type before you can use a computer well.

You should be willing to mark up your early drafts so much that you may be the only person who can make sense of them. But when your work goes out to readers, it should be neat and clean and correct. The appearance of your work will tell them whether to take it seriously or not.

12. *A good essay concludes swiftly and gracefully.*

Conclusions are difficult, and all writers have trouble with them. When you have trouble concluding, you may simply stop. Being abrupt is better than dragging the conclusion out so that your essay becomes a late-night guest who lingers at the door in the cold and will not say good-bye.

Like an introduction, a conclusion may be a story. An article in a recent *National Geographic* about the riches of the Egyptian desert ends with a little story and a short commentary on the story and the rest of the essay:

> Near the end of our journey we sat close to Abu Simbel on the shores of Lake Nasser. The governor remarked that we had never discussed one important item: petroleum.
>
> I explained that the dearth of data about the vast desert had delayed any significant exploration. The situation is changing, I told him. One U.S. oil company is evaluating seismic studies in the Great Sand Sea west of Farafra. His face beamed.
>
> I knew the smile. It was the same hopeful glee I had seen on Sheikh Mehedi's face on the northern fringes of the desert. As Mehedi would say, this ancient desert, like old men and date palms, is about to give more.[9]

[9] Farouk El-Baz, "Egypt's Desert of Promise," *National Geographic*, Feb. 1982, 220.

A final paragraph may draw some conclusions from the information presented in the rest of the article. In his book on late medieval culture, Johan Huizinga includes a chapter on the medieval fascination with death. Having described the literature and the images associated with death as well as many customs relating to death, Huizinga provides a final interpretation:

> The dominant thought, as expressed in the literature, both ecclesiastical and lay, of that period, hardly knew anything with regard to death but these two extremes: lamentation about the briefness of all earthly glory, and jubilation over the salvation of the soul. All that lay between — pity, resignation, longing, consolation — remained unexpressed and was, so to say, absorbed by the too much accentuated and too vivid representation of Death hideous and threatening. Living emotion stiffens amid the abused imagery of skeletons and worms.[10]

A quotation that seems to draw the essay together makes a good ending. A recent article in *Time* reported on an Italian competition to design uniforms for women in the police force. It ended with a humorous paragraph about other fields for fashion designers to explore:

> There is one further, relatively fresh field: clerical garb. Whether designer vestments would induce terror or pity in worshipers or boost morale and recruiting to the ministry remains uncertain. But there are dreamers. Biagiotti, a most honorable also-ran in the policewomen's sweepstakes, consoles herself with fantasy. "I'd like to design a nun's habit. I like fullness. And those beautiful black and white wools falling in folds. Lovely."[11]

Avoid the summary ending that outlines the essay you have just completed. Readers are bored and insulted if you tell them again everything you have just told them. Sometimes, as in a complicated essay, you may try to draw together the various thoughts you have developed. In such a summary you should try to distill the important conclusions from the evidence you have examined. Such conclusions often end scholarly articles in which the author has considered controversial and difficult matters. Here is Cleanth Brooks giving some final thoughts to an analysis of William Faulkner's definition of evil:

[10] Johan Huizinga, *The Waning of the Middle Ages*, trans. F. Hopman, (New York: St. Martin's Press, 1949; New York: Doubleday, Anchor Books, 1954), 151.

[11] *Time*, Jan. 16, 1984, 65.

To try for a summary of a very difficult and complicated topic: Evil for Faulkner involves the violation of the natural and the denial of the human. As Isaac's older kinsman says in "The Bear," "Courage and honor and pride, and pity and love of justice and of liberty. They all touch the heart, and what the heart holds to becomes truth, as far as we know truth." A meanness of spirit and coldness of calculation which would deny the virtues that touch the heart is by that very fact proven false. Yet Faulkner is no disciple of Jean-Jacques Rousseau. He has no illusions that man is naturally good or that he can safely trust to his instincts and emotions. Man is capable of evil, and this means that goodness has to be achieved by struggle and discipline and effort. Like T. S. Eliot, Faulkner has small faith in social arrangements so perfectly organized that nobody has to take the trouble to be good. Finally Faulkner's noblest characters are willing to face the fact that most men can learn the deepest truths about themselves and about reality only through suffering. Hurt and pain and loss are not mere accidents to which the human being is subject; nor are they mere punishments incurred by human error; they can be the means to the deeper knowledge and to the more abundant life.[12]

A good conclusion nearly always bears a clear relation to the introduction. A good way to test the coherence of an essay is to put the last paragraph under the first paragraph and see if you can discern a relation between the two without having to read what comes between them. Here are the introductory and concluding paragraphs from the second chapter of the book *Civilities and Civil Rights* by William H. Chafe, the story of desegregation in Greensboro, North Carolina. The first paragraph:

To those who believed that Greensboro might lead the rest of the South toward racial justice, the early response to the school board's desegregation resolution provided hope and reassurance. On May 19, 1954, the morning newspaper applauded the school board's willingness to face facts. "How one felt or what one did about segregation before Monday . . . has become relatively academic now," the Daily News editorialized. "Segregation has been ruled out and the responsibility now is to readjust to that reality with a minimum of friction, disruption, and setback to the public school system." A few days later, the Greensboro Jaycees–the largest chapter in the state—endorsed the school board's resolution by a margin of four to one. The same day, the Greensboro Ministerial Alliance added its support.

---

[12] Cleanth Brooks, *The Hidden God* (New Haven, Conn., and London: Yale University Press, 1963), 43.

The last paragraph:

> In the end, therefore, North Carolina's progressivism consisted primarily
> of its shrewdness in opposing racial change. The state's leaders failed to
> broaden the beachhead that the *Brown* decision had established. Instead,
> with the Pearsall Plan as its instrument and token desegregation in places
> like Greensboro as a primary defense, North Carolina set out to forestall
> integration. As one Little Rock school official wrote to an associate in
> North Carolina: "You North Carolinians have devised one of the cleverest
> techniques of perpetuating segregation that we have seen."[13]

Here it is easy to see that the key words in both paragraphs are
Greensboro and *segregation*, and you can guess from comparing these
two paragraphs that the chapter itself deals with how a promising beginning to desegregation in Greensboro gave way to dogged resistance.

Test your own opening and closing paragraphs in the same way,
and study professional essays to see how experienced writers make their
essays coherent by clearly relating their first and last paragraphs to each
other.

CONCLUDING REMARKS ON THE ESSAY

The essay form will be useful to you throughout your life as you
write memos, business letters, reports, and articles. One of the best
habits you can develop is that of studying the essays you find both enjoyable and informative. You can check a lot of the advice in this
chapter by sitting down with a good essay and seeing how it is put
together. As you become more aware of the habits of good writers, you
will develop those habits yourself. When you read with your own
writing in mind, your prose will almost always reflect something that
you have seen in your reading. Study the form of the essay as you encounter it in your reading, and you can throw this book away.

---

[13] William H. Chafe, *Civilities and Civil Rights* (New York: Oxford University Press,
1981), 42, 70. Copyright © 1981 by Oxford University Press, Inc. Reprinted by permission.

THREE

The Writing Process

Now that we have our goal—the essay—in mind, we need to think about how we can reach it. It is not an easy road. Shakespeare is said to have written his plays without erasing a line. The rest of us are not Shakespeare. Most writers revise and revise and revise. They cross out and write variations in the margins of their manuscripts. Sometimes they cut drafts apart with a pair of scissors and paste them together again in a new form.

Word-processing programs make some of the physical labor of writing less burdensome. But the writers who use word-processing programs still print out drafts and toil at them, scratching out words to be deleted, writing words, sentences, or whole paragraphs in the margins so that they can insert these additions onto the computer's data disk.

Writers often despair because despite their frequent revising, they remain dissatisfied with their work. Many writers say they never finish revising a piece; they merely abandon it and let a publisher take it away.

How much time you spend on your writing will depend on how serious you are about it. For the serious writer, writing is not merely an assignment. It is a way of life, an everyday habit.

When I get a writing assignment, I begin filling notebooks. I can look up from where I now sit and count twelve notebooks on my bookshelf. Another notebook lies here on the desk beside me. Another is in the waterproof nylon case that I carry over my shoulder as I ride my bicycle back and forth to my office every day. Writing is hard for me—by far the hardest thing I do. But I do a lot of it, and my notebooks help me along. I am always scribbling ideas, trial sentences, and random thoughts in them. All the examples in this book come from my notebooks, for they are passages that I have enjoyed in my general reading or else (as in some of the bad examples) passages that have dismayed or amused me.

You must find your own writing process. Mine is all wrapped up in notebooks, and I urge it on you. A notebook is portable. It is durable and efficient since you are unlikely to lose pages that are bound together. A friend of mine carries a small pack of three-by-five cards in his shirt pocket. The practice is hard on his shirts, but it lets him jot ideas down throughout the day and use them at night. Vladimir Nabokov wrote his novels in pencil on such cards, and later somebody typed his manuscript from them. If you prefer to carry three-by-five cards around in your pocket, do it. You can keep them together with rubber bands, and later on you can arrange them in the approximate order in which you might use them in writing an essay.

If you use a notebook, don't be afraid of letting it get messy and disorganized. You are the only one who will look at it. You don't have to be afraid that someone will think less of you if it looks sloppy.

When you read something interesting that relates to a topic you may write about, jot down paraphrases and copy direct quotations. Some people write direct quotations on one page and their own observations on the facing page. Make lists. Write down questions to yourself having to do with what you read. You may not be able to answer some of these questions, but they will help direct your thinking as to whether you can answer them or not. Unanswered questions may drive you to seek more information, and if after a search you still cannot answer a question, you will have learned something important about the limitations of knowledge on a subject. Acknowledging our ignorance helps to keep us honest.

INVENTING

Keeping a notebook will get you in the habit of considering your own thoughts as ideas to be written down. Most people have interesting thoughts, but they usually do nothing with them.

Jotting down ideas helps you to remember and develop your ideas. It will also help you in several steps of the writing process. For example, it can help you decide what the subject of an essay should be. Every writer must come up with a topic, and writer's block is frequently a paralysis that occurs before the necessity of defining a topic to write about.

Always choose a topic that you can handle well in the span of an essay. You cannot do an elaborate psychological analysis of Henry VIII in five pages. You cannot use the simple title "*Moby Dick*" for a ten-page library paper; it would imply that you intended to consider every aspect of the huge novel *Moby Dick* in your ten-page essay. You cannot write a good paper on the topic "Henry James wrote some interesting novels."

You must limit your topic to something you can do well in the space at your disposal.

As you gather evidence and make notes about it, you should always be asking yourself the following questions. Write them down in your notebook, and provide answers to them.

1. What do you observe? In looking at a text, this question becomes, "What do the words say?"

A close reading is the first step in understanding a text. Read every line of your evidence to see what it says. You will often be surprised. When I gave my students a collection of primary sources for the battles of Lexington and Concord and asked them to write a narrative of those battles, a biology major, accustomed to minute examination of evidence, read Paul Revere's own account of his participation in the events of April 18 and 19, 1775, and reached an astonishing conclusion. He realized that Revere himself had the lanterns posted in the tower of the Old North Church in Boston, as a signal that the British were about to move troops to Lexington and Concord, and only after the lanterns were displayed did he have himself rowed across the Charles River so that he could ride through the dark and give warning to the Minutemen asleep in their houses. In Longfellow's famous poem we have Revere waiting in the dark *across the river* when the lanterns are posted. Most people have read Longfellow, and most members of this class, with Revere's own words in front of them, still wrote their narrative according to the words Longfellow had put in Revere's mouth:

> And I on the opposite shore will be
> Waiting to ride and spread the alarm
> Through every Middlesex village and farm.

Just one student read Revere's words carefully and realized that Revere had the lanterns posted because he was afraid he might not be able to get across the river himself. But then he did get across, rowing undetected under the bow of a British ship, and went off on his famous ride, following other riders who also were spreading the alarm.

See what is in a text, and compare what you see with what other people have seen. Write the comparisons in your notebook, and you may discover that you have seen something new.

At some point you may have an important idea, one that seems to make everything you are reading make sense. Good papers come from such synthesizing ideas, ideas that seem to explain what a writer is doing or why a character in a book or a play acts the way he does. You can write down such ideas in your notebook to make them clear. Once you have done that, find the textual evidence to support the idea.

2. What can you infer from what you observe?

When you infer, you look beneath the surface of a text or an occurrence. When you infer, you often ask the question "Why?"

Suppose your teacher tells you to write a five-page paper on Shakespeare's *King Lear*. You will bore any English teacher if you summarize the plot. Your teacher has read the play fifty times and knows it by heart. Papers that tell readers what they already know are always boring. The assignment is to write a paper, and we write papers to inform, to tell others things they don't know or perhaps to make them see something familiar in a new way. If you give a plot summary, you have made a subtle and lethal change in the assignment: you have changed the assignment into an examination. We take examinations to prove that we know something that our teachers know already. Papers that become examination forsake interest and embrace tedium.

You can ask some questions about *King Lear* that lead to inferences — seeing what is below the surface of the text. What is this play about? Is it about pride? Is it about fathers and daughters? Is it about greed? Is Lear the only proud person in the play? Isn't Cordelia as proud as her demanding father? Why is pride destructive? Why do Christians and Jews and ancient Greek writers consider pride one of the great sins? Is there any way for a play like this to have a happy ending? Why is it tragedy? Is Lear's fool really a fool? Does Lear go mad in the play, or has he been mad all along? Can anyone be trusted? Can interesting people be trusted?

These are questions that you can answer only after you have studied the play carefully, thought about it, and tried to look below the surface. Jotting down these questions starts you thinking about them. And if you start trying to answer them, you will discover that some of them can coalesce into a good paper, a paper that informs your readers of something you have discovered for yourself.

Sometimes you can classify your questions. The classifications will then help you to look beneath the surface of a text you are studying or an event or group you are observing. In journalism schools aspiring reporters are taught the five Ws — who, what, when, where, and why. Who did it? What was it? When did it happen? Where did it happen? Why did it happen? In covering some events — such as a murder, for example — these questions arise naturally:

John Bailey, third-year chemistry student, was arrested last night by Cambridge police for the murder by poison of his roommate, James Klein. Klein died after drinking strawberry wine that had been laced with strychnine. "I couldn't stand his one Beatle record," Bailey said. "He played 'I Want to Hold Your Hand' all day long and all night. It was the only record he owned, and I couldn't stand it any more."

If you walk through this paragraph, which follows a typical newspaper format, you can see answers to all the five questions, and the story to follow will develop those questions that are most interesting to the reporter and to readers.

The same questions can help you see a literary text more clearly and help you formulate topics for a paper. For example, ask the question "Who?" of the short story "A Rose for Emily" by William Faulkner:

Who is Miss Emily Grierson?

She is a woman grown from beautiful youth to ugly old age in a changing Mississippi town.
She is the only daughter of a protective and tyrannical father.
She is a member of a family that has pride in its reputation and does not want her to marry beneath her station.
She is a woman with little money.
She is lonely.
She is unloved.
She is a monument and a curiosity in the town.
She is a failure in all her personal relations except that with her black servant.
She is a murderer.

The list can go on and on. And as you write down all the responses you can think of to the question "Who?" you begin to see things in the story that you may have overlooked or misunderstood in your first reading. The same process would work for the four other questions. And as you write down the answers to those questions, you will begin to see other questions you had not thought of before.

3. What connections can you make between what you observe or read and other things you know?

When you read a short story or a novel, ask yourself these questions: How is this piece like other things I know? How is it different?

Both these questions can have many different formulations. For example, you may read Hemingway's *For Whom the Bell Tolls* and look carefully at the woman character Pilar, the wife of Pablo, the guerrilla leader in the hills. How is Pilar like other women in Hemingway's fiction? How does she resemble women in Faulkner's stories? What do you think she would have to say to some of the women in the fiction of Henry James? What would a modern feminist have to say to or about Pilar?

Some of these questions are playful, and you cannot answer any of them so completely that no one will dispute your judgment. But always remember that few interesting subjects can be treated in such a way that your conclusions about them will be beyond dispute. Your job is to build a plausible case, something that may be believed because of the evidence you present. You should ask the questions, and you should jot down possible answers in your notebook. As you ask and answer, you may find a good limited topic for a paper.

By comparing one thing with another, you may see both things more clearly. In this way you help to integrate your own experience and understand it better. You may know vaguely that you like Faulkner's women better than the women who appear in Hemingway's works. (Or you may discover the reverse.) Working out the reasons for these emotional reactions can make for a fascinating paper. But a paper will not even be interesting if you limit yourself to telling your readers merely that you like Faulkner's women better than you like Hemingway's. Unless you are a great authority, people will not care about your naked opinions. You must give your readers reason to care, and that reason will come from your reading of different texts and your intelligent comparison of them.

4. Are there any contradictions in the evidence you are studying?

Every reporter learns to interview people with an ear open to ways they contradict themselves. In a good press conference the reporters will ask questions that get the speaker to consider these contradictions. "Mr. President, how do you reconcile your statement that you support education with your budget, which cuts federal money paid out to schools and cuts student loans?" Some candidates for the presidency have ruined their chances for election by contradicting themselves again and again in the course of the long campaign. Good reporters always study the words and deeds of a president to see if he is wobbling around on issues according to the whims of public opinion.

You can also find contradictions in written evidence that you may be collecting for a term paper. These contradictions often make good subjects for a paper. The contradictions may be of two sorts. One kind of contradiction may be found within a writer's various works. For example, in his *Utopia*, written in 1516, Thomas More said that his mythical Utopians practice religious toleration. They demand only that people believe God exists, that He rewards and punishes people in an afterlife for deeds done on earth, and that He guides the world by His providence. Utopia is an imaginary island off the coast of the New World, and people usually say that the book More wrote about it expresses his ideals for what society ought to be. But when the Protestant Reformation burst on the European scene and spread to England, More wrote many books vehemently demanding that heretics be put to death, and while he was lord chancellor of the realm, he was responsible for having several Protestants burned alive for their religious beliefs. What do we do with the contradiction between what More wrote in *Utopia* and what he wrote and did when the Protestants started making converts in England? You can probably find such contradictions in any interesting author. Sometimes they can be reconciled; sometimes they cannot be. You can point them out and puzzle over them if nothing else. Such puzzling can make an excellent, thoughtful paper.

Another kind of contradiction in written evidence occurs when different writers disagree with each other. One of my students once did a fine paper comparing essays written through the years on *The Age of Jackson*, a book by Arthur Schlesinger, Jr. He showed that when the book first came out in 1945, scholars all over America praised it. But after this first enthusiasm cooled, scholars took a second look and began to argue that the work was badly flawed. My student read about ten reviews of the book written over a period of some twenty years and sketched his findings in an interesting and original paper. Most interesting topics draw attention from writers; if you survey those writers' different opinions on a topic and try to discover why they hold those opinions, you may make an important contribution to knowledge.

Another of my students went through microfilm copies of newspapers from the year 1947 to see all the different ways in which reporters wrote about the coming of Jackie Robinson to the Brooklyn Dodgers. Robinson was the first black player in baseball's major leagues. This student found a lot of subtle differences in how sportswriters covered the story and how headline writers dealt with it.

Both these students were doing papers about contradiction. They found that different people wrote about the same things in different

ways, and those different ways—those contradictory approaches—
revealed something important about the subject. Both students came
up with fine essays.

5. What came out, or what may come out, of a subject you are studying?

We love to know how things turn out. A good paper can develop a
relation of cause and effect. As you will see in the chapter on argument,
the relation of cause and effect is often more difficult than it may seem
at first glance. But it is still worth pointing out.

In 1898 the United States fought a war with Spain. What were the
consequences? We became more deeply involved in Asia. We took over
the Philippine Islands and Puerto Rico. We made Cuba independent.
We reunited this country, which had been emotionally split by the Civil
War. We created a crisis of conscience in our theory of democracy because a great part of the American tradition had been against imperial-
ism. And so it goes. You can extend the consequence from any event into a list, and for a manageable essay, you can choose one or two things
from the list that you would like to develop.

Sometimes questions about cause and effect may stir up "what if"
papers. What if the British had won the American Revolution? What if
the United States had not made the Louisiana Purchase from Napoleon? What if Shakespeare had died in 1600? What if Ernest Hemingway had been a woman? What if Martin Luther had been killed by the
lightning storm in 1505 that frightened him so much that he became a
monk? We can never answer the "what if" question to our complete
satisfaction, but asking it often helps us see more clearly what actually
did happen, or it helps us understand an interesting issue. Virginia
Woolf has a great "what if" piece in her book *A Room of Her Own*: What
if Shakespeare had had a sister as gifted as he and as ambitious to be a
playwright? The question allowed Woolf to make a vital critique of how
women have been traditionally treated in Western society.

The "what if" question is a good, playful one to ask when you are
preparing to write a paper. It makes you break up some old forms in
your mind and replace them with new ones, and the breaking of old
constructs is one of the best ways to original thought.

Your notebook offers you a place to play with all these questions
and with others that you may find useful as you prepare to write a
paper. What goes down in the notebook may be disorganized, even

chaotic. But your mind will do a lot of organizing as you write your disorganized words, phrases, sentences, and paragraphs. Your notebook may be a mess, but it is a kind of compost heap of the mind, and ideas will grow in the mess and take on the ordered appearance of fruitful plants.

WRITING DRAFTS

Finally the moment comes to sit down and begin your first draft. It is always a good idea at the beginning to make a list of the points you want to cover. A list is not a formal outline. In making your first list, which you should write in your notebook, you should not bother to set items down in the order of their importance. Your mind will order things as you decide to include them in your essay. Perhaps you will make one list, think about it a little while, and make another one, this time approaching the order you intend to follow in your essay.

Here again, as in every part of the writing process, you must commit yourself to the task at hand. Sit down, and do not get up until you have written for an hour. Write down your thoughts as quickly as you can. Let one sentence give you an idea to develop in the next. But don't be disturbed if you feel things start to unravel. Organization, grammar, spelling—the individual words are not nearly as important in this first draft as getting it down, putting it on paper, getting yourself a form to work with. No matter how desperate you may feel, keep going. Your mind organizes as you write.

Keep your notebook beside you on the desk, opened to the place where you made your last list. Sometimes you may turn back through your notes to pick up a fact or a thought or one of the trial sentences you wrote earlier. But keep writing steadily. Cover several pages of paper—more than the assignment demands. Keep going until you think you have said everything you want to say. Keep going and going and going.

Always keep your mind open to new ideas that may pop into your mind as you write the first draft. Let your list help you, but don't become a slave to it. Writers often start an essay with one topic in mind, only to discover that another topic pushes the first one aside as they work. Ideas you had not even thought of before you began to write may pile onto your paper, and five or six pages into your first draft you may realize that the paper is going to be about something you did not imagine when you started.

If such a revelation comes to you while you write, be grateful for it and accept it. But don't immediately tear up your draft and start over again. Make yourself keep on writing, developing these new ideas as they come to you. If you start all over again, you may break the train of thought that has given you the new topic. Let your thoughts follow your new thesis, sailing on that new tack until the wind changes.

When you believe you have said everything you can say in this draft, get up from your desk and go sit in a chair somewhere else and read what you have written without trying to correct anything. Then put it aside, preferably overnight. It is an excellent idea to read a rough draft just before you go to sleep. Again and again tests have shown that sleeping on an intellectual problem helps the mind organize it, and if you study a draft just before you go to bed, you may discover that you have new ideas in the morning.

In your second draft be willing to make radical changes. If your thesis changed while you were writing your first draft, you will obviously want to base your second draft on your new subject. Even if your thesis has not changed, you may need to shift paragraphs around, eliminate paragraphs, add new ones. Inexperienced writers often suppose that revising a paper means only changing a word or two or adding a sentence or two. This kind of editing is part of the writing process, but it is not the most important part. The most important part of rewriting is in the willingness to turn the paper upside down, to shake out of it those ideas that interest you most, to set them in a form where they will interest the reader too.

I mentioned earlier that some writers cut up their first draft with a pair of scissors. They toss some paragraphs into the trash; others they paste up with rubber cement in the order that seems most logical and coherent. Afterward they type the whole thing through again, smoothing out the transitions, adding new material, getting new ideas as they work. The translation of the first draft into the second nearly always involves radical cutting and shifting around. Now and then you will get the order of your essay in your first draft, but most of the time you will settle on an organization only in the second draft.

Always be brave enough to cut out interesting thoughts, stories, and examples that have nothing to do with your thesis. Cutting is the supreme test of a writer. You work hard to create a smashing paragraph, and you succeed. Then you discover that it does not fit the paper you have decided to write. You may develop six or seven examples to illustrate a point in your paper and decide that you need only one.

You can digress now and then and journey off into pleasant little valleys apart from the main line of your argument. But you can't jump the track. If you digress too often, your readers will probably not follow you. It is a painful truth about harried modern life that most readers get impatient with the scenic route; they want to take the most direct way to their destination. So to appeal to most of them, you will have to cut things that do not pertain to your main argument.

In your third draft you can sharpen sentences, add information here and there, cut some things, and attend to other details that heighten the impact of your writing. In your third draft, writing becomes a lot of fun. By then you have usually decided what you want to say. Now you can work at words and sentences to be sure you are speaking as well as you can.

Should you make an outline before you write? Probably not. A good list is probably sufficient. Some people do make elaborate outlines, and if a complicated outline helps you, use it. But a simple list remains looser than the familiar outlines you see in textbooks on writing. These textbooks present outlines in which the major points and the subpoints are carefully put together in a symmetrical whole so that if you have three points under part one, you should have three points under part two. Real writing does not conform to such rigid systematizing, and such rigid designs for papers may block the creative action of the brain.

The main message of this chapter is not that you must follow any single writing process. All writers develop processes of their own, something that works for them and lets them produce. One of my friends tells me that his writing process consists of writing a sentence, agonizing over it, walking around the room, thinking, sitting down, and writing the next sentence. It seems unnecessarily painful to me to bleed out prose in that way, but it works for him. Several of my friends tell me they cannot compose at a typewriter and say that they must write a longhand draft first. These are the people most likely to cut up their drafts with scissors and paste them together in a different form. My way has been to get a book or an essay into being by writing through a first draft as quickly as I can. Then I have gone back and typed each page over and over again, getting it right before going on to the next page. Now that I am using a word processor, I print out drafts, take them downstairs to my kitchen table, make myself a big pot of coffee, and go over the drafts, writing in changes that I can then make on the computer before printing out the next draft. But even with a word processor I feel better typing all the way through the final draft, from beginning to end, letting all the words come through my fingers one last times. I have typed this book from beginning to end four times, making substantial changes each time.

The main thing is to keep at it. B. F. Skinner has pointed out that if you write only fifty words a night, you will produce a good-sized book every two or three years. William Faulkner outlined the plot of his Nobel Prize–winning novel A *Fable* on a wall inside his house near Oxford, Mississippi. You can see it there to this day. Once he got the outline on the wall, he sat down with his typewriter and wrote, following his outline carefully until he got to the end. He kept at it. And if writing an outline on a kitchen wall helps you keep at it, do it. You can always paint the wall over again if you must.

Whatever you do, always think of writing as a process. Don't imagine you must know everything you are going to say before you say it. Don't demean yourself and insult your readers by making your first draft be your final draft. Don't imagine that writing is easy or that you can do it without spending time on it. And don't let anything stand in the way of your doing it. Let your house get messy. Leave your magazines unread. Put off getting up for a drink of water. Don't make a telephone call. Don't straighten up your desk. Sit down and write. And write and write and write.

FOUR

Paragraphs

Paragraphs are a modern invention. Greek and Latin writers did not use them, and until the nineteenth century written English scarcely noticed them. The word *paragraph* originally meant a mark placed at the head of a section of prose to announce that that section slightly changed the subject of the discourse. After the mark the new section might go on for several pages. Eventually the paragraph mark was replaced by a new, indented line. Even then the indentation might introduce a long section of unbroken prose. The paragraphs of John Stuart Mill and Charles Darwin, both great nineteenth-century prose writers, might go on for several pages. Only gradually did the paragraph assume its modern form — a fairly short block of prose introduced by an indentation, closely organized around a limited subject.

Paragraphs help writers and readers alike. They order our thoughts and make our writing easier to follow. They break our ideas down into manageable units that we can treat efficiently. They let us arrange an essay one step at a time, and they allow readers to follow our thoughts along the stairway we have built for them.

Paragraphs give readers the sense that a piece of prose is going somewhere. They also provide relief for eyes that rebel against long columns of type. Nothing looks quite so forbidding in print as the unbroken columns in an early nineteenth-century newspaper. (Indeed, the most probable cause of the paragraph's popularity was the expansion of literacy fed by the penny press. Ordinary people who had a hard time reading wanted their newspapers to be more manageable, more readable.) We hesitate to start reading unparagraphed material because we secretly believe that we cannot get through it. By breaking down a piece of writing into blocks that we can handle, paragraphs make us think that we can absorb it. We accumulate all our knowledge a step at a time; paragraphs let us use this same process as we read.

THE TOPIC SENTENCE

A lot of nonsense has been written about paragraphs, and much of it is confusing advice. Much of it is wrong. Every paragraph should develop a central idea. Sometimes that idea will be stated in a summary sentence, usually placed at the beginning. Most textbooks call this sentence the topic sentence or the theme sentence.. This sentence makes a generalization, and the other sentences in the paragraph provide some reason to accept the generalization.

In paragraphs that explain an idea, a topic sentence at the beginning may help you and your readers. It presents the idea, or a part of it, with such clarity that it causes you to think of ways to support it in the sentences that follow. Clear ideas are helpful not only to readers but also to writers, for once writers know precisely what they want to say, they naturally have an easier time saying it. Here is an almost classic paragraph that begins with a topic sentence, the opening paragraph of a chapter called "The Long Habit" from Lewis Thomas's little book *The Lives of a Cell*:

> We continue to share with our remotest ancestors the most tangled and evasive attitudes about death, despite the great distance we have come in understanding some of the profound aspects of biology. We have as much distaste for talking about personal death as for thinking about it; it is an indelicacy, like talking in mixed company about venereal disease or abortion in the old days. Death on a grand scale does not bother us in the same special way; we can sit around a dinner table and discuss war, involving 60 million volatized human deaths, as though we were talking about bad weather; we can watch abrupt bloody death every day, in color, on films and television, without blinking back a tear. It is when the numbers of dead are very small, and very close, that we begin to think in scurrying circles. At the very center of the problem is the naked cold deadness of one's own self, the only reality in nature of which we can have absolute certainty, and it is unmentionable, unthinkable. We may be even less willing to face the issue at first hand than our predecessors because of a secret new hope that maybe it will go away. We like to think, hiding in the thought, that with all the marvelous ways in which we seem now to lead nature around by the nose, perhaps we can avoid the central problem if we just become, next year, say, a bit smarter.[1]

Thomas's paragraph starts with a general statement, and the rest of the paragraph builds on that statement and makes several cogent state-

[1] Lewis Thomas, *Lives of a Cell* (New York: Viking, 1974), 47.

ments about it. Most of the other paragraphs in this chapter of Thomas's book begin with a similar general statement and provide some sentences that make us believe this generalization.

When you explain ideas, you may find it helpful to write down a list of proposed topic sentences for paragraphs. Such a list may help you analyze a play or relate the significance of some item in the news or discuss an ethical or philosophical point. If you write about a controversial subject, such as abortion, the military draft, prayer in public schools, or government aid to religious colleges, you will be presenting assumptions, ideas, ruminations, and arguments that you will break down in a series of paragraphs. You may introduce many of these paragraphs with a general topic sentence.

BUILDING IDEAS IN PARAGRAPHS

Many paragraphs—probably most paragraphs, in fact—are not introduced by general statements. Here, for example, is a paragraph from Joseph Kastner's book *A Species of Eternity*, a history of America's early naturalists. This paragraph describes some of the Revolutionary War experiences of Charles Willson Peale, a patriot as well as an artist and a naturalist:

> In 1776, Peale moved himself and his family to Philadelphia, the center of colonial culture, and plunged promptly into the war. As an officer in the militia, he fought under Washington at Princeton and proved himself a highly practical commander. When his men went barefoot, he used his old skills as a saddle-maker and made shoes for them. When some of the soldiers broke ranks to steal fruit from an orchard, he kept discipline simply by ordering the whole company to fall out so all could join in the foraging. His paints and palettes went with him into battle, and the scenes he sketched provided backgrounds for two portraits of General Washington. During the winter at Valley Forge, he became a friend of the young Marquis de Lafayette.[2]

You could summarize the paragraph in a general topic sentence like this one: "Peale joined the Revolutionary army and had many interesting experiences." But such a sentence would be boring and unnecessary. As Kastner tells us what Peale did, event by event, we easily

[2] Joseph Kastner, *A Species of Eternity* (New York: Alfred A. Knopf, 1977), 146.

follow along. We see the unity of the paragraph as we read it. But how *do* paragraphs work? What do paragraphs with general topic sentences have in common with paragraphs that lack such sentences? Much debate rages about these matters, and the conclusion most people make is one already stated above: paragraphs have unity. But how do writers attain this unity?

I believe that the most plausible way to unify your paragraphs is to concentrate on building each one on a thought expressed in the first sentence. We have already seen that in Lewis Thomas's paragraph about death there is a first sentence on which the rest of the sentences in the paragraph are built. The same thing is also true of the paragraph from Kastner's book, although that paragraph has no topic sentence.

At the risk of some tedium, let us run through Kastner's paragraph again, one sentence at a time:

> In 1776, Peale moved himself and his family to Philadelphia, the center of colonial culture, and plunged promptly into the war.

Think a moment of all the possibilities in this sentence. We are writing about an artist who fought for American independence in the Revolutionary War. We have several key thoughts—the date, 1776; the move to Philadelphia, which is called "the center of colonial culture"; and the news that Peale "plunged promptly into the war."

The next sentence develops the information that Peale plunged into the war. It tells what he did as an officer in the militia:

> As an officer in the militia, he fought under Washington at Princeton and proved himself a highly practical commander.

Now we have the thought that Peale was a "practical" commander. How was he practical? The next sentence tells us:

> When his men went barefoot, he used his old skills as a saddle-maker and made shoes for them.

Now, we say to ourselves, that is real practicality! And the next sentence gives us yet another reason for believing that Peale was practical:

> When some of the soldiers broke ranks to steal fruit from an orchard, he kept discipline simply by ordering the whole company to fall out so all could join in the foraging.

Peale could have been a strict disciplinarian. He could have punished the soldiers who broke ranks to pick fruit. But then he would have made his men unhappy and lowered their morale. He kept discipline by letting them all go pick fruit. He avoided a confrontation and maintained himself as a leader.

The next sentence reaches back to the first sentence in the paragraph. Peale plunged into the war. What did he do in the war? He was a practical officer, but he also painted:

> His paints and palettes went with him into battle, and the scenes he sketched provided backgrounds for two portraits of General Washington.

Then we have a concluding sentence:

> During the winter at Valley Forge, he became a friend of the young Marquis de Lafayette.

This paragraph neatly summarizes Peale's wartime experiences. Kastner then turns to his chief interest, Peale as naturalist. The paragraph draws its unity from its general theme and not from a topic sentence. The first sentence gives us that theme with its announcement that Peale "plunged promptly into the war." It does not make a general statement, and we could write the paragraph in a different way if we wanted. Suppose, for example, that we chose to write this paragraph:

> In 1776, Peale moved himself and his family to Philadelphia, the center of colonial culture, and plunged promptly into the war. His wife and children remained in the city and were little affected by the conflict. Peale had already made enough money to let them live comfortably, and they scarcely felt the hardships supposedly endured by the Americans in that time. While he was stationed at Valley Forge during the terrible winter of 1777, Peale regularly came into the city to visit with them, and he appears to have remained warm and dry while the common soldiers in Washington's army suffered.

I do not know if these details about Peale's family are true. I have made them up only to show that a writer choosing to emphasize another idea in that same first sentence might have done so with the appropriate information. I picked up the idea of the family in Philadelphia and developed it. I might have picked up the idea of the date and produced a paragraph like this one:

In 1776, Peale moved himself and his family to Philadelphia, the center of colonial culture, and plunged promptly into the war. It was a stirring year for the Revolution. King George III of England had decided to repress the uprising by main force, and he and his ministers left no doubt that the American leaders would be hanged if they could be caught. The English Parliament was divided over the war, but a majority supported the government. Seeing no hope for reconciliation or for the redress of grievances, delegates from the various colonies met at Philadelphia in July and signed a Declaration of Independence drawn up by the Virginian Thomas Jefferson. Peale was not a delegate, and he did not sign the declaration. But he heartily approved of it.

You can see in these examples three different ways of developing paragraphs from the same first sentence. What makes them different? The different purposes of the writers. Each paragraph says something to develop an idea expressed in the all-important first sentence. The writer, in setting down that first sentence, is making a commitment to develop some word or phrase in it as he proceeds to the second sentence and to the third and to the fourth. The best way to preserve paragraph unity is not to worry about making a topic sentence; it is rather to decide to take some idea in that first sentence and go on with it.

THE QUALITIES OF A PARAGRAPH

Sometimes when you write, you will make your paragraphs almost spontaneously, without thinking very much about what you are doing. I have always found that when my students write rapidly in class about something that has happened to them recently, they make good paragraphs without much effort. They do so because they are naturally picking out ideas in each sentence to develop in succeeding sentences. If you follow the advice given earlier in this book and write your first draft rapidly, you may find that your own paragraphs flow spontaneously.

This book is addressed at least in part to those writers who want to reflect on what they are doing as they write. Some of you may have a lot of trouble doing what others do easily. When you do sense trouble in your paragraphs, give special attention to the first sentence in each one. See if it mentions something that is taken up by the second sentence, and see if the third sentence mentions something that was present in the first or the second sentences.

Professional writers always write down a sentence to begin a paragraph and then develop a second sentence that builds on some thought expressed in that first one. That first sentence may be a general topic sentence, but it may not be. For example, a narrative recounts events that happen one after another in time, and such events seldom need to be organized by a general topic sentence. Here is a paragraph from *Elizabeth the Great*, a biography of Queen Elizabeth I of England written by Elizabeth Jenkins. Jenkins here describes some of the events caused by an attack of smallpox suffered by the queen early in her reign. A doctor gave her a potion that made the disease erupt, lessening its threat and usually ensuring the patient's survival:

> The bringing out of the eruptions saved the patient's life, and the scabs left her face without permanent blemishes. She had been nursed by Robert Dudley's sister, Lady Mary Sidney, who took the disease and suffered the horrible disfigurement Elizabeth had so much dreaded. Sir Henry Sidney wrote after seeing his wife for the first time since her recovery: "I left her a full fair lady, in mine eyes at least, the fairest, and when I returned I found her as foul a lady as the smallpox could make her, which she did take by continued attendance on her Majesty's most precious person."[3]

Jenkins wrote in the first sentence of this paragraph that smallpox left the queen's face "without permanent blemishes." In previous paragraphs we learned about the attack of smallpox and the doctor's treatment of the queen. Now in this paragraph we turn to the effects of the disease. The key word in the first sentences is *blemishes*. Jenkins develops the thought not by repeating the word itself but by passing on to the sad case of "Lady Mary Sidney, who took the disease and suffered the horrible *disfigurement* Elizabeth had so much dreaded." *Disfigurement* is a synonym for *blemishes*, and by it we are given to understand that Lady Mary was left with the deep red scars on her face that smallpox often left on its victims when it did not kill them. The last sentence in the paragraph is a report of the comment Lady Mary's husband made when he saw this disfigurement.

Jenkins's paragraph needs no general topic sentence. A summary sentence would be in the way. But the sentences that follow the first sentence are built on a thought contained in it, and no reader has any trouble seeing the unity of the paragraph itself.

All good paragraphs show a similar development. The first sentence presents several thoughts. The second picks up the one the

[3] Elizabeth Jenkins, *Elizabeth the Great* (New York: Coward-McCann, 1959; New York: Pocket Books, 1960), 105.

author wishes to develop and goes on. Quite often student writers let
their paragraphs go slack because they forget to carry that development
from the first sentence through all the other sentences in the
paragraph. They write in a kind of shorthand that leaves out some
necessary thoughts. Feeling that something is left out, readers must
leap from sentence to sentence like agile children jumping from steppingstone to steppingstone over a stream. What readers want—and what
you should provide—is a smooth bridge that will carry them to their
destination without causing unnecessary strain. The most frequent
cause of unnecessary strain within a paragraph is the lack of development from sentence to sentence. Always look to see if your sentences in
a paragraph pick up an idea mentioned in a previous sentence and
develop that idea. If you look at a sentence and discover that you cannot
find mention of any of its ideas in a previous sentence in the paragraph,
you probably have a disorderly paragraph.

Sometimes paragraphs begin with a broad, general statement in the
first sentence, then follow it with a second sentence that limits the
general statement. The rest of the paragraph builds on the second,
limiting sentence. Most textbooks would call that second sentence the
topic sentence since it expresses the idea developed by the rest of the
paragraph. But it seems far more sensible to think of the first sentence
as setting the stage for the rest. When you read such paragraphs, you
can easily imagine the writer setting down that first sentence, then com-
mitting himself to developing the most important thought he finds in it.
Here is such a paragraph:

> Erosion of America's farmland by wind and water has been a problem
> since settlers first broke the virgin prairies and grasslands in the 19th cen-
> tury. A mainly invisible menace, erosion forced itself into the national
> conscience in the dust bowl days of the 1930s, when dry winds lifted the
> red, drought-stricken soil of Texas and Oklahoma in huge rolling clouds
> and deposited it hundreds of miles away. In a few years, wind and water
> erosion damaged 282 million acres of American farmland. The abandon-
> ment of the land by thousands of farmers driven into bankruptcy left
> fields untended and ever more susceptible.[4]

The first sentence introduces the general topic of erosion in
America, making a statement as to how long erosion has been a problem. The next sentence repeats the word *erosion* and grows naturally

[4] James Risser, "A Renewed Threat of Soil Erosion: It's Worse than the Dust Bowl,"
Smithsonian, March 1981, 122.

out of the first. But the second sentence is much more limited than the first, narrowing attention to the erosion in the great American dust bowl in the 1930s. The rest of the paragraph dwells on the crisis of the dust bowl during the terrible years of the Great Depression, when half the American continent seemed ready to blow away.

This kind of paragraph occurs often in professional writing. The first sentence provides a general introduction; the second limits the thought of the first, and the rest of the paragraph builds on the second sentence. *That second, limiting sentence must depend on some idea expressed in the first sentence.*

UNITY AND DISUNITY IN A PARAGRAPH

Disunity in paragraphs usually occurs because the sentences do not flow naturally from the first sentence. Writers fall into disunity when they are not sure what they want to say or when they have lost track of what they have said already. Sometimes they write a first sentence, take a long time to write the second, and in the interval forget what they have said in the first. If you have trouble with paragraph unity, check your first sentence carefully. See what ideas it contains. Then see if your next sentence takes up one of those ideas and develops it.

You can often check the unity of your paragraphs by seeing what happens when you leave out one of the sentences you have written. This is especially true in paragraphs that argue, explain, or narrate. In such paragraphs a second sentence usually develops a thought mentioned in the first sentence, and then a third sentence develops a thought expressed in the second sentence, and so on. To remove a sentence usually disrupts the flow that marks a unified paragraph. Here, for example, is an explanatory paragraph from David Attenborough's book *Life on Earth*:

> The marine iguanas follow a daily routine that maintains their bodies at the most efficient temperature. At dawn they assemble on the tops of lava ridges or clamber onto the eastern faces of boulders, lying with their flanks broadside to the riding sun and absorbing as much heat as possible. Within an hour or so their temperature reaches its optimum level, and they turn to face the sun. Now their flanks are almost in shadow, and the rays strike only their chests. As the sun climbs higher and higher, the risk of overheating grows. Although reptile skin has the crucial quality of relative impermeability, it does not possess sweat glands, so the iguanas

cannot cool themselves by allowing sweat to evaporate. Indeed even if they could, this might not be a practical technique in an environment where water is scarce. But they have to find some way of preventing themselves from simmering inside their skins.[5]

This paragraph moves smoothly from one sentence to another, and it would be quite difficult to remove any sentence and keep the paragraph harmonious. Everything after a removed sentence would seem out of order. You might take out the sentence, "As the sun climbs higher and higher, the risk of overheating grows." But then you would lose the transition from the daily routine of the iguanas to the danger of the central problem, that of their inability to sweat. When you have trouble with paragraph unity, see if you can leave a sentence out without damaging the whole. If you can, you may need to work some more on the paragraph.

You cannot always test paragraph unity by leaving out a sentence. Some paragraphs make a general statement in the first sentence and follow it with a list of statements that support the generalization. You can sometimes change the list around or even leave part of it out, and the paragraph will still hold together. Here is a paragraph from *Time* dealing with problems in Nigeria:

In a continent of nations still suffering 25 years later from the pains of birth and persistent poverty, Nigeria has a special significance. Its population, estimated at 90 million, is greater than that of any country in Western Europe. One of every five or six Africans is a Nigerian. Because of its oil resources, which have made it the third largest supplier of petrolem to the U.S. (after Mexico and Britain), Nigeria is the wealthiest nation in black Africa, with a gross national product that is more than half as large as that of the other black African nations combined. Unlike many other African countries, it has a sizable class of educated men and women who are well trained to run its government, industry and armed forces. And notwithstanding the occasional clampdowns imposed by the military, Nigeria has had a tradition of boisterous free speech, free-wheeling politics and an unbridled press.[6]

You could leave out the sentence "One of every five or six Africans is a Nigerian," and the paragraph would make perfect sense. You can rearrange the order of the sentences without doing great damage to the

[5] David Attenborough, *Life on Earth* (Boston: Little, Brown, 1979), 152.
[6] "The Light that Failed," *Time*, Jan. 16, 1984, 24.

meaning, though if you follow the sentences through carefully you can detect a rational development. Descriptive paragraphs have many of the qualities of lists. You can change the order of the sentences or leave some sentences out altogether, and you will not disturb the thought or the unity of the paragraph.

Sometimes paragraphs organize material in clumps of sentences that follow the first sentence. The sentences in each clump are closely related to each other. But the clumps themselves may be rearranged or even eliminated from the paragraph without disturbing the harmony of the whole. (In a good paragraph, the elimination of a clump of sentences would reduce the richness and dilute the thought.)

Here is a paragraph organized in clumps of sentences broken down in a schematic way. The paragraph comes from William Manchester's survey of American history from 1932 to 1972, *The Glory and the Dream*, and it describes the space journey of John Glenn, the first American astronaut to orbit the earth:

The temperature in the capsule had risen to 108 degrees, he noted, but the air-conditioning in his suit kept him cool.

He had been instructed to explain his every sensation—the audience, after all, was paying for the trip—and he began by reporting that he had no feeling of speed. It was "about the same as flying in an airliner at, say, 30,000 feet, and looking down at clouds from 10,000 feet."

Over the Atlantic he spotted the Gulf Stream, a river of blue in the gray sea.

Over the West Coast he made out California's Salton Sea and the Imperial Valley, and he could pick out the irrigation canals near El Centro, where he had once lived.

His first twilight was awesome: "As the sun goes down it's very white, brilliant light, and as it goes below the horizon you get a very bright orange color. Down close to the surface it pales out into a sort of blue, a darker blue, and then off into black."

The stars were spectacular. "If you've been out on the desert on a very clear, brilliant night when there's no moon and the stars just seem to jump out at you, that's just about the way they look."

Approaching Australia he radioed, "Just to my right I can see a big pattern of light, apparently right on the coast." From a tracking station below, Astronaut Gordon Cooper explained to him that this was the Australian city of Perth. Its 82,000 inhabitants had turned on all their light switches, to welcome him and test his night vision. Glenn replied, "Thank everybody for turning them on, will you?"[7]

The clumps of sentences in the preceding paragraph are arranged chronologically. You could leave any clump out without substantially damaging the unity of what is left. You could even rearrange some of the clumps without making readers feel that they had lost anything.

We can summarize paragraphs with a couple of diagrams:

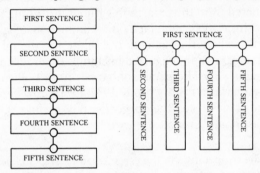

Some more complicated variations are of course possible, but these two are the fundamental forms of paragraph organization.

TRANSITIONS BETWEEN PARAGRAPHS

Paragraphs should not only hold together within; they should also allow smooth passage from one paragraph to the next. To ensure this smooth flow, pay attention to the transitions within your paragraphs. Transitions are words or phrases that look backward, tying the paragraph to what has come before, and look forward, binding the first sentence of your paragraph to what comes afterward. Good transitions make life easier on readers; they also help writers with their own thinking, for they set up relations within a piece of prose that are essential to its shape and unity.

You will use two kinds of transitions. The more obvious and somewhat clumsy are the clear, transitional words that tell your reader in no uncertain terms that you are moving from one idea in your paper to another. Words like *therefore, however, moreover, furthermore, nevertheless,*

---

[7] William Manchester, *The Glory and the Dream* (Boston: Little, Brown, 1974), 931.

and many others say to your reader, "Give me your hand; we are about to make a leap from one paragraph to the next."

Sometimes we must use these unambiguous transitions. But when we start to use one, we should hesitate just long enough to see if we can avoid doing so. They are careful words, plodding words, words that leap quickly to mind when we are stuck. When we use them too frequently to hold an essay together, they leave the rivets in our writing showing.

We can easily become addicted to such transitions. They help us smooth out rough prose. But the best transitions do the job without calling attention to themselves. Here as always you should study the work of professional writers to check my advice. You can go for pages and pages without seeing a *thus* or a *therefore* in the pages of *The New Yorker, Popular Mechanics,* or *Sports Illustrated.* In a good, lively book on a serious topic, you will seldom find such words. You don't see the rivets in such essays; you see paragraphs smoothly welded together so that you are not troubled by lumps and cracks.

One good device in making transitions is to use a word in the last sentence of one paragraph that you repeat in the first sentence of the next paragraph. Look at the following example from Edward Abbey's *Desert Solitaire.* Abbey is describing the arid country of Utah, where he spent a summer as a National Park ranger:

> And whenever it rains in this land of unclothed rock the run-off is rapid down cliff and dome through the canyons to the Colorado.
> Sometimes it rains and still fails to moisten the desert—the falling water evaporates halfway down between cloud and earth.[8]

The transitional word is *rains,* mentioned in the last sentence of one paragraph and repeated in the first sentence of the next.

Now in the following example we have a pronoun, mentioned in the last sentence of one paragraph and repeated in the first sentence of the next, serving as the transitional element:

> *He* would at times lose control of the battle, allowing generals to make mistakes *he* could not correct.
> Now *he* waited for the sun to dry the rain-damp ground.[9]

Sometimes a noun in the last sentence of a paragraph will be represented by a pronoun in the first or second sentence of the next:

[8] Edward Abbey, *Desert Solitaire* (New York: McGraw-Hill, 1968; New York: Ballantine Books, 1977), 130.

[9] John J. Putnam, "Napoleon," *National Geographic,* February 1982, 181.

Eskimos ticked to a different kind of clock, the chief driller said, and so there were all sorts of bad feelings.

Whaling season was the worst. In spring and fall, *they* would just up and take off for Barrow or Point Hope.[10]

You can often make a good transition by using an adverb in the first sentence of a paragraph that identifies the action of that sentence with something said in the previous paragraph. The adverb serves as a pivot to carry the flow of the narrative from the previous paragraph to a slightly different place in the writer's thought. The following paragraphs are about Henry James's return to America from Europe in 1904:

American architecture regularly disappointed him. The many-windowed skyscrapers of New York appalled him with their vulgarity and sameness, and the great new Boston Library, which houses the "so brave decorative designs" of Abbey and Sargent which he had watched develop in London, was—apart from a splendid staircase—"mere chambers of familiarity and resonance." Still, he rationalized weakly, the decorated public places in Italy served the "graceful common life," and "Was it not splendid . . . to see in Boston, such large provisions made for the amusement of children on rainy afternoons?"

After Boston, New York, and Philadelphia, James was the guest of Henry Adams in his house on Lafayette Square in Washington.[11]

The adverbial phrase beginning with *After* moves the action from Boston to Washington and helps the reader get easily from one place to another in the text.

No book can show all the possible transitions in good writing. But with what you have learned in this chapter, you should be able to study the paragraphs in a magazine or book you enjoy and see how the transitions work. An excellent exercise is to locate the transitions that bind paragraphs together in something you have enjoyed reading. You will see that every transition looks back to something that has been mentioned before and looks forward to a thought about to be developed. In all good writing, the key element in transitions is the repetition of a word, a phrase, or a thought, and good writers seldom use the mechanical transitional words like *thus, therefore, moreover, furthermore,* and *however.* Well-constructed paragraphs usually do not require these rivets. Learn to connect your paragraphs without them.

[10] Joe McGinnis, *Going to Extremes* (New York: Alfred A. Knopf, 1980), 55.

[11] Stanley Weintraub, *London Yankees* (New York: Harcourt Brace Jovanovich, 1979), 129–130.

THE LENGTH OF A PARAGRAPH

How long should a paragraph be? No single answer exists to that question. Journalists break their paragraphs every couple of sentences. Newspapers and magazines are often printed in narrow columns, and copy editors indent frequently to break up the long lines of type. In academic writing paragraphs may run on for a page or more. In student papers, I like to see about two indentations on each page of typewritten copy. My experience tells me that when inexperienced writers run on and on without an indentation, their thoughts may be rambling or fuzzy.

No sure rule can guide us. Some long paragraphs are just right; some short ones are incoherent. The flow of one sentence into another makes a better measure of the unity of a paper than does the length of its paragraphs. If you make your sentences develop ideas one after the other, you may indent almost at will. I sometimes look at a page in my own writing and decide that I want to divide a paragraph that has become too long for my taste. I can almost always find a place to make a new indentation.

Whatever the length of your paragraphs, observe the first-sentence rule: make your first sentence the introduction. Take one of the thoughts from it, and develop that thought in the next sentence — and then choose whether you want to make the third sentence develop a thought in the second sentence or whether you want to make the third sentence refer to something you said in the first sentence. Always keep in mind that an essay develops thoughts. Nearly every sentence in a good essay looks backward and forward. Something in the sentence refers to some word or thought you have previously mentioned; something in the sentence — some word or thought — will be mentioned in a sentence to come.

CONCLUDING REMARKS ON PARAGRAPHS

If you have trouble with paragraphs, your first attempts at building paragraph unity will require much effort on your part. But as you get the hang of analyzing your own sentences, the going will be easier. Writing can be like dancing: learning the first new steps requires concentration, and you will almost certainly step on your partner's feet or else — in more modern dancing — collide with somebody on the floor.

But suddenly it comes, and you will keep time to the music with your feet as if you were born to do so. When you write, pay attention to how your sentences develop thoughts previously mentioned and how they reach to thoughts you will mention later on.

And to repeat a previous piece of advice: cram your head with knowledge of the subject you are going to write about. You must know something if you are to develop thoughts. Write your first draft as quickly as you can. When you keep your pen — or, preferably, your typewriter or word processor — going, paragraphs come naturally. Slow, laborious writing of a first draft often makes your paragraphs sprawl all over the place without shape or unity. The rapid writing students do nearly always shows a natural unity, and once you create that natural unity in your paragraphs, you can shape them to carry your essay smoothly along.

FIVE

Writing
Sentences

Sentences make statements or ask questions. We learn to make sentences naturally when we learn to talk because we have to make statements if we are to be understood by members of the community where we live. Although some people imagine that they do not speak in complete sentences, we in fact nearly always do unless we are answering a question or adding information to a sentence we have already made. To say that a sentence is complete is only to say that it makes a comprehensible statement.

Most sentences make their comprehensible statements by naming a subject and by making a statement about that subject. Clauses, phrases, and other kinds of modifiers may amplify the basic statement just as harmonies may amplify the theme of a melody. Everything in the sentence should serve the basic, central statement. When you write a sentence, you should know exactly what that basic statement is. Are you telling how somebody acts? Are you explaining that something exists in a certain way? Are you saying that something happens? If you do get confused with one of your sentences, stop and ask yourself what is the most important statement you are trying to make in that sentence. Name the subject, and as simply as you can, tell what you want to say about it. Once you have arrived at that thought, revise the sentence so that it clearly conveys what you want to say.

Sentences like this one are common in the first drafts of most writers:

> Since the Japanese, a people whose artistic care for the common things of the daily life has always excited Americans, live crowded together on their small islands, they have been forced to construct social customs to help them endure living so close together, which are the basis for much of their art, including their love of miniaturization.

This sentence gets lost in its own words. In the second draft the

65

writer should decide what the main statement of the sentence should be. It would probably be something like this:

> The Japanese have made art out of the necessity of living close together in their crowded islands.

A writer can then do several things with this core statement. She can add some elements:

> The Japanese, whose artistic care for the common things of the daily life excites Americans, have made art out of the necessity of living close together on their crowded islands — an art that includes social customs and miniaturization.

I find that version a little cumbersome, and I prefer to break up the first-draft sentence into several statements, all of them closely related to each other:

> The Japanese have made art out of the necessity of living together on their crowded islands. Part of that art has been a set of social customs that provide careful forms for the daily life. Another part has been miniaturization. Americans have always been fascinated by Japanese art — probably because its dedication to the small is so different from their own.

You can play with these examples yourself and see many different possibilities. You will notice that as you clarify your main statements in your sentences, you will add some thoughts and delete others. Your mind is rearranging the material, both simplifying it and filling it out.

Always when you write a sentence, force yourself to make a simple, main statement. What is happening? Who is acting? Who is receiving the action? Be sure that statement forms the heart of the sentence. Don't write sentences in which several equally important statements are competing for attention. Give each of your statements a separate sentence. Don't confuse your readers by trying to pack too many important statements in a single sentence. Brevity in writing is splendid as long as you do not try to condense things so much that nobody can follow your thought.

English sentences make three kinds of statements. A sentence may tell us that the subject does something:

1. *Mr. Pinkerton* crashed through the glass door.

The subject is *Mr. Pinkerton.* In this sentence the subject has acted, an action shown by the active verb *crashed.*

2. *He* was baffled, angry, and bleeding.

The subject of this sentence is the pronoun *He,* and the sentence describes a condition.

3. He *had been cut* in the face by flying glass.

Again the subject is *He,* but now the subject is joined to a passive verb phrase, *had been cut.* Something is done to the subject. Sentence 1 answers the question "What did the subject do?" Sentence 2 answers the question "In what condition was the subject?" Sentence 3 answers the question "What was done to the subject?"

WRITING GOOD SENTENCES

Here are some principles of writing good sentences. Study them, and put them into practice.

1. *The strongest sentences are usually those in which the subject does something.*

We say that sentences in which the verb acts (or the verbs such sentences contain) are in the active voice; that is, the subject acts through the verb. In a sentence in the passive voice, something is done to the subject. Although the passive is a good and necessary part of the English language, if you use it too much, you will deaden your style.

We seldom use the passive when we speak. We don't say, "Jack's car was driven into the reservoir Saturday night." We say, "Jack drove his car into the reservoir Saturday night." We want to know who does things. The passive does not tell us who is responsible for the act a sentence reports. That is why so many government publications use the passive — the passive voice evades responsibility. We read something like this:

An oversupply of ten thousand blackboard erasers was ordered for the city school system.

We learn that the city school system now has enough erasers to last five hundred years. But who ordered them? The passive permits the writer to avoid saying that the brother of the school superintendent was in the school supplies business and nearly bankrupt, and the superintendent decided to help him out by placing a big order. The passive voice does not tell us who ordered the erasers; it makes the whole thing sound like a misprint on somebody's computer.

Inexperienced writers often use the passive because they think it sounds impressive. But the passive nearly always sounds impersonal, voiceless.

> It has often been noted that writing is important.

> It has long been recognized that life is short.

> Minor characters in Shakespeare's plays have often been studied.

But who has studied the minor characters in Shakespeare's plays? Unless you tell us, we may think you have nothing to say and are simply trying to fill up space.

Use the passive when you have a clear need for it. If the recipient of the action in your sentence is the most important part of the statement, use the passive:

> In the United States, a president is elected every four years.

> My Uncle Mike was hit by a bicycle as he left the saloon Saturday night.

> The Mona Lisa was once stolen from the Louvre.

Probably the most common use of the passive arises in paragraphs that make a series of statements about a person or an object. The writer wishes to keep attention fixed on one spot. To do so, he may use the passive as Robert Caro does in this paragraph from his biography of Lyndon Johnson. Caro describes Johnson's first congressional campaign in Texas:

> These speeches *were* generally *delivered* on Saturday: traditionally, rural campaigning in Texas *was* largely *restricted* to Saturdays, the day on which farmers and their wives came into town to shop, and *could be addressed* in groups. On Saturdays two automobiles, Johnson's brown Pontiac and Bill Deason's wired-for-sound gray Chevy, would head out of Austin for a swing through several large towns. On the outskirts of each town, Johnson would get out of the Pontiac ("He thought it looked a little too elaborate for a man running for Congress," Keach says) and walk into the town, while the Chevy would pull into the square, and Deason or some

other aide would use the loudspeaker to urge voters to "Come see Lyndon Johnson, your next Congressman," and to "Come hear Lyndon Johnson speak at the square"; to drum up enthusiasm, records *would be played* over the loudspeaker.[1]

The passive verb phrases—italicized in this paragraph—allow Caro to keep his focus. Now and then, as in the first sentence, he might have changed to the active: "Johnson generally delivered these speeches on Saturdays," but Caro probably supposed he was repeating Johnson's name too often in his book (it is a huge book) and shifted here into the passive to give his readers some relief.

Try to use the active whenever you can. When you do use the passive, have a clear reason for doing so. The active voice should be your normal way of writing a sentence.

2. *Whenever possible, make your verbs assert action rather than tell a condition.*

You can say this:

> It would appear that voters in Massachusetts are in favor of capital punishment, at least for convicted murderers, given the results of yesterday's referendum on the subject.

Or you can say this:

> In yesterday's referendum, Massachusetts voters approved capital punishment for convicted murderers by almost two to one.

Stating the action gives you a more vivid sentence. It also usually helps you to make a statement in fewer words.

A form of the verb *to be* often states a condition. Look for the overuse of *to be* verbs, and see if you can make sentences using them more vivid by changing to active verbs. You can say this:

> Massachusetts voters *are* in favor of capital punishment.

But it is more vivid to say this:

> Massachusetts voters *favor* capital punishment.

[1] Robert A. Caro, *The Years of Lyndon Johnson: The Path to Power* (New York: Alfred A. Knopf, 1982), 413.

You can say this:

> Many Americans *are* of the opinion that foreign cars are more durable than American cars.

Or you can say this:

> Many Americans *believe* that foreign cars last longer than American cars.

Sometimes you can check your use of *to be* verbs—*is, am, are, was, were*—by circling them on a page. If you have a lot of them, you will see a lot of circles, and you can rethink some of those sentences. Don't be a fanatic about it; *to be* verbs are part of the language, and you must use them sometimes, but too many of them will make your prose dull.

> 3. *Be sure that everything in your sentence supports your core statement. Don't digress in the middle of a sentence.*

Sometimes inexperienced writers throw needless information into a sentence to show how much they know or because the information is interesting, and they want to share it whether it has anything to do with their main point or not.

Remember that you should gather much more information while you prepare to write than you can use once you start writing. You should always have so much knowledge of your subject that you must cut out some interesting things. So don't write a sentence like this:

> Napoleon Bonaparte, who some people now think may have been poisoned when he was in exile on St. Helena Island, invaded Russia on June 21, 1812.

If you are writing an essay about Napoleon's campaign in Russia, stick to that point. The theory that Napoleon died by poisoning may have turned up in your research, but leave it out when it becomes a digression from your main point.

As I have said earlier, digressions in a first draft may be not only harmless but useful. Such a digression may lead you to a subject much more interesting than the one you had in mind when you started writing. Digressions in first drafts can be creative and wonderful, but once you have firmly decided on the topic you will discuss in your essay, stick to that subject. Make all your sentences support it. Be sure every sentence has a clear main statement and every part of the sentence helps make that statement.

4. *Combine thoughts when you can to give your sentences a sense of pace, and build to keep your readers aware of where you are taking them.*

Now and then we all read choppy sentences, and sometimes we write them, especially in our notes, when we are gathering information for an essay. Choppy sentences trouble us not because they are short but because they give us a sense of unnecessary stopping and starting and, sometimes, the feeling that the writer cannot tell the difference between the more important thoughts and the less important thoughts in a piece of prose. Consider these two versions of the same thoughts:

> The soldiers had a year in Vietnam. Sometimes they had a little less. Over and over they counted each day gone. They counted all the days left to get through. They counted all the time. They told you fifty days were left. They told you ten days were left. They told you three days were left. The army counted everything else. The army insisted that all things be counted. The numbers meant nothing. But still the counting kept on.

Where are we going in these sentences? They bore us with their repetition, and we may lose the point very quickly, especially if we must read page after page of sentences like these. But look at what careful combination can do:

> The soldiers had a year in Vietnam, sometimes a little less. Over and over they counted each day gone and all the days left to get through. They counted all the time and told you fifty days were left, ten days, three days. The army counted everything else, insisted that all things be counted, until the numbers meant nothing—but still the counting kept on.[2]

Now you can break these sentences down into a few core statements that help order every thought in the group:

1. The soldiers had a year in Vietnam.
2. They counted each day.
3. They counted all the time.
4. The army counted everything else.

---

[2] Gloria Emerson, *Winners and Losers* (New York: Random House, 1976), 65.

Gloria Emerson, author of this piece, reduced her thoughts to two distinct subjects, the soldiers and the army. She combined several actions taken by the soldiers—the actions of counting—and by way of contrast threw in the simple, final statement about the army. When you express different actions done by the same subject, you can often combine thoughts to make one active sentence instead of several choppy ones.

5. Avoid the proliferation of dependent clauses in a sentence.

Dependent clauses help us write with a mature style. All good writers use them to amplify thought in a sentence:

> *After he had done all his Christmas shopping for the many people who expected presents from him,* he bought a large gift for himself, wrapped it up, put it under the tree, and told visitors *that it was from his best friend.*

The italicized words in this sentence represent three dependent clauses. The first, beginning with *After,* is an adverbial clause modifying the verbs *bought, wrapped, put,* and *told* in the independent clause. That adverbial clause includes an adjectival clause, *who expected presents from him,* which modifies the noun *people.* The final dependent clause, *that it was from his best friend,* is a noun clause, the direct object of the verb *told.* So this sentence has one example of each of the three general classes of dependent clause.

Dependent clauses can clutter your thought if you try to stuff too many of them into a sentence. Don't put a dependent clause into every sentence you write. One dependent clause in a sentence rarely makes trouble—so long as you don't have a dependent clause in every sentence. When you put two dependent clauses in a sentence, a warning flag should be raised in your mind. When you have three, that flag should start waving back and forth, and you should reexamine the sentence to see if you can simplify it. Now and then it is perfectly all right to have three dependent clauses in a sentence. But don't let such practice become a writing habit.

This sentence gives us no trouble:

> American coin collectors eagerly gather pennies, although the value of the penny is sometimes less than the copper that goes into making it.

But this one begins to lose its focus:

> American coin collectors, who are not a completely rational group, eagerly gather pennies, although the value of the penny is sometimes less than the copper that goes into making it.

And this one begins to get confusing:

> American coin collectors, who are not a completely rational group, eagerly gather pennies, although the value of the penny is sometimes less than the copper, which fluctuates wildly in price, which goes into it.

In the rush of doing a first draft, you may produce many over-crowded sentences in which the main ideas get confused with a lot of subordinate related thoughts stirring around in your head. When you revise, pull out distracting dependent clauses. Make them into sentences of their own, or eliminate them altogether.

Like so many of the other rules in this book, this one is observed with wide variations among different writers. Weekly news magazines have developed a startling ability to keep dependent clauses to a minimum. They substitute various kinds of phrases for the clauses, and they arrange sentences so that dependent clauses are infrequent. This style lends itself to swift reading and ready absorption. You can make your own survey, but here are the results of one that I made myself. Each digit below represents a sentence. The number itself refers to the dependent clauses in that sentence. The digit 0 indicates no dependent clauses; the digit 1 indicates one dependent clause, and so on.

A long article in *Newsweek* on child abuse:

$$2,0,0,1,0,0,0,2,0,0,0,3,2,0,1,2,1,1,1,1,1,0,0.$$

A long article in *U.S. News and World Report* on cosmetic surgery:

$$0,0,0,0,0,0,0,0,0,0,0,2,1,2,1,1,0.$$

A movie review by Pauline Kael in *The New Yorker*:

$$0,0,2,1,0,0,0,2,1,1,0,3,0,2,0,0,0,0,1,0,0,0,0,1.$$

I chose these articles at random, and they do not prove much by themselves. I began at the first sentence in each article and checked the dependent clauses in successive sentences, counting as two sentences any two independent clauses joined by a semicolon.

You would expect popular journalism to be more streamlined than writing intended for a specialized audience. A serious book intended for serious readers may have a larger percentage of dependent clauses in its sentences.

Here is a reading of a passage chosen at random from the first volume of Robert Caro's biography of Lyndon Johnson:

0,1,0,3,0,1,0,3,1,0,2,1,0,2,1.

It contains two sentences with three dependent clauses, two sentences with two dependent clauses, five sentences with one dependent clause, and six sentences with no dependent clause. Caro instinctively places his more complicated sentences next to fairly simple sentences. For example, the first sentence with three dependent clauses is bracketed by two sentences with no dependent clauses.

A random paragraph chosen from Richard Ellmann's biography of James Joyce shows the following pattern of dependent clauses in sentences:

0,0,2,0,0,2,0,0,2,0,0,0,0,0,0,1,1.

You can see that Ellmann uses a smaller ratio of dependent clauses to sentences than Caro does. In fact, Ellmann is close to the ratio used by most journalists.

It is usually (but not always) a bad idea to make a dependent clause modify something in another dependent clause. Avoid constructions like the following:

> The auto-parts company that went bankrupt last year because high interest rates made its business fall off is trying to pay its debts.

The adverbial dependent clause *because high interest rates made its business fall off* modifies the verb *went* in the dependent clause *that went bankrupt last year.* This piling on of dependent clauses removes attention from the core statement of the sentence, which is that the auto-parts company is trying to pay its debts. Too many sentences with dependent clauses modifying elements in other dependent clauses will suffocate your prose.

6. Begin most sentences with the subject.

The normal pattern for sentences is *subject + predicate.* Experienced writers follow this pattern. Look through a copy of almost any book or magazine, and you will discover that two-thirds or more of the sentences begin with the subject. In a recent column of prose chosen at random from *National Geographic,* I discovered that fourteen of twenty-two independent clauses began with the subject. In a column and half chosen at random from *Sports Illustrated,* nineteen of twenty-eight independent clauses began with the subject.

The normal pattern of speech is to declare a subject and make a statement about it. Writing should usually do the same. When we read one sentence after another that does not begin with the subject, we sense that the writer is straining for effect, and we become uncomfortable. We begin to wonder how the writer will begin the next sentence; we should be asking ourselves what she is going to say.

7. *When you do not begin a sentence with the subject, you should usually open with some form of adverb — a word, a phrase, or a clause.*

In most English prose, about a fourth of the sentences begin with adverbs.

> *One day, when the hunters were absent,* a band of armed Indians blocked the wagon, and apparently wanted payment of some kind for the privilege of crossing their country.[3]

> *Surely,* music (along with ordinary language) is as profound a problem for human biology as can be thought of, and I would like to see something done about it.[4]

> *Because smallpox and measles are especially spectacular when they attack virgin populations, and because plague remained spectacular in its incidence always,* these diseases almost monopolize literary references in those cases when it is possible to surmise what infection caused some sudden and large-scale die-off.[5]

8. *In general, avoid participial sentence openers.*

A participial opener is built around a participial form of a verb and used as an adjective to modify the subject of the sentence to follow. Occasionally professional writers use participial openings to compress information:

[3] Dee Brown, *The Westerners* (New York: Holt, Rinehart & Winston, 1974), 127.

[4] Lewis Thomas, *Late Night Thoughts on Listening to Mahler's Ninth Symphony* (New York: Viking, 1983), 79.

[5] William H. McNeill, *Plagues and Peoples* (New York: Doubleday, Anchor Books, 1976), 144.

Riven by tribal factionalism since independence, Nigeria established a deliberate policy aimed at breaking down old tribal hostilities.[6]

A participial opener allows a writer to invert a sentence, putting the subject after the verb, to obtain a pleasing variety:

> *Standing uninvolved for the moment but nevertheless carefully observing these practices* was the young Providence pitcher Monte Ward, who, before his time was out, would do much to revolutionize the whole player-owner relationship.[7]

Again and again studies of professional writing have shown that participial openers are rare. They make prose unnatural. We rarely use them when we speak. We don't say, "Having been out in the cold wind all day, I'm stiff and nearly dead." We say something like this: "I've been out in the cold all day, and I'm nearly dead."

Participial openers should always modify the grammatical subject. Otherwise we get confusing sentences like this one:

> Aged in barrels for five years, he discovered that the wine had a pleasant, woody taste.

The most common misplacing of a participial opener occurs in constructions like the following:

> Flying every week between Boston and New York, it was hard for her to maintain her fear of airplanes.

A careful writer would say this:

> She could hardly maintain her fear of airplanes since she flew every week between Boston and New York.

9. *In general, try to avoid beginning sentences with* There is, There are, There were, *and* There was.

These openers can be useful, and we all use them sometimes. But they can substitute vague description for action. Not:

> There were several reasons he refused to smoke.

---

[6] "A Continent Gone Wrong," *Time,* Jan. 16, 1984, 29.

[7] Robert W. Creamer, "First Inning: 1876-1901," in *The Ultimate Baseball Book,* ed. Daniel Okrent and Harris Lewine (Boston: Houghton Mifflin, 1981), 14-15.

But:

> He refused to smoke because he feared cancer, his wife and children objected to the smell, and he remembered how he nearly died once by catching his bed on fire with a lighted cigar.

10. Be economical with adjectives.

Adjectives are vital to good writing because they add qualities to nouns and pronouns. We cannot do without them. But we should use them only when they are necessary. Too many of them can clog our prose and blur the core statement we are trying to make in a sentence.

Here are paragraphs from two good nonfiction writers. See how few adjectives they use. Notice how the core statements in the sentences stand out clear and sharp:

> Through the *first* snowfall, Beverly's father held *firm*. But when the river froze up, he relented to an extent. He still would not help them find jobs, but he did let them known that there was an *old* house *available* at the edge of the river downtown. He was, of course, convinced that winter would drive the "hippies" away. But he figured he would just as soon see it happen without also seeing his daughter freeze to death.[8]

> They had been together for years and assumed they would remain together until the end of their enlistments. Sergeant Sullivan's death shattered that assumption. It upset the sense of unity and stability that had pervaded life in the battalion. One-Three was a corps in the *old* sense of the word, a body, and Sullivan's death represented the amputation of a *small* part of it. The corps would go on living and functioning without him, but it was *aware* of having lost something *irreplaceable*. Later in the war, that sort of feeling became *rarer* in *infantry* battalions. Men were killed, evacuated with wounds, or rotated home at a *constant* rate, then replaced by *other* men who were killed, evacuated, or rotated in their turn. By that time, a loss only meant a gap in the line that needed filling.[9]

11. Don't use nouns as adjectives.

Much supposedly official language from bureaucracies groans under the tyranny of nouns pretending to be adjectives. Proper nouns can sometimes serve as adjectives. You can talk about the *Gettysburg* Address, the *Marshall* Plan, or the *Bowery* Bank. Some words have the

---

[8] Joe McGinnis, *Going to Extremes* (New York: Alfred A. Knopf, 1980), 146.
[9] Philip Caputo, *A Rumor of War* (New York: Holt, Rinehart & Winston, 1977), 163.

same form whether they are nouns or adjectives, such as *volunteer,*
deputy, savage, poor, and many others. But most common
nouns—especially those ending in *tion, sion, ism,* and *ness*—seldom do
well as adjectives.

A careful writer will avoid constructions like the following:

> They worked hard in skills acquisitions.
> She was expert in writing improvement practices.
> He was a jaded secretary retraining expert.
> The reporters learned scrutiny thoroughness.

These sentences sound much better when they are revised using
idiomatic English:

> They worked hard to acquire skills.
> She was an expert at improving writing.
> He helped retrain secretaries who had become jaded at their work.
> The reporters learned to be thorough.

12. Avoid long strings of prepositional phrases.

Prepositional phrases make nouns act as adjectives and adverbs, and
they add vigor and grace to prose. But beware of tying long strings of them
together. A sentence like this one makes your main statement fuzzy:

> The cemetery on the hill with the church near the woods of thickly grow-
> ing oaks with tall branches against the sky was a quiet place.

A sentence like this does well in a first draft. You are visualizing the
details of a scene. In your later drafts you should revise such sentences
so you will not smother your core statement.

13. For sentence variety, occasionally use free modifiers and absolutes.

A free modifier is usually a participial phrase that is placed at the end
of a sentence and modifies a subject. Free modifiers can often replace
dependent clauses. The free modifiers in these sentences are in italics:

> The house collapsed, *broken by the terrible storm.*
> She raced up the street, *sprinting for the bus.*

You can sometimes place several free modifiers at the end of a sentence. Here is a paragraph from Bruce Catton's book *The Coming Fury*. Catton is describing the preparations to defend Fort Sumter in Charleston harbor at the beginning of the Civil War:

> The soldiers had not yet been called into action, but they were busy, and the materials to force a decision were piling up—in Fort Sumter, and on the mud flats that surrounded it in Charleston harbor. Major Anderson was doing what he could to perfect his defenses, *mounting additional guns on the barbette, making his walls more solid by bricking up embrasures that could not be manned, removing stone flagging from the parade ground so that shells that might be thrown into the fort would bury themselves in the sand before exploding.*[10]

The series of participial phrases in italics carries a sense of simultaneous action that Catton wishes to convey, showing us a busy commander going about the business of protecting his post, doing many things at the same time.

Participial phrases acting as free modifiers may also carry a sense of progression, showing one thing happening after another, leading to a climax:

> Slowly she inched her way up the face of the cliff, *feeling* for holds in the rock, *moving* with infinite care, *balancing* herself delicately step after step, not *daring* to look down, *breathing* hard, *fearing* exhaustion, *going* on, *wallowing* at last onto a shelf of rock and safety at the top.

You can extend a series of free modifiers almost indefinitely because each modifies the same thing—in the preceding example the pronoun *she*.

Absolutes share many qualities and advantages of free modifiers. An absolute phrase includes a noun and a participle and usually modifies the whole clause or sentence in which it appears:

> The police rushed to the scene, [core statement]
> their sirens screaming, [absolute]
> their guns drawn, [absolute]
> their faces twisted with fear. [absolute]

Absolutes are common in modern writing since, like the free modifier, they speed up the pace of prose and lend themselves to describing fast action:

[10] Bruce Catton, *The Coming Fury* (Garden City, N. Y.: Doubleday, 1961), 247.

Then she fled beneath his fist, and he too fled backward as the others fell upon him, swarming, grappling, fumbling, he striking back, his breath hissing with rage and despair.[11]

In this example William Faulkner uses both absolutes and free modifiers, providing a sense of swift, violent action.

14. Occasionally use compound verb phrases for variety.

Compound verbs compress action and quicken the pace of prose. They offer an efficient device to move readers along.

The triple compound verb has become especially common in the modern American style. A single subject controls three verbs:

> From 1600 on, when modern warfare developed in Europe, the German states (even with the rise of Prussia) *spent* fewer years at war than any other nations except Denmark and Sweden, *engaged* in fewer battles, and *suffered* fewer casualties.[12]

> To signify his right to punish, the Prince twice rejected a good price offered by towns to buy immunity from sack. His letters express only a sense of satisfied accomplishment. His raid *had enriched* his company, *reduced* French revenues, and *proved* to any wavering Gascons that service under his banner was rewarding.[13]

> The attack on the Fascist redoubt which had been called off on the previous occasion was to be carried out tonight. I *oiled* my ten Mexican cartridges, *dirtied* my bayonet (the things give your position away if they flash too much), and *packed* up a hunk of bread, three inches of red sausage, and a cigar which my wife had sent from Barcelona and which I had been hoarding for a long time.[14]

15. Use appositives to speed the pace of your sentences.

An appositive is a word or phrase that is written after a noun and renames or otherwise defines the noun. The simplest appositives are single nouns:

[11] William Faulkner, *Light in August* (New York: Random House, 1932), 147.

[12] Kirkpatrick Sale, *Human Scale* (New York: Coward, McCann & Geoghegan, 1980), 129.

[13] Barbara Tuchman, *A Distant Mirror* (New York: Alfred A. Knopf, 1978), 139.

[14] George Orwell, *Homage to Catalonia* (Boston: Beacon, 1955), 86.

His car, a *Chevy,* was not as fast as my Buick.

Sometimes an appositive may be a long phrase:

> An age of faith is almost certain to become an age of quarrels among the faithful. They divide into bitterly hostile sects, *each with its own leader and each hoping for support from one group or another among the infidels.*[15]

The appositive may be a clause set off by dashes:

> On the other hand, the animals that feed on the plants of the reef or on the sessile invertebrates like corals and sponges—prey that can't leave, hide, or run away—can most easily feed during the day, when they can see best.[16]

You can often revise dependent clauses into appositives. A dependent clause:

> Abraham Lincoln, *who was born in 1809,* moved around as a boy and never developed a great attachment to one state.

An appositive:

> Abraham Lincoln, *born in 1809,* moved around as a boy and never developed a great attachment to one state.

16. *When you must write long sentences, balance them with short sentences to give your readers some relief.*

Readers search for the core statement that every sentence should make. The longer the sentence, the more difficult it is to find that core statement. We can all understand this sentence although it is fairly long:

> Although the rain fell hard enough to strip the leaves from the trees, leaving the air thick with the smell of shattered foliage, the drought had been so severe that we still needed water after the storm had passed on up the valley.

If we had several sentences of such length running together on a page, we would have to slow down to absorb all of them. Since readers usually

---

[15] Malcolm Cowley, *And I Worked at the Writer's Trade* (New York: Viking, 1978), 100.

[16] Walter Starck and Alan Anderson, Jr., *The Blue Reef* (New York: Alfred A. Knopf, 1979), 103.

read at a constant pace, they will most likely keep their eyes moving whether they understand what they are reading or not. They look for what they can understand, and they often skip what is hard for them. So when you write one long sentence after another, you are probably not communicating as well as you should. It would be a good idea to follow the long sentence above with a short one, perhaps this:

An inch below the surface, the ground was dry.

No one can make an ironclad rule about the length of sentences. All readability surveys show that short sentences are more readable than long ones. The core statement in short sentences is much easier to find than it is in long sentences. But no one should write short sentences exclusively. They make for a monotonous style. The point is to give your readers a break by providing them with a short sentence that allows them to catch their breath after they have worked to absorb one or two long ones.

CONCLUDING REMARKS ON SENTENCES

You can teach yourself much more about sentences by observing how experienced writers make them. Pay attention especially to writing you like to read. Try to incorporate into your own writing some of the things you observe in books and magazines that you enjoy. Always remember that the main job of the sentence is to make a statement your readers can understand. Be sure that each of your sentences makes that clear statement. You can write foggy sentences in your first draft, but even then you can help yourself by thinking as you write each sentence, "What is the most important thing I want to say here?" You should be able to answer that question with a simple statement, and that statement should be prominent in the sentence that follows.

SIX

Figurative Language

Figurative language is the use of words in any but their literal sense. If I say, "She floated easily on her back in the pool," I am using the verb *floated* in its literal sense. If I say, "She floated easily from person to person at the party and never paid any real attention to anyone," I am using the verb *floated* in a figurative sense. If I say, "The water boiled for tea," I am using the word *boiled* in a literal sense; if I say, "My blood boiled," I am using the same word in a figurative sense. Figurative language engages the experience of readers, calling up fragments of their memories and making them imagine the things the writer wants them to see. Figurative language often helps readers remember what they have read.

Figurative language must do three things. It must draw on some common experience that binds a writer to her audience; it must be fresh and engaging — often surprising; it must be appropriate to the context the writer is developing.

A good simile or metaphor can be a powerful tool in explanation since it makes our audience see an idea clearly. In the writing program that I direct, we have a metaphor for a certain kind of research paper that comes to us filled with quotations, demonstrating hours of hard work by the student yet lacking any ideas from the writer herself. We say that such a paper is like a plastic model of the *Titanic*, the ship that sank after striking an iceberg in the North Atlantic. You can buy such a model at a hobby store and spend hours or even weeks putting it together until you have an impressive object to put on your table, but you will have contributed nothing to the model except the careful labor of putting it together. We say that we want papers that show careful labor, but we also want some honest, original thinking that comes out of the writer's own ruminations on the material she is studying. We want our student writers to do more than paste sources together; we want them to design the papers they write. The metaphor helps our students understand the difference between writing a paper that is formally correct and writing one that shows some hard thought and originality.

Let us first get some terms clear. Throughout this chapter we are going to be talking about metaphor. Grammarians often make an unnecessary distinction between *metaphor* and *simile*. A metaphor speaks of something as if it were something else: "Johnson was a bulldog in argument." We make a metaphor and call Johnson a bulldog. We know that our readers suppose that the major characteristic of a bulldog is stubborn tenacity. To emphasize Johnson's qualities in argument, we make a metaphor.

We could say, "Johnson is like a bulldog in argument," or we could say, "Johnson is as tenacious as a bulldog in argument." Then we would be using similes, because similes make comparisons by using *like* or *as*. Such is the conventional distinction between metaphors and similes.

The distinction between metaphor and simile is more formal than real, and in this chapter I often use the term *metaphor* to include both of these figures of speech. They both make us see connections between things that are not obviously alike. They take one part of our experience—something that is common to us as writers and to our readers—and they join it to part of our experience that our readers do not know so well. When I say, "Johnson is a bulldog in argument," I assume that my readers know something about bulldogs or at least that they *think* they know something about bulldogs. (Bulldogs are in fact gentle creatures.) I assume that they need to be told something about Johnson—that he is tenacious. So I lead them from what we both think we know about bulldogs to what I know about Johnson.

This use of a shared experience or perception to communicate an idea that readers do not share with us is essential to all metaphor. Whenever we use metaphors, we must think hard about what our readers have experienced. If they have not had the experience that the metaphor requires of them, it will be dead language as far as they are concerned. It will not engage them in our prose. If our readers did not share with us some knowledge about the reputation of bulldogs, my statement about Johnson would make no sense. Suppose I said, "Johnson is an aardvark in argument." Most readers probably know the word "aardvark" only because it turns up in crossword puzzles. They do not immediately think of qualities in the aardvark that might apply to Johnson. Or suppose I made a metaphor of something my readers do know although they cannot see the relation between that and something else I see. Suppose I say, "Johnson is a salmon in argument." Most readers cannot see anything about salmon that would apply to arguments, so the metaphor does not work. I could say this: "Johnson is a salmon in argument; he starts in one place and goes all around the world and comes back to where he began, no matter what we say against his point of view." Then the metaphor might work a little better because readers can see why I made it. But it is still clumsy. Good metaphors work a little like the punch line of a joke—they make a sudden and vivid impression. Jokes and metaphors that have to be explained are usually awkward. Like good jokes, good metaphors depend on common experience. We have all had the experience of not getting a joke that everybody else in a group laughs at. We don't get the joke because somehow we have escaped the common experience that makes everyone else laugh. And unless we make metaphors that depend on the common experience of our readers, the attempt to use metaphor fails.

Whether you use metaphors or similes depends on your taste, rhythm, style, subject, and perhaps the mood of the moment. Sometimes you will want to say, "Johnson is a bulldog in argument," and at other times you will want to say, "Johnson is like a bulldog in argument."

THREE KINDS OF METAPHOR

Metaphors may be divided into three types. The first kind helps us understand one concrete object by reference to another concrete object; the second kind helps us understand an abstraction by reference to a concrete object; the third kind, the embedded metaphor, makes language more vivid by substituting metaphorical terms for literal reporting. Metaphors that help us see one concrete entity by reference to another help us describe things. Metaphors that use a concrete reference to illuminate an abstraction help us explain ideas. Embedded metaphors help make our language more vivid in subtle ways.

The Descriptive Metaphor

Descriptive metaphors help us imagine scenes. D. H. Lawrence wrote:

> At the edge of the wood the bluebells had flowed over into the field and stood there *like floodwater.*[1]

John Gardner wrote:

[1] D. H. Lawrence, *Sons and Lovers* (New York: Modern Library, 1962), 239.

But the curve was free, and the truck rushed on, past Webb's and Burkmeister's and Ford's and Mahoney's, the motor screaming *like a buzz-saw cutting through ironwood,* the rattles from every hinge and every bolt filling the cab with a noise *like chattering leaden bells of wasps stirred up to rage.*[2]

Ralph Ellison wrote:

I heard the sharp intake of breath, *like a toy balloon suddenly deflated.*[3]

Always the descriptive metaphor uses something readers know to help them see better something they do not know. In Lawrence's metaphor, for example, we have not seen the field and the flowers he describes, but we can imagine the flowers flowing thickly onto the field because we have seen ground flooded after rain and know how the waters creep out along the contours of the land. The image of the flood helps us see both the profusion of the flowers and their well-defined limit.

The Abstract Metaphor

A different kind of metaphor helps us explain ideas. It attributes a concrete reality to an abstraction and makes the abstraction more manageable to readers. Such metaphors have been used for centuries. The Psalmist, feeling the blessings of God, wrote, "My cup runneth over." The cup is a metaphor for the life that can receive God's goodness. In the book of Proverbs we read, "The candle of the wicked shall be put out." The "wicked" walk by a manmade light that will be extinguished, leaving them in darkness. And we speak of "bearing a cross," meaning a suffering we endure through no fault of our own. Sometimes we speak of death as a person, recalling both the apostle Paul's personification of death in his epistles and the figure of the Grim Reaper with his scythe that has been with us since the Renaissance.

This kind of metaphor easily translates into the political cartoon. Hunger becomes an emaciated skeleton devouring the world. War becomes a cruel warrior in classical Roman armor. The Republican party becomes an elephant; the Democratic party, a donkey.

Such metaphors have a long history in our own political life. When Southerners claimed, before the Civil War, that every state had the

[2] John Gardner, *The Sunlight Dialogues* (New York: Ballantine, 1972), 197.
[3] Ralph Ellison, *The Invisible Man* (New York: New American Library, 1952), 49.

right to interpret the United States Constitution without reference to any other state or to judgments of federal courts and that states could nullify laws made by Congress, Daniel Webster replied that if Southerners were correct, the federal union was no more than "a rope of sand." Abraham Lincoln, some years later, used a biblical metaphor when he spoke ominously of a country part slave and part free, declaring that "a house divided against itself cannot stand." In our own century, when Franklin D. Roosevelt proclaimed that his administration would give a "New Deal" to the American people, the phrase *New Deal* became one of the most powerful metaphors in American history. Millions of Americans felt that they had been dealt an unlucky hand by the Great Depression and that some bad luck beyond their control was responsible for all their suffering. The image of a New Deal made them think that now they might have another chance. The metaphor suffered the fate of many good metaphors: it became a cliché, and now when we use the term *New Deal* we think not of a card game but of the Roosevelt administration.

A good metaphor may help us think. As aids to thinking, metaphors find an important—we may say a necessary—place in modern science. Some might argue that without metaphor some current scientific thinking could scarely go on. Albert Einstein's theory of relativity deals with phenomena so removed from common-sense experience that most people can scarely begin to understand it. Indeed the *London Times* once called Einstein's theory "an affront to common sense." In consequence of its difficulty a legion of metaphors has been called up to explain it—that is, to translate a difficult abstract theory into language that we can visualize according to our own experience, to turn the theory into something that we can "remember" in the way I spoke of memory in Chapter 1.

Einstein himself tried to imagine how the universe would look to someone traveling at the speed of light: he made a pictorial leap in his mind similar to the kind of leap we make when we read a good metaphor. He began with the notion that the speed of light is constant, seen from any vantage point in the universe, whether the light is moving toward us or away from us. This bizarre idea called forth from Bertrand Russell, the English philosopher, this metaphorical utterance:

> Everybody knows that if you are on an escalator you reach the top sooner if you walk up than if you stand still. But if the escalator moved with the velocity of light you would reach the top at exactly the same moment whether you walked up or stood still.[4]

[4] Bertrand Russell, quoted in Ronald W. Clark, *Einstein: The Life and Times* (New York: World, 1971), 87.

Einstein had hit on the idea that anything in motion at the speed of light has a set of relations with other objects that is radically different from those of anything in motion at a lesser speed. Since we ourselves sense motion at much, much lesser speeds than that of light, the non-mathematicians among us require figurative language if we are to have any comprehension of Einstein. Here a metaphor has been valuable in helping to communicate at least part of the truth of a painfully complex set of ideas.

The Embedded Metaphor

The third kind of metaphor is much more common — so common in fact that we often do not recognize it as metaphor. This is the embedded metaphor, the metaphor that uses a verb or a noun in such a way that it gives added coloration to the reality we are describing.

Suppose I write, "The fire devoured the house." I might say, "The fire burned the house down," or "The fire destroyed the house." When I use the verb *devoured,* I am using an embedded metaphor that suggests a ravenous animal eating something up without hesitation or mercy, with a voracious appetite, as if I were attributing life to the fire.

Joe McGinnis, describing his experiences in Alaska, writes:

> Even now, in fact at 6:30 P.M., new clouds were moving in and beginning to blanket the high, sharp mountains that rose above the oil tanks around the harbor.[5]

We take the word *blanket* for granted since we use it so often as McGinnis does here, but it is an embedded metaphor. A *blanket* lies across our bed to keep us warm in cold weather. By extension, *blanket* becomes a metaphor for anything that covers something else with a layer.

W. P. Kinsella writes:

> I glance up at the water tower that *watches* over the town like a benevolent alien.[6]

He is using two kinds of metaphor in the same sentence. The simile *like a benevolent alien* goes with the embedded metaphor *watches,* which personifies the inanimate object, the water tower. The verb gives the

---

[5] Joe McGinnis, *Going to Extremes* (New York: Alfred A. Knopf, 1980), 204.
[6] W. P. Kinsella, *Shoeless Joe* (Boston: Houghton Mifflin, 1982), 139.

tower life and makes it a character in the scene. Obviously we are not to believe that the water tower has real life; the metaphor gives us the author's feelings toward the scene and conveys to us his sense of the scene. At times all of us feel that physical objects have some kind of personality, that they are threatening or friendly or merely present as something more than inanimate matter, and that sense is just what Kinsella conveys when he tells us that the water tower watches over the town.

METAPHORS AND ATMOSPHERE

Atmosphere is the complex and sometimes only partly conscious emotional response that a piece of writing conveys. How do you feel when you read something? Metaphors may have a lot to do with the answer to this question. Suppose you want to call attention to how thin someone is. With one kind of metaphor you can create an impression of unhealthiness:

> Mr. Murray was taller than most men and so thin that he looked a bit like a patient in a terminal cancer ward.

With a different metaphor we can create a more positive impression:

> Mr. Murray was taller than most men and so thin that he looked like a long distance runner able to win two marathons a day.

The different feelings we get from reading these two sentences contribute to the atmosphere of the pieces where they appear. Mention of a cancer ward makes us see Mr. Murray's thinness as dangerous; mention of two marathons a day makes us feel that his thinness is a benefit.

Some writers command metaphor with stunning effectiveness to create atmosphere. Study the metaphors (in italics) in the following passage by Joseph Conrad, a master of the metaphorical art. They shift somewhat from one to the next, but they remain consistent, and together they create a mood of awe and foreboding:

> You know how these squalls come up there about this time of year. First you see a darkening of the horizon — no more; then a cloud rises *opaque like a wall*. A *straight edge* of vapour lined with *sickly* whitish gleams *flies up* from the southwest, *swallowing* the stars in whole constellations; its

shadow *flies* over the waters and *confounds* sea and sky into one *abyss* of obscurity.[7]

Few writers today would dare try to duplicate this rich and subtle use of metaphor. We have a cloud rising *opaque like a wall*. We have a *straight edge* — a ruler — of vapor lined with *sickly whitish gleams*, as if the stormy sky were a person sick with some tumultuous disease. Then we have the vapor flying up so that we easily imagine some monstrous bird *swallowing the stars in whole constellations*. Then *its shadow flies over the waters*, giving us another image of a bird of prey swooping over the sea after something — perhaps a ship — that it may find floating there. Afterward we have a swell or two of the sea running *like undulations of the very darkness*. Those in the audience familiar with the first chapter of the book of Genesis, as most literate people were in Conrad's day, remember the chaotic darkness at the beginning, when "the earth was without form and void, and darkness was upon the face of the deep," an image we are prepared for with the words *confounds* and *abyss*, which recall that primordial universe before God created light.

Conrad in effect gives us two worlds, the world of the storm on the sea and the eerie world of imaginary association called up in his mind and ours by the storm. The association includes in it not only what we may have experienced of violent tempests but also what we have read and thought of the biblical story of creation, where God struggles against the chaos at the dawn of time. Conrad creates in us something of the primitive fear, probably lurking in the subconscious of most of us, a legacy of the terror felt by our remote ancestors in the face of the forces of nature. Without this string of metaphors, Conrad would not accomplish these effects. The metaphors are numerous, but we accept them because they are consistent, and they work together to create an atmosphere of foreboding and awe. It is a different view of a storm from that which we might see on the evening television news in our own time, with the brightly made-up meteorologist gesturing and grinning at a map to show us that rain is coming.

In his inaugural address of January 20, 1961, young President John F. Kennedy delivered a series of metaphors that gave his speech an aura of vigorous energy and, by extension, conveyed a like feeling to the administration he was about to lead and to his ideal of America. He said:

> Let the word go forth from this time and place, to friend and foe alike, that the torch has been passed to a new generation of Americans,

[7] Joseph Conrad, *Lord Jim* (New York: New American Library, 1965), 80. First published, 1899.

born in this century, tempered by war, disciplined by a hard and bitter peace, proud of our ancient heritage, and unwilling to witness or permit the slow undoing of those human rights to which this nation has always been committed, and to which we are committed today at home and around the world.[8]

We have the image of a torch passed, and we think of the Olympic runners carrying the flame from one to another across a country until they arrive at the place where the games are held. The new generation of Americans is described as *tempered*, the process of making steel stronger by first heating it and then plunging it into cool water. We are told that these Americans have been *disciplined* by a hard and bitter peace, and we think of soldiers trained by hardship to do their duty.

So it goes through the speech, one vigorous metaphor after another, conveying an image of strength, vitality, endurance, and courage. Presidents always convey some sense of what they themselves think of their administration when they use metaphors. You can read their speeches and easily come to some kind of understanding of what they believe about their own leadership. In your own writing the metaphors you use will tell readers much about yourself and what you think of them.

Metaphors should make one point sharply. Extended metaphors seldom interest readers. You may think it clever to create an extended metaphor that likens getting a college education to climbing a mountain. Admission is like arriving at the base; enrolling in your first classes is like putting on your helmet and climbing tentatively over the first rocks; social life is like rain on the side of the mountain, since a little of it is refreshing but too much may wash you off the cliffs. You can go on and on with such metaphors until you liken graduation to getting to the top. But readers will find such an extended metaphor contrived and boring, and by the time you have gotten to the top, they will have turned the page and gone on to something else. The British call the use of extended metaphors "making a metaphor walk on all fours." It is a scornful expression, referring to the heaviness and tedium of metaphors that try to do too much.

Extended metaphors can give a misleading impression of reality if people take them too literally and begin to read too much into them. A writer argues that because some figure resembles something else in several details, we can study the figure and understand that other thing. For example, the so-called organic metaphor has long been popular in

[8] John F. Kennedy, Inaugural Address, 1961.

the study of history. Plants and other organisms are born; they enjoy youth; they pass into maturity and then into old age; and finally they die. Sometimes the organic metaphor provides a useful way of talking about certain ages in history. Edward Gibbon's *Decline and Fall of the Roman Empire*, an account written in the eighteenth century, accustomed several generations of literate readers to thinking of the final centuries of the Roman Empire in the West as a decline, much like the aging of a human being.

More recent historians such as Oswald Spengler and Arnold Toynbee fell so in love with the organic metaphor that they made it an argument. Metaphors may illustrate arguments, but no metaphor can be a sufficient argument in itself. From the organic metaphor of history, these men constructed elaborate patterns that human history was supposed to follow, and both of them frequently twisted the historical evidence to make events conform to the design that they had imposed on the past. Spengler in particular wrenched history into a plantlike shape whereby all civilizations were made to pass through the same stages, and every stage might be likened to a similar stage in the development and decline of an organism. He provided his readers with a design for human history in which no individual striving could make much difference and no collective effort could change the implacable pattern of things. He saw history repeating itself just as the life cycle of a plant repeats itself again and again in the individual members of a species. Since he believed that the twentieth century represented the last stage in the organic life of western civilization, he provided no hope for the future. Toynbee was more tempered in his judgments, but his conclusions resembled those of Spengler.

Metaphors may be helpful to thought and expression, but they should not take over our minds or our writing. We should think hard about reality, about things as they are, and we should think equally hard about how we should express reality in metaphors. We should avoid confusing the vehicle of our expression with what the vehicle is supposed to carry — although at times making a distinction between the two may be difficult. My best advice is to use caution.

Also, avoid packing your prose with so many metaphors that they become confusing. Using too many metaphors may produce ludicrous results. "By keeping his nose to the grindstone, he climbed the ladder of success." Or, "My high school English teacher was always prepared to water any spark of genius, and as a result many of her students grew from acorns into stout oaks of knowledge." A university memo I saw some time ago urged the faculty "to grapple with the burning issues." I wondered if we were to use gloves while we did this grappling.

How do we cultivate metaphor in our own prose? The first step is to believe that you can use metaphor effectively. That takes a little daring and a willingness to make some mistakes, to laugh about them, and to try again. You can begin to develop the talent by doing some exercises. If you keep a notebook, note down qualities in the things and the people you observe. Make metaphors from those qualities. You will make some ridiculous combinations, but be dauntless. Keep at it, even when the results are not rewarding, and after a time you may discover some gold in the sand.

Here is the kind of exercise I mean:

As calm as:

a pond at noon on a hot summer day.
snow on a field at midnight under
   the full moon.
granite.
a blackjack dealer in a casino.
the face of George Washington on
   a dollar bill.

As white as:

a set of new false teeth.
a paper cup.
vanilla ice cream.
a hospital shower curtain.
a priest's collar.
the sun at noon.

As out of place as:

grief in an undertaker.
a dump truck on the Indianapolis
   Speedway.
a Republican on food stamps.
humility in a TV meteorologist.

You can experiment by writing metaphorical descriptions of things you observe. Again, the results will vary. Some of your metaphors will be terrible; a few will be good. But the point is to get your mind working in the mode that makes metaphor possible:

The trees stood guard in the night, a thin, dark line of still sentinels between the sleeping house and the lonely highway.

The trees stood like a congregation of bereaved faithful after the death of summer, their naked branches lifted skyward in prayer for spring after the long winter.

The trees in the early dusk of winter gave the eerie impression of a party of otherworldly creatures, gathered down there to discuss the best plan of attack before advancing through the gloom against the house.

The trees stood like a group of giant friends idly holding hands at the bottom of the field and whispering secrets to each other in the tireless way of gossips who love the talk as much as the tale.

You get the point. You can make a pleasant and diverting game out of making metaphors in the privacy of your notebook. Make some howlers, give yourself some prizes, and the little game will help you develop a way of looking at language and the world that will make your writing more vivid.

APPROPRIATE METAPHORS

Metaphors should be appropriate to the topic you are discussing. This is a matter of taste, and some writers may feel comfortable using some metaphors and similes that would annoy others. I would not want to read that General Robert E. Lee's theory of battle was to crash into his foes as if he were trying to drive a bulldozer through a brick wall by taking a running start. General Lee never saw a bulldozer in his life, and a careful reader considering the incongruity of such a simile would probably be annoyed by it.

In making similes and metaphors fit your subject, use your wit. Here is an instructive simile from an article in *Time* magazine about computer software:

> A computer without software is like a car without gasoline, a camera without film, a stereo without records.[9]

At times you may use a series of metaphors if they do not clash with each other. Here is Irving Howe describing the Jewish immigrant housewife in turn-of-the-century New York City:

[9] Alexander L. Taylor III, "The Wizard Inside the Machines," *Time*, April 16, 1984, 56.

It was from her place in the kitchen that the Jewish housewife became the looming figure who would inspire, haunt, and devastate generations of sons. She realized intuitively that insofar as the outer world tyrannized and wore down her men, reducing them to postures of docility, she alone could create an oasis of order. It was she who would cling to received values and resist the pressures of dispersion; she who would sustain the morale of all around her, mediating quarrels, soothing hurts, drawing a circle of safety in which her children could breathe, and sometimes, as time went on, crushing her loved ones under the weight of her affection.[10]

Howe's metaphors come so naturally that we may not recognize them as metaphors until we think about them. But then we see "oasis of order," "circle of safety," and the metaphorical phrase "crushing her loved ones under the weight of her affection."

Always match your metaphors and similes to the tone of your essay. These examples drawn from Howe nicely fit his subject, the development of the Jewish mother. It is a serious subject but not a somber one. His metaphors fit into that tone.

And here is John Gardner in a somewhat lighter mood:

We met at the Wallace, and John showed us the armor. He stood huge and wild-headed, *an enormous bird with diamond eyes,* his sportcoat *tattered like an anarchist's.* He pointed out the ornamentation on swords and pistols, so finely wrought that it might have been carved by intelligent spiders. Sometimes he'd bend over, bringing *his huge beak* an inch from the glass, *like a nearsighted eagle* in front of a mirror, his eyes *screwing up like a jeweler's,* and he'd say, "Exactly!"[11]

You should not force metaphors until they become overwrought and unnatural. You may not wish to use a lot of them. But you should use them sometimes. As you write, making metaphors will become easier.

CLICHÉS

Figurative language should make your writing vigorous; the opposite of vigorous writing is prose filled with clichés, expressions as pre-

---

[10] Irving Howe, *World of Our Fathers* (New York: Simon and Schuster, Touchstone Books, 1976), 174.

[11] John Gardner, *The King's Indian* (New York: Alfred A. Knopf, 1974), 127.

dictable as a funeral sermon. A good metaphor surprises us and makes us respond to what the writer is saying to us. When we hear the first couple of words of a cliché, we know how the expression will end. The plan was as dead as a _____ before it could be voted on. We hear the words, *as dead as*, and we know that it was as dead as *a doornail*.

But what is a doornail, and why should it be dead? We do not know. It is a word that has the advantage of beginning with the letter *d*, so that when we say "dead as a doornail," we get to repeat a strong consonant sound. We like such repetitions in English. If we were to speak the expression, we might get some power into it, and we might make it effective. But it does not mean anything special, and it creates no pictures in our minds.

The author of the piece *waxed eloquent* on the economic benefits of deficits.

Why do people *wax eloquent*? No one seems to know. They do wax eloquent more often than they wax anything else. Wax means "to become" or "to grow." People in the sixteenth century used to *wax old*. And the moon still *waxes and wanes*. But now people only wax eloquent — perhaps because eloquence seems somehow slick and dangerous.

The *cold hard facts* are these: *it will be a cold day in July* before you see me *pull his chestnuts out of the fire*.

Why must disagreeable facts always be cold and hard? The expression must have had some power once. Facts must have seemed like cold pieces of steel, and unpleasant facts must have made someone think of this expression. It caught on, and other people started using it, thinking that it said something special. Now everybody trying to sound bold and strong and worldly-wise uses the expression *cold, hard facts*. We have heard the expression so often that it makes us think more of laziness than wisdom.

So it is also with *a cold day in July*. That expression might have seemed funny once to someone living in one of the valleys of Tennessee, broiling in the sun of July 4 while politicians stirred the hot air with speeches producing more of the same. It would not seem odd or expressive to anyone in northern Vermont where wood fires often blaze on hearths on July evenings.

And who has ever pulled chestnuts out of a fire, risking burned hands or a burned face, for someone else? Chestnuts are still around, and a few people may roast them in fireplaces, but does the expression mean anything? Probably not.

A writer uses clichés out of weariness or uncertainty or hesitancy. He sits at his desk, struggling to put something on paper, realizing, as we all do, that the physical process of writing is hard work. A cliché pops into his mind, and he writes it down quickly because it is easy. Perhaps he does not know it is a cliché. Because he has heard it so often, he may suppose it is valuable. We are all timid when we begin to write, and clichés often give timid writers a feeling of security: they are familiar; they make a point; they take up space; they are not taxing; they seem like writing. But all these are reasons that make any piece of writing dull.

A young reporter covers a congressional hearing and listens to the president of a coal mining company explain the economic value of opening a strip mining operation in Yellowstone National Park. The reporter writes that the president of the coal company "had his own ax to grind." Neither the reporter nor the reader will think of the company president, bringing his own ax to the community grindstone, forgetting all the other tools in the village, concentrating only on his own interest. No reader of this story has ever ground an ax; the reporter may never have held an ax in his hands. But the phrase pops into her mind, and it feels comfortable. She knows that it refers to those who are motivated by greed to advocate high causes.

Most clichés convey meaning, but they do not convey images. So down goes the cliché on paper, where it becomes a dead metaphor, one that conveys meaning without stirring up any image in anybody's mind, language we have heard so often that we never think of being stirred by it in any way. If we used it ourselves, we would never imagine being proud of it.

Here is probably the worst sin of the cliché—the laziness it forces on writers and readers alike. The cliché makes readers suppose that the writer either would not or could not imagine any original way to express a thought. And readers may assume that the writer scarcely bothered to think at all. Clichés make reading a passive act, something that tranquilizes the mind and leaves it unable to take the material seriously. They open no windows, provide no revelations, give us nothing to remember. And they are quickly forgotten.

Good, vivid writing gives an impression of a bright mind, of someone who has thought seriously about a topic and is saying something worth reading, and we heed such writing because we enjoy it. Clichés irritate us, grind our pleasure down to boredom, and erode our respect for the writer. She has not worked hard to engage our attention; why should we work hard to read what she has to say to us?

TWO KINDS OF CLICHÉ

Clichés come in two packages. Some are dead metaphors and similes, vainly trying to call up an image; some are common phrases, including fad words, that sound like formulas. Dead metaphors include *tight as a drum, fit as a fiddle, sound as a dollar, white as snow, blue as the sky, sharp as a tack, neat as a pin,* and legions more. Common phrases that are clichés include such expressions as *to add insult to injury; pick and choose; tried and true; poor but honest; a deep, dark secret; an undercurrent of excitement; the agony of suspense; a bustling city; a brutal murder; a tragic death;* and row on row of others stacked up like fool's gold in the vaults of our minds.

Fad words come and go through our society like pockets of unpredictable air turbulence. Suddenly people start using them to show that they know what's going on and that they enjoy the superior culture of those who have discovered superior expressions. *Parameter* pops up on the page instead of *limit* or *perimeter.* People suddenly start talking about *the bottom line,* and they get *feedback* when they submit their *input* to a group discussing a problem. Football coaches tell us that *the name of the game* is defense or that *the name of the game* is quickness. And we supposed naïvely all along that the name of the game is football. Of course they tell us that *when the going gets tough, the tough get going.* When a lineman makes a solid hit on a quarterback, the TV announcer tells us that that lineman *came to play,* and when somebody works hard to play well, we are told that *he gives 110 percent.* Since so many of us are using computers, we hear that the scholars in the English department must *interface* with people who teach writing. We also hear that some people are *programmed* for success and that others are *programmed* for defeat.

We live immersed in such clichés. They pour through newspaper columns, academic essays, student papers, and memos that pass from office to office. They gush out of TV talk shows. They litter conversation.

You will seldom find clichés in the slick-paper magazines you buy on newsstands. These magazines must be carefully edited if they are to survive, and editors know that clichés kill prose and that dead prose will not sell. Here is another place where we may look to the good journalists and essayists in our society.

How do we know when we are using clichés? They are so pervasive in our society that all of us stumble into them at times. Some inexperienced writers cannot recognize them. I have already given one clue. Some clichés identify themselves by being so familiar that when we hear the first word or two of the phrase, we know how the phrase will end. When you start to use a phrase that so readily identifies itself as a cliché, pause and try to think of some other words that can carry your thoughts.

The best way to eliminate clichés is to be sure that you clearly understand every expression you use and that it says exactly what you want to say as efficiently as possible. We read in the morning paper that somebody was gunned down in the street by a thug, and we are told that it was a *brutal murder.* The reporter wishes to convey her sense of horror and perhaps outrage at a violent death. But do we need the worn-out adjective *brutal?* Can we imagine a *gentle* murder? Perhaps a gentle murder is committed by putting poison in somebody's hot milk, but even that does not seem gentle to most of us. Murder is murder; *brutal murder* is a phrase not far removed from *flowering flowers* or *criminal crimes.*

What of those letters of recommendation that tell us that somebody is a *personal friend?* Are there *impersonal* friends? And what of those historians who in describing the Renaissance tell us about the *bustling cities* to show that the urban centers of the time were busy? The term is used so frequently in history texts that we may gain the impression that cart drivers, merchants, bankers, lawyers, and courtiers and Renaissance princes pushed through the crowded streets shouting, "bustle, bustle, bustle," at each other.

Couples who are dating may tell us that they have a *meaningful relationship,* and when they break up, they tell us that their love affair was a *learning experience.* People who learn their profession by apprenticeship are said to have *hands-on* experience. And since the televising of the Watergate hearings in 1973, we have referred to any given moment as *that point in time.* We hear that personal computers are *selling like hotcakes,* and we do not stop to think that in this day of chemical preservatives and freezers we have probably never seen people line up to buy hotcakes.

All this is to say that our writing requires concentration. We must examine every word, measure every sentence, and tailor our expressions to fit our thought exactly and engagingly. We may write clichés in our first drafts, especially if we write rapidly to get a piece of prose into being so we can later tinker with it. But when we go back and revise, we should slash our clichés ruthlessly from our texts.

The simplest way to deal with a cliché is to change it into ordinary language. We can say that cities of the Renaissance were thriving or that they were growing or that commerce gave them a busy life they had never enjoyed before. Then these cities do not have to bustle. We can describe a murder with enough detail to allow readers to know the kind of murder it was. Then we can leave it to them to decide whether it was brutal or not.

The tedious commonplace phrases that seem obligatory in modern casual speech have moved powerfully into our written language, and we find them difficult to resist. The word *feedback* is here to stay, though only a short time ago it referred primarily to the electronic shriek that came out of a loudspeaker poorly matched with a microphone. I like *response* better, but I am in a minority. Some friends of mine object to the word *normative* because it says nothing that *standard* does not say, but *normative* now seems embedded in popular speech. And how do we fight against the unrestricted use of *hopefully* and *relationship?* I cringe at both words because they have so few roots in the literary language. Through slow evolution the literary language has proved itself to be a magnificent tool for our thought, but now, thanks to radio and television, the spoken language is dominant, and the literary language is becoming much more open and colloquial as a result.

No book like this one can settle the question of dead language for every writer. But I do say that to be a good writer, you must try to make your words stir something in the minds of your readers. Good figurative language can often create a vivid picture in your mind and in the minds of those who read your work. Dead language with its clichés and its worn-out expressions cannot create that response. Now and then you may use a cliché without being guilty of a capital literary crime. Too many clichés will suffocate your prose, and your readers will conduct their own sort of funeral by refusing to read your work.

In the back of this book is a short appendix of clichés. You will not find every English cliché there, but you can open the book to those pages when you are tempted to use a phrase and do not know whether it is a cliché or not. If you find the phrase in my list, try to think of another expression.

CONCLUDING REMARKS ON FIGURATIVE LANGUAGE

Try to use figurative language when it seems appropriate, but try hard to make it something that comes out of your experience, not something you put on paper just because everybody seems to be saying it. If you learn to reflect on your experience with a notebook in hand, you can develop a talent for figurative language. It takes time. But so does everything else about writing.

SEVEN

False Rules and What Is True About Them

English has many rules that you must observe if you are to make yourself understood and respected. Break those rules, and you make it hard for your readers and for yourself. Your readers will falter if you use a plural verb form with a singular noun or if you use a double negative, and they will think you are ignorant for breaking the rules.

Unfortunately, many people, straining to do the right thing, complicate matters by making up false rules that they adhere to when they start to write. These rules burden style and often make prose sound stilted and somehow wrong. They are "rules" regularly violated by professional writers.

Yet the false rules have a vigorous life. Writing is a complicated business, one of the most difficult acts of the human mind. False rules seem to grant security, to reduce the process to a formula that anybody can understand, so that it becomes much less threatening. Many people would like to believe that they will become good writers if they obey the rules, and the false rules seem just fancy enough to be guarantees of survival. So they hang onto these rules as though to life preservers in a stormy sea—and sometimes they wonder why nobody will publish what they write despite its grammatical correctness. Writing is not a matter of obeying the rules; it is a matter of observation and imagination. The multiplication of false rules is much like welding armor onto a car; in the end the car may be perfectly safe, but it is also too heavy to run. Some textbooks on writing include chapters attacking false rules, but often the authors of these books consider only the extremes of the rules, the absurdities that all true writers can recognize in an instant. Often these authors are a little too jubilant for my taste, at times giving the impression that English has no rules at all and that the false rules have grown up out of perversity or absurdity.

You should not be bound by the false rules. But you should also remember that they did not leap into the world like aliens from outer space without any relation to anything that has gone on before. The false rules evolved out of genuine needs in writing. They became false rules because some people started giving them more value than they gave to the strong, natural expression that we should all cultivate when we write. Although the rules are falsely expressed, they do have some substance, and we should take that substance into account even as we are rejecting the silliness and the pedantry of the extremes.

COMMON FALSE RULES

Here are some of the most common false rules with a few notes about what may be true about them.

1. Don't say "I" or "we."

Every college freshman knows this one. Many high school teachers have told their students not to say, "I think," or "I believe," or "we see." So instead of the first person, we get impersonal, stiff constructions like these:

It is the opinion of this writer that . . .
This writer would be forced to agree . . .
This writer has shown . . .
The reader is made to feel . . .
The audience reacts in a predictable way . . .
This writer was hit by a truck when she . . .

Despite the almost unanimous rule against the first person, only a little attention to professional writing shows that the first person turns up in many books and magazines. Newspaper reporters visiting a war zone or a natural disaster use the first person when they describe their observations. The author of a report will use the first person, especially if the report considers several courses of action and concludes with a recommendation by the author.

Some classic reflective pieces about experience are written in the first person. Montaigne used it in his essays. James Baldwin's "Stranger in the Village," most of E. B. White's essays, Richard Henry Dana's *Two Years Before the Mast*, Mark Twain's *Life on the Mississippi*, and dozens of other prose works use the first person.

Writers of movie and book reviews frequently use the personal pronoun *we* and sometimes the singular pronoun *I* to avoid the tedious repetition of clumsy phrases such as *the reader, the audience,* or *the viewer.* A few people say they dislike having a reviewer write:

> In the end, we somehow sympathize with Macbeth despite his great evil because we see how he has been led astray by temptations that might seduce any of us.

These readers resent being included in opinions they do not share. They would prefer to read:

> I think Macbeth gets exactly what he deserves, and I don't sympathize with him at all.

The first person is always preferable to tiresome repetition of phraseology like this:

> In the end the audience somehow sympathizes with Macbeth despite his great evil because the audience sees how he has been led astray by temptations that might seduce anyone.

Hardly anything dulls the mind more in a review than the merciless repetition of the phrase, *the reader, the reader, the reader.*

In formal writing about matters in which the writer is not intimately involved, the first person is more rare. Edward Gibbon used it now and then in his *Decline and Fall of the Roman Empire,* but he is something of an exception. Modern historians seldom use the first person unless they write an autobiographical narrative of events they have been involved in. They express opinions and make judgments, stating them without hesitation in declarative sentences. Bruce Catton, writing of the lack of industry and of a transportation network in the South at the beginning of the Civil War, says:

> These problems, indeed, were so grave and pointed so surely toward final defeat that one is forced to wonder how the founding fathers of the Confederacy could possibly have overlooked them.[1]

He might have said, "that *we* are forced to wonder" rather than "that *one* is forced to wonder," but he did not.

But in his biography of Samuel Johnson, Walter Jackson Bate feels no compunction at using the first person plural:

[1] Bruce Catton, *The Coming Fury* (Garden City, N.Y.: Doubleday, 1961), 435.

Even if we knew nothing of the state of mind he was forced to battle during this psychological crisis, the edition of Shakespeare — viewed with historical understanding of what it involved in 1765 — could seem a remarkable feat; and we are not speaking of just the great *Preface*. To see it in perspective, we have only to remind ourselves what Johnson brought to it — an assemblage of almost every qualification we should ideally like to have brought to this kind of work with the single exception of patience; and at least some control of his impatience, if not the quality of patience itself, might have been possible if this period of his life had not been so distressing.[2]

Surprisingly enough, the first person is fairly rare in serious journalism. In a recent *New York Times Magazine* picked up at random from the pile here by my desk, I found four feature articles that did not use the first person and one that did. The overwhelming majority of articles in an informal journal such as *Sports Illustrated* will not use the first person. A writer can say, "Dick Williams looked at me across his desk and told me that the most important thing a manager can do is keep up with statistics," but most writers will say, "Dick Williams says that the most important thing a manager can do is keep up with statistics."

In many essays, using the first person is like throwing yourself at the legs of your readers to trip them up on their way to understanding. Are they supposed to be reading about you or about the events you report? Professional writers do not say, "In my opinion, the Middle East is the most dangerous place in the world." They say simply, "The Middle East is the most dangerous place in the world." If a writer signs her name to an article, every reader with common sense will recognize that the assertions in the article represent the writer's considered opinion and not some universal truth carved in stone by the finger of God.

Wayne C. Booth's "implied author" — mentioned in Chapter 2 — should come to mind here. We should never be cute or domineering in our prose. We should not be show-offs; we should avoid drawing attention to ourselves since readers should be much more interested in what we say than they are in us as persons. Most of the time we should keep ourselves out of the spotlight and stick to the business of telling our readers what we want them to know about our subject. From how we write they can infer some things about us if they wish to do so; but when we blatantly insert ourselves into a story we are telling, we are like thoughtless people who invite friends to a movie and then spend so much time talking that they are not allowed to enjoy the show.

We should also avoid giving the impression that when we say, "I

---

[2] Walter Jackson Bate, *Samuel Johnson* (New York and London: Harcourt Brace Jovanovich, 1977), 395.

think," we install ourselves in an impregnable fortress, immune to any counterargument. Many people today believe that all opinions are equal and that those who express themselves vehemently enough and sincerely enough deserve respect. We seem to be guilty of bad taste if we disagree with opinions strongly spoken or strongly written. Many an argument ends with the offhand and sometimes surly remark, "Well, you have your opinion, and I have mine." The speaker declares that she will not argue any more, telling her adversary that *he* should not argue any more because it will not help; she will not change her mind. She may also be saying that she does not have any other arguments to muster to her cause and that she does not want to be upset by the evidence. She has an opinion. Her opinions are sacred. Trying to get her to change an opinion is like trying to get her to change her religion.

We are fortunate to live in a society in which people have the right to say just about anything they please. They may be dull, brilliant, foolish, or simply ordinary. This freedom does not confer equality on all opinions. Educated people know that if they are to win any respect among thinking readers, they must support opinion with evidence. They must give some good reason why they have that opinion and persuade others to accept it or at least to believe it is worthy of respect.

Command of the evidence allows you to make statements without using the first person. Eugene D. Genovese, in his classic book about slavery in the South before the Civil War, writes this about the music of slaves:

> The slaves' talent for improvisation, as well as their deep religious conviction, drew expressions of wonder and admiration from almost everyone who heard them sing.[3]

He is not compelled to place an "I think" before this opinion; he assembles evidence to show that it is so, and the evidence convinces us without a needless first-person pronouncement that would call more attention to Genovese than to what he is saying.

Barbara Tuchman, discussing the ineptitude of the American ambassador to China in 1945, Patrick J. Hurley, writes:

> It happens that Hurley was a man whose conceit, ambition, and very vulnerable ego were wrapped up in his mission to the point of frenzy.[4]

[3] Eugene D. Genovese, *Roll Jordan Roll* (New York, Random House, Vintage Books, 1976), 249.

[4] Barbara Tuchman, *Practicing History* (New York: Alfred A. Knopf, 1981), 196. Copyright © 1981 by Alma Tuchman, Lucie T. Eisenberg, and Jessica Tuchman Matthews. Reprinted by permission of Alfred A. Knopf, Inc.

She makes her case by assembling piles of evidence, and she does not have to preface her opinion with a feeble "I think."

When you deliver yourself of an "I think" before a judgment in writing, you seem to be granting that other people can think anything they want. But if you present evidence for your assertions, you can convey an impression of confidence that will make your audience take you seriously and perhaps assume that your views must be true.

So the false rule about the first person contains some truth, and you should avoid using the first person except when it is clearly called for. The following are some places where it may be in order.

When you deliberately assume a conversational tone as in a regular newspaper column, a letter, or a book like this one, you may use the first person. The conversational tone may help you create a sense of intimacy with your readers. Most books about writing share the assumption that we all perform the same task and that the author has something to share with others who write. Most books like this one are chatty—perhaps too much so. Some subjects lend themselves to informality; some do not. You will not find a chatty book on brain surgery or leukemia. For such subjects, informality would be in bad taste.

For serious subjects, use the first person only if your experiences are essential to your essay. If you report on research that you have done alone or with colleagues, you may use the first person or the passive, depending on your own taste. In general, experimenters use the passive in their reports:

> One thousand people were questioned about their preferences for automobiles. They were asked whether performance was more important than economy, whether they needed a large back seat, and whether color might influence their choice of a new car. They were asked whether they had more confidence in American cars or in Japanese makes.

Some writers will use the first person in such reports, and the first person may be more lively:

> We asked one thousand people about their preferences for automobiles. We asked them if performance mattered more than economy, whether they needed a large back seat, and whether color might influence their choice of a new car. We also asked them if they had more confidence in American cars or in Japanese makes.

Magazines such as *Consumer Reports* and *Road and Track* generally use the first person in reports of tests they make of products. The first person is always more readable and clearer than the passive. Still, scientific journals generally use the passive instead of the first person because they prefer to seem more formal.

You may want to use the first person in reporting interviews, although many successful interviewers such as Studs Terkel and the writers who conduct the *Playboy* interviews usually avoid the first person.

If you sign your name to a formal essay or report, you may venture an occasional comment in the first person. You may wish to assert your own choice among conflicting opinions when the evidence for each seems evenly distributed. You may, for example, do an essay on studies of the relation between drinking coffee and cancer. Medical researchers are divided on whether too much coffee can cause cancer, and an honest article on the subject would sum up the evidence on both sides. You may wish to conclude such an article with the remark, "But I am going to stop drinking coffee." The first person is not necessary here, but you can use it without harm.

You cannot use the first-person singular if you have not signed the essay. If you write a memo to represent the views of your university on a controversial issue like investments in South Africa, you may use the editorial *we* to show that your opinions represent the official policy of your institution. But you cannot say "I" since no one knows who you are if your name is not on the piece.

It is always easier to use the first-person plural than it is to use the first-person singular. *We, us, our,* and *ours* are easier to use than *I, me, my,* and *mine.* In a literary paper you can avoid the tedious repetition of phrases like *the reader* by using the first-person plural. Don't say, "William Faulkner tells the reader that those who do the worst things are often to be the most pitied." Say rather, "William Faulkner tells us that those who do the worst things are often to be the most pitied." Or simply say, "William Faulkner believed that those who do the worst things are often to be the most pitied."

2. *Never write a sentence fragment.*

This false rule should be amended to read, "Never write a sentence fragment unless you know what you are doing." If you cannot tell the difference between a sentence and a sentence fragment, you should get yourself a good English handbook and work on the problem until you beat it. But good writers who know what they are doing use sentence fragments for special effects. Here is E. B. White:

The whole thing was so familiar, the first feeling of oppression and heat and a general air around camp of not wanting to go very far away. In mid-afternoon (it was all the same) a curious darkening of the sky, and a lull in everything that had made life tick; and then the way the boats suddenly swung the other way at their moorings with the coming of a breeze out of the new quarter, and the premonitory rumble. Then the kettle drum, then the snare, then the bass drum and cymbals, then crackling light against the dark, and the gods grinning and licking their chops in the hills. Afterward the calm, the rain steadily rustling in the calm lake, the return of light and hope and spirits, and the campers running out in joy and relief to go swimming in the rain, their bright cries perpetuating the deathless joke about how they were getting simply drenched, and the children, screaming with delight at the new sensation of bathing in the rain, and the joke about getting drenched linking the generations in a strong indestructible chain. And the comedian who waded in carrying an umbrella.[5]

White's sentence fragments provide a rapid pace for his prose, and pace is the reason most writers use fragments. They are especially effective when they occur in the context of a series of events or thoughts or described objects. If the context is clear, fragments are both readable and efficient. They get readers quickly from place to place. Here is Robert M. Pirsig in his book *Zen and the Art of Motorcycle Maintenance*:

> At the top of the plateau at Grangeville, Idaho, we step from the blasting heat into an air-conditioned restaurant. *Deep cool inside*. While we wait for chocolate malteds, I notice a high-schooler sitting at the counter exchanging looks with the girl next to him. She's gorgeous, and I'm not the only other one who notices it. The girl behind the counter waiting on them is also watching with an anger she thinks no one else sees. *Some kind of triangle*. We keep passing unseen through little moments of other people's lives.[6]

Pirsig could have written complete sentences, or he could have attached his two fragments to the previous sentences by using a comma before the first and a dash before the second. He chose to use fragments because they stand out like signposts, drawing attention, strongly making his point.

Fragments are common in fiction and in nonfiction. Sometimes you can begin a paper with a series of fragments. But most of the time

---

[5] "Once More to the Lake," in *Essays of E. B. White* (New York: Harper & Row, 1977), 202.

[6] Robert M. Pirsig, *Zen and the Art of Motorcycle Maintenance* (New York: William Morrow, 1974; New York: Bantam Books, 1976), 282.

your fragments depend for meaning on the sentences that come immediately before them. They can usually be joined to the immediately preceding sentence by a comma, a dash, or a colon. Instead of telling you never to use them at all, teachers should tell you to use them with care. Care means seeing to it that the fragment does not become tiresome as a result of your using it too often.

3. Don't split infinitives.

Before we talk about split infinitives, we should be sure we know what they are. An infinitive can be split only by inserting a word or phrase between the infinitive marker *to* and the verb that makes the infinitive. The split infinitives below are in italics.

> Coach Clemm told his fullback *to speedily pocket* the money from the booster club.
>
> He planned *to deliberately insult* his boss so he would be fired from the job his mother made him take.
>
> She hoped *to really do* better this year.

These are not split infinitives:

> *To be truly understood,* Paul wanted his life to be an open book.
>
> Unfortunately, the pages were far too dull *to be carefully read* by anyone with taste.

Many people who know nothing else about grammar know about split infinitives and know that they do not like them. In most languages the infinitive is one word. *Hacer, faire,* and *facere* are infinitives in Spanish, French, and Latin respectively, and they are all one word. Rigorists insist that the infinitives in English should always be considered one word and that to split one is barbaric. Their reasoning seems confirmed by our use of infinitives in English, especially by our habit of referring to an infinitive with the pronoun *it*: "To write was everything to her, and it was a compulsion that sometimes alarmed her friends." The pronoun *it* refers to the infinitive *to write*, a singular entity used as a noun. To split an infinitive violates—in the minds of some—an integrity of the noun the infinitive represents.

Nevertheless, common sense tells us that English infinitives are not one word but two, and common observation shows us that good writers occasionally split infinitives. Here is a paragraph from *Time* about the

disappearance of the Japanese explorer Naomi Uemura, who vanished
on a mountain-climbing expedition:

> He became a national hero in 1970 when, as a member of the first
> Japanese team to successfully climb Mount Everest, he was the first to
> reach the 29,028-ft. peak.[7]

Writing is now governed by a general set of standards that are de-
termined by what editors will publish. Split infinitives fall within that
standard now, and writers should feel less guilty about splitting infinitives now and then.

Still moderation is in order. Although many professional writers occasionally split infinitives, they do so *only* occasionally. Three or four split
infinitives in a short essay will begin to sound clumsy. A large number of
split infinitives seems to break down the natural rhythms of speech that
make for clear writing and easy reading. We rarely split infinitives when
we speak. We should be moderate in splitting them when we write.

Beyond rhythm is efficiency. Most split infinitives are not bad because
they violate a sacrosanct rule of grammar but because the adverb that does
the splitting is unnecessary. If you write, "He wanted to really work hard,"
you can drop the *really* and have a better sentence. It is a pointless intensifi-
er. The same is true of most split infinitives; the adverb that does the splitting is usually unnecessary, and dropping it makes the sentence stronger.

You should remember that some people vehemently object to the
split infinitive and vigorously reproach writers who use it. If you want to
win those people to your side in an argument, you had better avoid the
split infinitive.

I don't split infinitives. I don't know why, but I do not feel comfortable splitting. Split infinitives seem to disturb some delicate sentence
balance I am aware of when I write. Perhaps the feeling is an illusion.
Perhaps it is a lingering memory from my seventh-grade English
teacher. Perhaps it is only the consciousness of how much split infinitives annoy some people whom I respect. Whatever it is, my own feeling
against the split infinitive is so strong and so habitual that I do not fight
it. I revise sentences to eliminate split infinitives, and something old-
fashioned in me makes me notice when other people split them. You
are much more likely to find split infinitives in journalism — newspaper
and magazine writing — than in trade books. The more time editors have
with a manuscript, the more likely they are to eliminate split infinitives.
But the split infinitive is so common nowadays in so many things we

[7] *Time*, March 4, 1984, 47.

read that writing teachers become a little foolish in trying to combat split infinitives in the name of some grand principle.

4. *Don't end a sentence with a preposition.*

Prepositions are small words that never change their form no matter how they are used; they connect nouns or pronouns in prepositional phrases that serve as adjectives or adverbs in a sentence. The importance of prepositions is that they allow the strength of nouns and pronouns to modify other elements in a sentence:

> *In the night* he dreamed *of horses.*

The prepositional phrase *In the night* works as an adverb modifying the verb *dreamed*; so does the prepositional phrase *of horses.*

> The umbrella *in the hall* was left here by a guest.

The prepositional phrase *in the hall* works as an adjective to modify *umbrella.*

Putting a prepositional phrase before its object helps to follow the general rule of English syntax that related elements in a sentence should be as close to each other as possible. If a preposition comes at the end of a sentence or a clause, it obviously cannot have its object after it, and this apparent disorder may be upsetting. But on occasion it seems awkward, stiff, and unnatural to be strictly formal in putting prepositions before their objects. We can easily say this: "That was the argument I fought against." We can change the sentence to read, "That was the argument against which I fought." But only a robot would talk like that. You can revise the sentence to read, "I fought against that argument"; but if you have been talking about several arguments and want to identify the particular one you have fought against, you may wish to say, "*That* was the argument I fought against."

In developing our style we make deliberate choices between alternatives that sometimes differ only slightly from each other. I can see an important difference in emphasis between the sentences, "That was the argument I fought against," and "I fought against that argument."

5. *Don't begin a sentence with a conjunction.*

Conjunctions are words that join sentence elements — words, phrases, or clauses. The common coordinating conjunctions — *and, but, for*, and *or*—join equal elements. Other conjunctions, such as *if*, *although*, *whether*, and *even*, join dependent elements.

I don't know the origin of the rule that sentences should never begin with a conjunction. It means a lot to some people. Any glance at a newspaper or magazine shows that professional writers frequently begin sentences with conjunctions. John F. Kennedy used conjunctions to begin fifteen sentences in his short inaugural address. E. B. White, one of the finest essayists of our time, uses conjunctions to begin many of his sentences. So does Lewis Thomas, one of our best writers about science. So the false rule would seem to have little validity among those who write English best.

Using a conjunction to begin a sentence emphasizes the connection between the thoughts of two consecutive sentences. With a conjunction at the start of a sentence you say something like this: "This sentence is closely related to the thought in the sentence immediately before it. But it is important enough to stand by itself, to begin with a capital letter, so you will have to take careful note of it."

Most sentences in English develop some thought in the sentence immediately preceding them. Although you may want to emphasize such connections now and then, your readers will become immune to the effect if you use the device of the conjunction too often. Too many conjunctions will start looking like a verbal tic, an eccentricity of style that can become as annoying as the steady kicking of a restless child against your seat in the movies. Used with circumspection, the device of beginning an occasional sentence with a conjunction can hold paragraphs together and make your prose a little more fluid.

6. *Never use the pronoun* you.

If you have read this far in this book, you know that I have violated this false rule again and again. This book is written in an informal, conversational style, and in conversations we address our readers with the second-person pronoun. We do the same in letters.

In more formal writing you should use the second person rarely if at all. The second person can be wordy, and often it is out of place. No one would write this sentence in a formal essay on cancer: "If you study cancer long enough, you will discover that it is not one disease but a large group of diseases that share certain lethal qualities." The writer would much more simply and directly say: "Cancer is not one disease but a group of related diseases." Nor would you use the pronoun *you* in an essay on history: "You have to sympathize with the Germans in World War I, facing as they did powerful enemies in both the east and the west." You will say something like this: "In World War I, Germany faced powerful enemies in both the east and the west."

Even in informal writing the second person should be sparingly used. No one can sensibly write a sentence like this one: "To serve in one of the first submarines, you had to be brave or foolish or both." Your readers did not serve in one of the first submarines, and you cannot meaningfully include them in the sentence. You have to say this: "Crew members on the first submarines had to be brave or foolish or both." Nor can you say this: "When you have been a famous athlete most of your life, you sometimes can't bear it when the cheering stops." Most of your readers have not been famous athletes all their lives. It is much better to write this: "Famous athletes sometimes can't bear it when the cheering stops."

7. Never use contractions.

Here much of the advice about the pronoun *you* can be repeated. Contractions do well in informal or semiformal prose — like the prose in this book. If your prose feels tight and difficult, you can perhaps loosen it by using contractions. Most teachers accept contractions in college papers, and contractions serve well enough in letters. We can easily write a friend, "I wanted to come to your party, but the snow was so thick that I didn't dare try to get the car out of the garage."

Contractions serve less well in formal essays. I feel uncomfortable using them in scholarly articles because I find them a little too conversational, a little too informal for a serious subject that I want to be taken seriously by the audience who will read the article. I have not seen contractions in dissertations, in formal books about history or philosophy or literary criticism, in business reports, or in articles in medical journals.

8. Use that *to introduce restrictive clauses,* which *to introduce non-restrictive clauses.*

Restrictive clauses add information essential to the main statement of the sentence; *non-restrictive clauses* add information that may be parenthetical, interesting and valuable but not essential to the meaning of the sentence. The restrictive clause in the following sentence is in italics:

The teacher *who gave me the worst grades* also taught me the most.

If we were to leave out the italicized clause, the sentence would not make any sense. Grammarians call the clause "restrictive" because it restricts the noun that it modifies. We are not talking about just any teacher; we are talking about the one teacher *who gave me the worst grades*. But here is a non-restrictive clause, one that does not restrict the meaning of the noun it modifies but merely adds some information:

> My English teacher, *who was also my next-door neighbor*, knew me from the time I was born.

Now we have a clause that can be deleted from the sentence without doing harm to the main statement. The clause is parenthetical; it adds interest, but it is not essential. It does not restrict the noun *teacher*.

Back in 1906, the English grammarian H. W. Fowler hit on the idea of using *that* to introduce restrictive clauses and *which* to introduce non-restrictive clauses. Fowler wanted people to write sentences like these:

> The song that Sam played in the Movie *Casablanca* was "As Time Goes By."

> The ocean, which we could see from our house, changed color according to the shifting light of the sun through the clouds.

Many people, especially academics over fifty years old, have taken Fowler's suggestion to be a rule of the language. Fowler himself knew better. Calling restrictive clauses "defining" and non-restrictive clauses "non-defining," he wrote the following:

> If writers would agree to regard *that* as the defining relative pronoun, and *which* as the non-defining, there would be much gain both in lucidity and in ease. Some there are who follow this principle now; but it would be idle to pretend that it is the practice either of most or of the best writers.[8]

Fowler was much more charitable than his modern disciples who have turned the that/which rule into a fetish. Few writers and editors care much about it. We use *that* or *which* according to some indefinable sense of which one sounds better in the sentence. It obviously cannot hold in who/whom clauses that may also be restrictive or non-restrictive, and it cannot help us in restrictive or non-restrictive phrases.

Yet it is important to make a difference between restrictive and non-restrictive clauses. The only sure way to do so is by proper use of

---

[8] H. W. Fowler, *A Dictionary of Modern English Usage*, second edition revised by Sir Ernest Gowers (New York and Oxford: Oxford University Press, 1965), 626.

commas. Restrictive clauses are not set off by commas; non-restrictive clauses are set off by commas. Sometimes the meaning of the sentence changes according to the way the writer places commas. Here is an example:

His novel, which he wrote in Virginia, sold more than 30,000 copies.

We are talking about the only novel he wrote. The non-restrictive clause, which is set off by commas, provides the additional information that he wrote the novel in Virginia.

His novel which he wrote in Virginia sold more than 30,000 copies.

Now we are identifying one novel among many. This is the novel *which he wrote in Virginia* as distinguished from the other novels he has written. The restrictive clause tells us something essential, and it is not set off by commas.

The that/which rule is false, and few writers pay attention to it. But you must follow the rule of using commas to set off non-restrictive clauses and not using commas to set off restrictive clauses. Otherwise you may not express the meaning you intend.

CONCLUDING REMARKS ON FALSE RULES

In considering the false rules, again you must think hard about your audience and the purpose of your essay. Consider the articles you read in the journals in which you would like to publish. Ask your teacher what she prefers in your papers. And use your head.

EIGHT

Good Diction

Diction is the choice of words we make when we write or speak, and good diction helps intelligent readers understand us, respect us, and believe us. Words have connotations, shades of meaning, associations with a long tradition of writing and speaking. If we call somebody an *opponent*, we mean one thing; if we call her an *enemy*, we mean another. If we say that a man is *charming*, we usually intend to compliment him; if we say he is *smooth*, we imply a slight insult; if we say he is *oily*, we mean a stronger insult, and perhaps we mean to warn people who may meet him.

THE QUALITIES OF GOOD DICTION

In good diction we use words efficiently. We do not pad our thought or inflate our utterances. A person may speak of *preplanning*, supposing that word to be more impressive than mere *planning*. And almost every bureaucrat nowadays speaks of *preconditions* for agreement when it would be much better to speak only of *conditions*.

In good diction we avoid words that might lead educated readers to suppose that we are ignorant of the written traditions of our language. The democracy of our society has extended to our language, and many popular words we hear on television or in the movies are now written easily in formal prose. Some words remain so questionable that you should not use them. You should not say this: "*Irregardless* of the cost, I am going to buy a new stereo." *Irregardless* is a double negative in a single word, since both the prefix *ir* and the suffix *less* convey a negation. You will never find the word in a published essay unless it occurs in a direct quotation. Nor will you find the word *ain't* in normal literate discourse, although you may find it in quotations. For some reason, *ain't*—a Cockney English word that originated in the eighteenth century—has never become part of our literary tradition. Perhaps it should have made the grade, since we don't have a contraction for *I am not* or *am I not*. It would seem efficient to say, "I ain't" or "ain't I?" But we do not say such things because the word retains its bad reputation.

THE CHANGING LANGUAGE

Language always changes, and nowadays it seems to be changing more rapidly than ever before. New words come into speech with amazing frequency, both because technology and urban life bring us so many different kinds of experience and because television and the daily newspapers have opened communication to so many people not acquainted with the literary and conservative tradition of language nurtured by readers and writers. Writers once controlled the language, and writers have nearly always been conservative in their use of language. But now talk-show hosts like Johnny Carson and Dick Cavett and the general run of sitcoms and police thrillers on television and in the movies affect the language far more than writers possibly can.

The spoken language may depend on tone of voice, on gestures, on conversational repetition. But the written language depends on words alone and on words that flow along without much repetition. When we read something, we do not have the author there to explain confusions or to repeat some difficult thought or to clarify some obscurity. So in the written language, words must be precise, used according to definitions educated people agree on.

These definitions are changing, and it is foolish and futile to withstand all these changes. Some changes show vitality and invention. One of my favorite books is entitled *9,000 Words: A Supplement to Webster's Third New International Dictionary*—a collection of words that have come into the English language during the past fifteen years. In it I find modern coinages such as *software, dunk shot, monokini, printout,* and *life-support system,* all of them signs of the nearly miraculous talent human beings have of finding names that help them describe and control their experiences. (Only a few years ago the ancester to that book was called *6,000 Words.*) When a baseball writer tells me that a shortstop is *showboating,* I find that word much stronger than the older term *showing off*. I don't suppose that I would like to read this sentence in a history book: "John Paul Jones was one of the great hot dogs of the American Revolution." But I don't mind reading a lighthearted sports story that tells me that a pitcher for the St. Louis Cardinals is a hot dog.

Not only do new words continually flow into the language, but old words just as continually change their meanings. In Shakespeare's day the word *shrewd* meant "wicked," not "clever" as it means today. *Courage* could mean "male sexual prowess," and a *queen* could be a prostitute. Only a few years ago novelists could write that a man *made love* to a woman while they rode along together in a carriage, and every reader knew that the man had proposed marriage to the woman. Modern readers would imagine a different and somewhat bizarre scene. In my own boyhood on a farm in mountainous east Tennessee, people still used *prevent* to mean "go before" or "announce," just as the word is used in the King James Version of the Bible, where the Psalmist tells us, "I prevented the dawning of the morning."

Some good words mysteriously pass out of the language altogether. When sixteenth-century Englishmen spoke of whispering, they used the word *rouning*. I like that word. It catches the low murmuring of some whispering, especially the kind that occurs in a crowd of people who do not so much whisper as grumble. But the word is gone. Our parents or grandparents talked about *swells*, persons who put on a great show of wealth. From it they derived the adjective *swell* and spoke of having a swell time at a party, meaning "a time befitting the rich." The word is all but gone now. Other words, like *spiffy*, *zany*, and *gosh*, are similarly in oblivion

Today the language is changing so swiftly that conservatives like me want to slow it down a little. Our language is a currency of meaning; currencies work best when their values remain constant. If words mean one thing today and another tomorrow, the possibility of communicating between generations is called into question. It is a great thing that an adolescent can read and enjoy Jonathan Swift's *Gulliver's Travels*, written over two centuries ago, and that the novels of Charles Dickens still live for readers more than a hundred years after Dickens died. The American democracy rests on a Constitution written generations ago, and it still makes sense to us.

In the novel *1984* George Orwell invented the word *newspeak* to stand for the terrifying loss of words' common meanings. When words lose precise meanings, thought becomes confused. Now we have the reprehensible use of the words *people's democracy* to describe harshly totalitarian states in which the people dare not dissent from government policy and where no election is honest and no voice represents the general will. And something called *national security* enables a government to invade the privacy of its citizens, perhaps burgle their houses or their offices, tap their telephones, limit their freedom of speech, and threaten them for having unpopular opinions.

Yet the conservative critics of language often express themselves foolishly. The critic John Simon has declared that language changes only because of ignorance. This is an opinion so ridiculous that we can scarcely take seriously anything else Simon has to say on the subject. But he is only the worst of a large group of linguistic purists who believe that the world is going to hell because some words' meanings have changed. While I deplore the bad temper and the blind outrage of these purists, I sympathize with their intuitions. The language should not be sterile; but it should be stable, not only because a stable language allows us to communicate across space in the present but also for the reason I have mentioned already: a reasonably stable language allows us to communicate across generations and provides a tradition that binds the living and the dead.

SOME LIVELY PROBLEMS IN USAGE

On the following pages I express my own thoughts about some lively problems in usage. When readers looked at the first draft of this book, several commented with dismay that I was far too conservative and that the strictness of some of my definitions might make writing more difficult for the inexperienced. I freely admit that my commentary on diction — like all such commentaries — reflects my own reading, experience, taste, and simple prejudice. I hope that I have read enough and thought enough about language to make my comments have some authority, but no informed reader will agree with all of them. I believe that the majority of professional writers and editors share my views.

Perhaps the greatest value of my list will be in its making you check my views against what you read. Look carefully at the prose in good magazines and popular nonfiction books to see how many times my rules are broken. This exercise will make you more conscious of language and more conscious of your own usage. To be aware that usage does offer problems is to start making the distinctions that make for clear writing.

All together/Altogether

If you say, "They gathered *all together* in one place," you mean that everyone was present at that place. If you say, "They were *altogether* mad," you mean they were completely mad. The adverb *together* always refers to some kind of collection; the adverb *altogether* always refers to some kind of completeness.

Alright/All right

The spelling *alright* is not acceptable to most editors although it turns up in thousands of student papers every year. Use two words: *all right*.

Amount/Number

The distinction is similar to that between *less* and *fewer*, which you will encounter later in this list. You have an *amount* of something not customarily divided into countable units. You have a *number* of things you can count:

A large number of people applauded her performance.

They left a large *amount* of litter on the floor.

Anxious/Eager

The debate about this pair of words goes back at least a century. It seems better to use *anxious* to indicate an element of fear in expectation, *eager* to show pleasure:

I am *eager* to attend the first baseball game in Fenway Park each April.

I am *anxious* that the Red Sox will fold in August as they always do.

Anymore/Any more

The adverb *anymore* should be used only in negative constructions after the negative statement. You can say, "He doesn't smoke *anymore*," and everyone will know he once smoked but stopped. Sometimes people say, "Anymore I drink tea rather than coffee." The speaker means she once drank coffee but now she drinks tea instead. A negation is implied, but the implication confuses most people accustomed to the convention that *anymore* must follow a negative. You can make a clearer statement like this: "I don't drink coffee anymore; I drink tea instead."

Always make a distinction between *anymore* and *any more*:

I never see her *anymore*. [adverb]

I don't want to see *any more* friends today. [adverb *any* + adjective *more*]

Apt/Liable/Likely

To say that someone is *apt* is to remark on a skill:

She is *apt* at finding exactly the right thing to say on any occasion.

To say that someone is *liable* is to remark on a legal obligation, usually an obligation for damages:

He was *liable* for all the costs of the accident.

To say that someone is *likely* to do something is to remark that she will probably do something:

If you frustrate someone continually, she is *likely* to get angry or discouraged.

As/Since

English writers commonly use these words as synonyms. Charles Darwin did so in *The Origin of Species,* and Charles Dickens did the same in his novels. The American practice of differentiating between the two words seems preferable. *As,* used as a conjunction, connotates contemporary time, something happening while something else is happening, too. *Since* gives the sense of something happening after something else, quite often causing the later event.

These sentences do not confuse:

He waved at me *as* the boat pulled away from the dock.

Since her mother became ill, she seldom goes out of the house.

But a sentence like this one can be confusing:

As I commute to work by bicycle, the cuffs of my pants sometimes get blackened by oil.

In isolation this sentence may convey the impression that commuting by bicycle causes my cuffs to get blackened by oil. In a paragraph it may appear that although the commuting and the blackening might occur at the same time, the bicycling is not clearly the cause of the blackening. *Since* conveys a stronger impression of causation than *as,* and the conjunction *because* conveys an even stronger impression:

Because I commute to work by bicycle, the cuffs of my pants sometimes get blackened by oil.

A while/Awhile

Awhile is an adverb used to modify verbs:

He stayed awhile.

While is a noun expressing an unspecified but usually short period of time. It is often the subject of a preposition:

He stayed for a while.

The sense of the two forms is so close that good writers often confuse them. The meaning given by most dictionaries for the adverb while is "for a while." Careful writers should make a distinction, and it is an easy matter. When while follows a preposition—usually in or for—you should make two words: a while; when while is used with a verb and without an intervening preposition, use awhile.

Between/Among

The standard rule is that between should be used to speak of two things; among, of more than two:

It was easy to make a distinction between the two words.

She moved gracefully among the people in the room.

The difference between the two words sometimes gets fuzzy. We don't speak of the infield on a baseball diamond as the space among the four bases, and we don't say that a treaty banning genocide was signed among most of the nations of the world. We say the treaty was made between the nations. If I am sitting with four friends at a table and wish to share a confidence, I say, "Just between us, I think his performance was terrible." I somehow don't feel comfortable saying, "Just among us, I think his performance was terrible."

The best rule seems to be to let literate people follow their inclinations. We should not fear using between with more than two when the intention is to show some kind of active participation of every party in response to someone's lead. And we should not fear using between to refer to an enclosed space and its boundaries, no matter how numerous those boundaries are. Even these rules are not sufficient to cover all the ways we can use *between* when we speak of more than two.

You should never write, "between you and I," or "between she and I," or "between she and he." *Between* is a preposition in these constructions, and the objects of prepositions should always be in the objective case. So you should say, "between you and *me*," or "between *her* and *me*," "between *her* and *him*." It is a common error to say, "between you and I," but literate people regard the usage as an error, and editors seldom accept it. True, Shakespeare used the construction "between you and I" in *The Merchant of Venice*, but a modern editor would blue pencil this usage.

You should also avoid the phrase *between each* in constructions like this one: "A wall was built between each of the rooms." *Each* is singular; *between* implies more than one. It does not make sense to say *between each* unless you add another parallel noun: "A wall was built between each room and the one adjacent to it." You would more likely change the construction entirely: "The rooms were separated by walls."

Co-equals

This is a redundancy like *irregardless*. Two captains in an army unit are not co-equal in authority; they are merely equal. But *co-* words are becoming common, probably in imitation of the word *copilot*. The problem is that we sometimes don't know whether *co-* signifies "equal to" or "assistant to." A copilot is an assistant to the pilot on an airplane. Some high school football teams have a captain and a *co-captain* who is like a *copilot*: that is, he takes over when the captain is unable to function or when the captain relinquishes his authority. Other teams don't have a captain at all and instead have co-captains supposedly equal to one another. The *co-* scene is a mess, and I think it better to abandon *co-* words entirely except when we have to speak of the copilot. Fortunately, we don't talk about copilots very often.

Common/Mutual

These two words have often been used as synonyms since at least the time of Shakespeare. Charles Dickens, no mean stylist, wrote a novel called *Our Mutual Friend*, and many people today use the word in a similar way in sentences like this one: "We were introduced by a mutual friend." But strictly speaking, *mutual* describes some reciprocal action, something going back and forth between two things or two persons. People can have a mutual affection or a mutual dislike for each other, meaning that each likes or dislikes the other. If they share something like an interest in photography, we should say, "They had a *common* interest in photography," or, "They shared an interest in photography."

The term *mutual friend* seems so established in the American habit of speech that it is foolish to fight it, and no one will hang you if you say, "You and I have a mutual friend." I still prefer to say, "You and I are both friends of Jack Wilcox."

Comprise/Include

Comprise means "to embrace." So we say:

Our country *comprises* fifty states.

This list *comprises* everyone in the county subject to jury duty.

The states in the United States do not comprise the country; they *make up* the country, or they *constitute* or *form* the country. So you should not say, "The fifty states comprise the United States"; you could not say, "The fifty states embrace the United States."

Comprise calls attention to all the parts. When you want to call attention to only a few of the parts that make up the whole, use *include*:

The United States *includes* Tennessee and Georgia.

The price *includes* a service warranty.

Conditions

The high frequency with which this word is used seems to originate with TV meteorologists. They talk about "snowy conditions prevailing in Minnesota" or "stormy conditions over New England." They cannot bear to say, "Snow is falling in Minnesota tonight," or, "Thunderstorms are flooding New Mexico." Now we have traffic conditions and economic conditions and housing conditions. When an Air-Florida jet crashed while taking off from Washington National Airport in 1982, one official was reported as saying, "Weather conditions are such that they are not conducive to rapid recovery." He apparently meant that it was too cold to recover the bodies swiftly from the icy Potomac River.

We should have snow, rain, weather, traffic, and housing, and we should use *conditions* to mean "requirements":

I made some *conditions* for letting him use the car: he had to carry out the garbage, clean his room, and stop being surly.

Yet conditions of all sorts come up in our prose, and now we have a further barbarism—*preconditions*: "Israel set certain preconditions for negotiations."

Contact

Many writers object to the use of *contact* as a verb. Strunk and White, in their classic little book *The Elements of Style*, advise readers to telephone, to write, or to get in touch with somebody but not to contact her. The objection probably arose because *contact* means "touch," and to use *contact* as a verb probably seemed vulgar to some because it is more blunt than *to get in touch with*. But professional writers have long since abandoned this rule, and few of us object to reading that someone will contact us about next week's meeting. The word means that some of us may be telephoned, others written to, and still others hailed on the street and reminded to come.

Continuous/Continual

Something *continuous* goes on without interruption; something *continual* goes on at intervals:

Water flows in a *continuous* whispering in the river.

Her life involved *continual* conversations.

Don't tell somebody that you expect to be with him continuously unless you never intend to let him out of your sight. It is all right to say that you hope to use the dictionary *continually* or that you will be in *continual* contact with someone over a business arrangement you are working out.

Cope

People often use this word to give the impression that they are saying much more than they really are. If you must use the word, say, "cope with," and follow the two words with some reasonable object:

I sometimes can't *cope with* mathematics in practical situations.

Some of us would prefer that you say, "I don't know how to figure compound interest," or, "I can't add up a bowling score." *Cope* carries with it (to my mind, at least) a vagueness that I don't like. But if you must use it, try to make it as specific as you can. To say, "I can't cope," is to admit some general debility, a frustration of some sort, but it does not locate the source of the frustration. It leaves readers and listeners and perhaps the person using the word in general confusion. Usually the expression is so mild that the confusion is unimportant, especially in casual speech. But in writing, you should eliminate unimportant and confusing locutions. Neither you nor your readers have time for them.

Couldn't care less/Could care less

The original idiom, which had a certain force in my adolescence, was, "I *couldn't* care less." It seemed straightforward and emphatic. It meant that someone cared so little for a person or a thing that he could not possibly feel a lower sentiment. "I couldn't care less about Jackson" meant that Jackson was so insignificant that you could not have less feeling about him no matter what he did.

Now the idiom has changed into the nonsensical, "I could care less." It seems to be everywhere. "I could care less about Jackson." If we take language seriously, this idiom now means that the speaker does care something about Jackson. Perhaps she adores Jackson. But for some unspecified reason she could care less about him. We wonder what that reason might be. With such an idiom as "I could care less," language has become not communication but incantation.

The problem can be avoided by using another, more simple, less hackneyed expression: "I don't like Jackson." At best, "I couldn't care less about Jackson" has become a cliché, and we may as well bury it. Even so, the cliché is better than the nonsensical phrase "I could care less."

Crafted/Handcrafted

These are advertising words with almost no meaning. They are in our language to stay, but we should realize how empty they are since that recognition may clean up our language a little. Supposedly *crafted* and *handcrafted* mean the same thing—that something has been made by hand and that the handwork guarantees a special quality. Often we say that writing is a *craft*, and we mean that writing is a manual activity, something we do carefully with our hands, and that we can polish it and make it better by spending more time on it.

In fact, many *crafted* items these days are made by machine. And a great many *crafted* or *handcrafted* items have to be made by hand, and things made by hand can be good or bad. If you buy a *handcrafted* shirt, for example, you may be sure that the stitching has been done by a sewing machine. Even if the pieces of the shirt were cut out by a machine, somebody had to operate the machine, so the salespeople can still speak of *crafting*. Much the same is true of shoes and most other items of clothing. We could speak of the *crafting* of automobiles since much of the work on assembly lines is done by hand, but we may get higher quality cars if robots do the work. Robots don't have hangovers on Mondays or feel the rush to quit early on Friday afternoons.

Different from/Different than

Most writers use *different from* and consider *different than* bad diction, although the distinction seems to be fading. Most writers I know prefer to say, "His tastes in literature are *different from* what they used to be," but some will say, "His tastes in literature are *different than* they used to be." Nearly everyone will say, "Her tastes are different from mine." I prefer *different from*, and I think most editors are still more comfortable with this form than they are with *different than*.

Differ from/Differ with

These two offer little trouble. If you *differ from* someone, the two of you have different qualities. If you *differ with* someone, you have a disagreement:

> I *differ from* him in age, appearance, and origin, but we were lifelong friends.

> I *differed with* her on the proposal for the new building. I thought the plans were beautiful, but she thought they were old-fashioned and foolish.

The difference between these phrases shows one of the glories and mysteries of English. Some uses of the same words have radically different meanings. Why these differences should occur may seem mysterious since there is little logic to them. The careful writer observes the differences. We know that there is a lot of difference between *making up with someone* and *making out with someone*, and we know there is a difference between *putting up* with someone and *putting on* with someone. These differences are part of idiom, the habits we use in conveying meaning. Knowing idiom is a part of writing well, and you should always be careful to use idiom according to the conventions of English.

Dilemma

Properly speaking, a *dilemma* is a vexing problem that presents us with two equally unattractive choices and requires us to make one. Confirmed cigarette smokers face a dilemma: they can give up a habit that provides them much pleasure and suffer discomfort, prolonged nervousness and irritability, and perhaps also a failure of concentration; or they can keep on smoking and run a high risk of lung cancer, heart disease, and emphysema.

Often now people use *dilemma* to indicate any serious problem, and the language is poorer in consequence. Your best bet is to use *dilemma* only when you are speaking of a necessary choice between painful alternatives. Once you have named the dilemma, you should immediately tell what the contrary choices are.

Disinterested/Uninterested

Disinterested may be one of those words we should retire from the language for a time, substituting the word *impartial*. Then, at least, we could avoid using the word improperly.

The *disinterested* person has nothing to gain or lose no matter who wins an argument or a contest. Juries, umpires, referees, judges, and teachers should be *disinterested*. Jonathan Edwards, the great American Puritan preacher of the eighteenth century, defined love as "disinterested benevolence," the kind of benign feeling toward others that does not demand anything from them in return. But a judge should not go to sleep with a murder trial going on under his nose; he should be *interested* and *disinterested* at the same time. To be *uninterested* is to have a lack of interest. I happen to be *uninterested* in chess.

The confusion of these words has been around for a long time, and it is not likely to disappear soon. Perhaps the best solution is to retire *disinterested* from the language and use the word *impartial* instead.

Dubious/Doubtful

Things are *dubious* when they cause doubt; people are *doubtful* about *dubious* things:

> His tale of how the ghost stood at the foot of his bed at midnight was *dubious*.

> I was even more *doubtful* when I discovered that he had been drinking all evening before he saw the apparition.

The distinction between these words has long been recognized in

English, but now it is wearing thin, and the two are often used as synonyms. It seems to be a distinction worth preserving, and careful editors and writers still maintain it.

Due to/Because

A journalism professor of mine years ago told his class that the only correct use of *due to* was in a sentence like this: "The train was *due to* arrive at two o'clock." *Due to* leads to clumsy constructions, especially when it is used for *because* at the opening of clauses: "She was late due to the fact that her car broke down." It is much simpler to say, "She was late because her car broke down."

Often the use of *due to* makes the statement of a sentence vague: "He got a life sentence due to the murder." Did he commit the murder? Probably, since he got the life sentence for it. But the sentence is so vague that it could imply that the judge and the jury made a mistake. So *due to* is one of those constructions that, while not wrong in itself, keep us from making a clearer statement.

Effect/Affect

A perennial problem! The word *effect* is usually a noun, as in the phrase *cause and effect*.

The *effect* of her decision was to create a boom in the computer business.

Affect is commonly a verb:

My attitude always *affects* my performance.

Occasionally *effect* is used as a verb meaning "to cause":

Luther's revolt against the Catholic Church *effected* a revolution in Western thought.

Effect used as a verb carries with it the connotation of completeness, of having done something to the full.

Ensure/Insure

Use *ensure* when you are making sure that something happens; use *insure* when you are talking about an insurance policy:

The only way we can *ensure* good writing is to require students to write continually as part of their education.

You should *insure* your car against theft.

Enthuse/Enthusiastic

It is still not widely acceptable among professional writers and editors to use the word *enthuse* as in the sentence, "They were all *enthused* at the prospects." It is much more common to use the adjective *enthusiastic*: "I am *enthusiastic* at the prospect of making the trip."

Factor

A much overused word, a verbal signal that a paper will be dull. Like other such words, its chief fault is not that it is wrong but that it prevents us from making a more specific statement. It allows us to shilly-shally. "His character was a factor in the breakup of our friendship." Writing such an ambiguous sentence keeps us from saying, "I discovered that he was a liar and a cheat, and so I ended our friendship," or, "He was much more successsful than I was, so I decided I disliked him."

Factor is one of those words that substitute easy writing for the hard work of finding words to express our thoughts exactly. Your best bet when *factor* leaps to mind is to ask yourself exactly what you want to say. Then say it and forget about *factor*.

Feedback

This word, like *imput*, has come into the language from the world of electronics. It originally denoted a circuit by which part of the output of a radio source was brought back to its origin. Sometimes this feedback was unintentional, and the result was a high, ugly howl in the loudspeaker. Now *feedback* is commonly used as a synonym for *response* when people talk about other human beings. It is becoming increasingly common in all sorts of bureaucratic writing, but it seldom appears in well-edited books and magazines. I strongly object to mechanistic metaphors to describe things human beings should do with their brains. *Feedback* makes us sound like robots.

Feel bad/Feel badly

We *feel bad* when something makes us sorry; we *feel badly* if we have burned our fingers or otherwise damaged our skin so that we have harmed our sense of touch. If I say, "Loretta *feels badly* because Leo lost their car in a poker game," I mean that Leo's rash stupidity took the feeling out of her fingers. If I say she *feels bad* about the loss, I mean she is sorry.

The verbs of sense used with several common linking verbs cause trouble because some writers and speakers mistake a predicate adjective for an adverb. A predicate adjective modifies the subject of a clause. We do not have any trouble with sentences like this one: "He looked healthy and happy." We understand that the meaning of the sentence is this: "He looked to be healthy and happy." Hardly anyone would write, "He looked healthily and happily." We also say, "She sat *still* in the house." We would not say, "She sat stilly in the house." And we say, "He felt *damp* after being caught in the rain." No one would say, "He felt damply after being caught in the rain." We write without difficulty, "He walked into the room *resolute* and *angry*," knowing that it is not his walking that is resolute and angry but that *he* is resolute and angry. We should close a door *tight* because we mean to close it until it is tight in its frame. If we close the door tightly, we imply that we are drunk — or at least *tight* — as we shut the door. We have our steak cooked *rare* because to have it cooked rarely would mean that most of the time we eat raw steak.

So we feel *bad* when something displeases us or when we do something foolish that we regret, just as we smell *bad* when we have not taken a bath in a while and smell *good* when we have just bathed with good soap. We feel *good* when our team wins, and we feel *bad* when it loses.

Flaunt/Flout

To *flaunt* something means to wave it proudly for everyone to see. The implication is that some people will be displeased for all that waving but the flaunter does not care:

Many bright freshmen *flaunt* their SAT scores.

Flout means "to disobey," "to scorn," or "to run in the face of some rule," and to do so flagrantly, proudly, openly, even arrogantly:

Boston drivers flout all the rules of the road.

Both *flout* and *flaunt* imply a certain pride or even arrogance. This pride in each is responsible for the confusion of the words, but the distinction is important and worth preserving.

Fortuitous/Fortunate

Something that happens *fortuitously* happens by chance or by accident and may be good or bad:

> Mr. Daley's election was entirely *fortuitous*; he happened to be the only candidate not yet in jail at the time.

We could not argue that Mr. Daley's election under such circumstances was *fortunate*. The collision of two cars is usually *fortuitous*. It is not fortunate; it is simply accidental. *Fortuitous*, like *disinterested*, seems to have lost so much of its strength that you should consider using another word instead of it to avoid misunderstanding. I would not now write this sentence: "He happened to be home sick that day, and so his presence in the house at the moment of the attempted burglary was entirely fortuitous." I would say, "He happened to be home sick that day, and so it was entirely by chance that he happened to be in the house when the burglars tried to break in."

Fulsome

Here is another word so often misused that its proper meaning has perhaps been irretrievably buried under confusion. Until recently the common meaning of *fulsome praise* was praise so flattering that it could not possibly be sincere. *Fulsome* meant "disgusting" or "obsequious" or even "nauseating," and anyone who received *fulsome praise* without protest was taken to be blindly arrogant. Anyone who would give *fulsome praise* was a boot-licking sycophant. But now *fulsome* often means "great" or "hearty" praise.

It is a shame that the distinction is being lost, for our language will be impoverished by the loss of such an ironic and useful term. *Insincere praise* carries none of the force of *fulsome praise*, but now the cult of exaggeration makes the simple offering of praise or *lavish* praise or *high* praise seem inadequate. All our expressions must be inflated until they are sound and fury, signifying nothing very much, depending on the exuberance with which they are delivered rather than on the plain meaning of words. The writers and speakers who exaggerate everything are responsible for turning *fulsome* into an inflated adjective, and in their eagerness for emphatic utterance, they have failed to see that the traditional meaning is the opposite of their intended meaning.

Hands-on

The expression is a current fad and may not be in use by the time

this book is published. It sounds like advertising hype, a barbarous combination that seems to be used most of the time as an adjective.
Somebody told me not long ago that teachers of architecture in a certain university had once run a *hands-on* program for their students but
that lately these professors had withdrawn, leaving the students to
teach themselves. I wondered why this person did not say that teachers
had once helped students with their work, talked to them frequently,
and supervised them carefully. All these expressions would have been
more specific than *hands-on*.

Head up

People now seldom *head* or *direct* or *lead* things. Instead they *head
up* committees, bands, groups, classes, or whatever. I don't know what
up adds to *head* except perhaps a specious bureaucratic importance.

Healthy/Healthful

Something is *healthy* if it enjoys good health, if it is strong, vigorous, and alive:

Jack kept himself *healthy* by eating well and running every day.

Marge had a *healthy* arrogance.

Something is *healthful* if it contributes to the health of something
else:

He took *healthful* exercise every day.

War is not *healthful* for any of us.

Hopefully/Hope

Hopefully seems to be an idiom that since about 1932 has come into the language as a synonym for *I hope* or *it is hoped*. The ninth edition
of the Merriam-Webster *New Collegiate Dictionary* offers a scornful
note against the "irrationally large amount of critical fire" drawn by the
word when it is used as a synonym for *I hope* or *it is hoped*, and it offers
analogies with *interestingly, presumably,* and *fortunately* which are often
used as "sentence modifiers," that is, modifiers of entire sentences.

While willing to admit that usage is king and that probably no great
good is accomplished by opposing *hopefully*, I must nevertheless state
some reservations that to me, at least, are compelling. For one thing, 76

percent of a usage panel assembled by Wright Morris, editor-in-chief of *The American Heritage Dictionary*, and Mary Morris, a distinguished authority on usage, said they would not use *hopefully* in the sense of *I hope* or *it is hoped*. That such a lopsided majority should oppose the word should give us some pause in using it.

The words *interestingly, presumably,* and *fortunately,* cited by the editors of the Merriam-Webster dictionary, offer little of the ambiguity of *hopefully.* If we say, "Presumably he joined the army," we know that the adverb does not modify the entire sentence but that it modifies the verb *joined,* and there is no ambiguity in the sentence. It is presumed he joined the army; we do not know if he did or not. But if we say, "Hopefully he joined the army," we are left in a dilemma. Thanks to today's usage, we do not know if he joined the army with hope in his heart—the obvious grammatical meaning of the sentence—or if the writer of the sentence hoped he joined the army. And it is in just this ambiguity that opponents of *hopefully,* including me, find the word offensive.

Other adverbs are equally ambiguous and equally offensive. "Briefly, the battle of Verdun lasted for ten months." People may use *briefly* in such a way to mean that they are going to be brief in their statement. But the statement would be far clearer if the authors of such sentences left the word *briefly* out. "Happily Robert Ford shot Jesse James before Jesse could kill anyone else." We do not know if Robert Ford shot happily or if the author of the sentence is happy because Robert Ford did the shooting.

So it is with *hopefully,* as in the sentence, "Hopefully the faculty will get a raise this year." Does the sentence mean that the faculty is certain to get a raise and that it will receive its bounty with hope in its collective heart? Or does it mean that the writer of the sentence hopes that the faculty will get a raise? The latter meaning is probably more in accord with current informal usage. The administration may hope with all *its* collective heart that the faculty will not get a raise. Is it too demanding to ask that writers tell where the hope is originating? "The faculty hopes it will get a raise this year." "I hope the faculty will get a raise this year."

To use *hopefully* in the novel, popular sense has another disadvantage: adverbs cannot be inflected; they have only one form. Consequently nobody can say, "Hopefully when I was young, I would be rich." We must say, "When I was young, I hoped to be rich." The verb *to hope* can be inflected to show when the hope goes on. In the past tense, you usually say, "I hoped." Why not use the verb in the present tense as well?

But the main objection to *hopefully* is that it makes something abstract that is in fact personal. Hope is not something that floats around in the air like nitrogen; hope is an emotion we feel as persons, and we ought to locate its source and the people who have it. I hope that readers will take seriously these comments on a common usage.

Illusion/Allusion

We make an *allusion* by referring to something without mentioning it specifically. We create an *illusion* by making an image that is not reality:

> When he told me that he wanted nothing more than to lie down in green pastures, he was making an *allusion* to the Twenty-third Psalm.

> In our society, movies cause *illusions* that often take our minds off our troubles.

An *allusion* is always indirect. It is not the same as a mention. Literary allusions often enliven writing by making us recall other things we have read. When we read, "All his ambitions were but sound and fury," we recall Shakespeare's Macbeth and the soliloquy in which Macbeth declares that life is a "tale, told by an idiot, full of sound and fury, but signifying nothing." A writer does not have to mention Macbeth by name; we would think him pedantic if he did so. So he makes an allusion.

Imply/Infer

Here is another confusion that has lasted for many centuries, and I can express only a majority opinion, not a unanimous verdict. We *imply* something by conveying a meaning in some way other than a direct statement; we *infer* a conclusion by reasoning out the evidence although that evidence may not deliver the solid proof we may wish.

> By his rudeness, Mr. Bradley *implied* that he did not wish to have lunch with me, although he did accept my invitation.

> I *inferred* from his hostility that I had done something to offend him.

Cognate words of *imply* and *infer* are *implication* and *inference*. Here we seldom find confusion. "There was an implication in his words that I could not quite understand." That is, he *implied* something that I could not grasp. "The inference that I drew was that she did not want to tell me everything." That is, I *inferred* that she did not wish to tell me everything she knew. We shall come back to inference in the chapter on argument.

Incredible/Incredulous

Something is *incredible* if we cannot believe it. We are *incredulous* when we cannot believe something incredible:

> His belief that taxes could be cut, military spending increased, and the budget balanced was *incredible*.

> Her remark that she had read all the works of Tolstoy in a week left me *incredulous*.

In recent years the adjective *incredible* has become an all-purpose exaggeration. We say that something was *incredibly* interesting or *incredibly* bad. The word is so overused that it has died, and it is far better to tell why something is interesting or why something is bad than merely to tell us that we cannot believe how interesting or how bad it is.

Indicate/Say

To *indicate* is much the same as *to imply*, though the connotation of *to indicate* is usually a little stronger. That is, something *indicated* is nearly always true, but something *implied* may be true or false. Even this distinction between the two words is not always observed. *Indicate* is often used to show that something is happening without any special intention on the part of the actor. *Imply* is customarily used when the actor of the verb wishes to convey some significance beyond the plain meaning of the words.

Smoke *indicates* fire. The smoke is impersonal; it has no intention. It is a sign that a fire is burning even if we cannot see the fire. A woman laughing *indicates* that she is happy. She may be laughing spontaneously without intending to show that she is happy, but she shows her happiness whether she intends to do so or not.

If someone says something directly and unambiguously, you should say so, using the verb *say*, not *indicate*:

> "Tuition is going up by 14 percent next year," the president *said*.

She did not *indicate* that tuition was going up; she made a plain statement of fact that should not be softened by the weaker word *indicate*. But you can say:

> The recent losing seasons by the football team, the disapproval voiced by the alumni, and the refusal of the president to speak to him in public *indicate* general dissatisfaction with the coach.

Individual

A much overused word. Use *individual* only when you make a deliberate comparison between a single person or object and a group:

> One of the great philosophical problems has always been to define the rights of the *individual* against the rights of the society as a whole.

It is stiff and pretentious to write, "At the parade, I saw three individuals I knew."

Sometimes the word *individual* is used for no good reason with the word *each*: "Each individual house on the block has a porch and a garage." Only a little thought shows that *Each individual* is a redundant phrase. You get the same meaning by saying "Each house."

Innovative

Why not say *original* instead? *Innovative* is a longer word, now so overused that *original* will sound original when you use it.

-ize

You can tack *-ize* onto just about any noun and make a verb, so that we *summarize* and *organize*, and increasingly, we *finalize*. A problem arises when we pass the uncertain boundary into writing that becomes tedious because we use *-ize* too much and rob English of its natural rhythmic beauty. Nowadays people *utilize* when the verb *use* expresses the same thought. Organists now *concertize* across America, and a recent newspaper headline urged me to *accessorize* my garden. A workman told me a year or so ago that he would *prioritize* my office when I complained that the temperature in there was forty-five degrees in January. I was tempted to tell him that I would prefer to have it thermalized.

Such frequent use of the suffix *ize* threatens to turn English into a species of pig Latin, and we should resist the trend.

Less/Fewer

Some authorities think this distinction has been lost, and in some professional writing it has indeed been blurred, but most careful writers still preserve it. The distinction is much like that of *amount* and *number* commented on early in this list. *Less* is used for quantities not customarily counted by unit; *fewer* is used for quantities that can be counted by unit:

There was *less* litter on the floor because *fewer* people used the room.

Still we use *less* in some idioms when we might at first suppose that *fewer* would be preferred:

She gave me *less* than ten dollars.

Today's high temperature was ten degrees *less* than yesterday's.

In these usages we sense a unity of quantity in the money and in the temperature, and we use *less* to express our sense of the wholeness of what we describe.

Lie/Lay

One of the most commonly violated distinctions. Both the verbs are irregular in the past and in the past participle — a major reason for the confusion they cause writers and speakers. To complicate things still more, the past tense of *lie* is *lay*. No wonder even educated people mess them up! *Lie* means "to recline"; *lay* means "to put" or "to place":

I *lie* on the floor to take a nap in the afternoon.

I *lay* a paperback book under my head as a pillow.

The past tense is more troublesome:

Yesterday I *lay* on the floor and took a nap.

I *laid* a paperback book under my head as a pillow.

The past participle can give trouble, too:

I have often *lain* on the floor to take a nap.

I have *laid* a paperback book under my head as a pillow.

The *lay/lie* affair gets more complicated when we consider some folk usages that come down to us from the time when English reflexive verbs were more common than they are now: "Now I lay me down to sleep; I pray the Lord my soul to keep." Obviously the prayer in modern idiom might be phrased like this: "Now I lie down to sleep."

Despite the confusions, you should learn this one carefully. The distinction is important, and people with an ear for language notice when others confuse the words.

Like/As

This distinction is changing before our eyes. The supposed rule, followed by most editors and writers, is that *like* should never be used as a conjunction to join two clauses. But in speech and informal writing many educated people have been using *like* as a conjunction for years. Charles Darwin wrote, "Unfortunately, few have observed like you have done,"[1] and not long ago N. R. Kleinfield wrote in the business pages of the *New York Times* about the decline of the audience for televised professional football games:

> One result is that disgruntled advertisers, complaining that they are not getting the audience for commercials that they expected have been banging on the networks' doors, looking for restitution. And it looks like they will be successful.[2]

A recent short story in *The New Yorker* contains this line:

> "They're not Swedes," I tell him. But he acts like he doesn't hear me.

Many authorities want *like* to govern only nouns, pronouns, or a noun substitute such as a gerund. No one should object to this sentence: "I felt like coming in the summer." *Coming* is a gerund, a noun substitute, and can be governed by *like*. But many will object if you write, "I felt like I would come in the summer." These objectors will prefer that you write, "I felt *as if* I would come in the summer."

You will be safe from attack if you use *as if* instead of *like* to introduce a clause. But to many ears *like* is more simple and even more pleasing, and this is a place in the grammatical rule book where you should make up your own mind, knowing that if you do use *like* as a conjunction, many people will be annoyed.

The confusion between *like* and *as if* is not nearly so disturbing to me as the ill-considered effort of some dislikers of *like* to purge *like* from the honorable place it has long occupied in our language. It is perfectly correct to say, "The party included some distinguished guests *like* the dean of the college and the president of the university." But the fastidious here substitute *such as* for like. There is nothing at all wrong with using *such as*; but there is nothing wrong with *like* here either. The

---

[1] Charles Darwin, *Life and Letters*, vol. VIII, p. 58 (cited in O.E.D.).
[2] N. R. Kleinfield, *The New York Times*, Nov. 23, 1983, C-1.

"rule" that writers follow in using *such as* is aptly phrased by one textbook which gives this advice: "When you are giving an example of something, use *such as* to indicate that the example is a representative of the thing mentioned, and use *like* to compare the example to the thing mentioned." This rule would give us these sentences: "The party included distinguished guests *such as* the dean of the college," and, "He wanted to be distinguished *like* the dean of the college." The rule is harmless for those who trouble themselves with it, but that number does not include many professional writers.

A somewhat more troublesome use of *like* is in comparisons like these: "She sings like a bird"; "he walks like an elephant." These sentences imply a verb following the final noun: "She sings like a bird sings"; "he walks like an elephant walks." So if the verb were written, the sentences would be formally incorrect. In fact the verb is not written, and we are permitted to let her sing like a bird if she can, and we may allow him to walk like an elephant if he must. It would be a false note to have her sing *as* a bird and heavy-footed indeed to have him walk *as* an elephant.

Literally

This word gives notice to your readers that you are not using metaphor or hyperbole. When you say, "My papers were *literally* scattered to the winds," you mean that a storm blew your papers in confusion down the street. When you say, "He *literally* did not have a dime to his name," you don't mean he was merely short of money; you mean he could not find as much as a dime in his house.

Avoid using *literally* merely to be emphatic when you don't mean what you are saying. Don't say, "My blood literally boiled" unless your temperature rose to 212 degrees Fahrenheit and you started giving off steam. Much of the time you can avoid the word altogether. Instead of saying "Literally thousands gathered to hear her speak," you should probably say, "Thousands gathered to hear her speak."

Masterful/Masterly

This distinction has been all but lost, and I regret its passing. *Masterful* once meant "domineering" or "overbearing"—acting like a master ruling his slaves. *Masterly* meant "with the skill of a master." If we say, "Coach Dixie did a *masterful* job preparing his team for the game with Alabama," we mean that he treated his team like a chain gang. If we say that he did a masterly job, we mean that he did everything a great coach is supposed to do to prepare a team for a big game. To confuse the words eliminates a fine distinction.

Me/I

We have already considered the phrase *between you and me* in the rubric dealing with *between*. The phrase should always be *between you and me*. *I* should never be a direct object or the object of a preposition in a sentence. You should never say, "He told Rocky and I that he would not fight the challenger," or, "She sent Jill and I to the library for the book."

Oddly enough, just as *I* has become misused in the objective case, *me* is now often misused in the nominative, or subjective, case. Many people say, "Me and Paul went to the movies Friday night," or, "Joan and me took a writing course last summer."

The misuse of *me* and *I* is a serious sign of illiteracy, and you should learn the differences between these pronouns and use them correctly.

Medium/Media

The word *medium* is a singular noun that signifies anything that enables something else to work or appear. Until recently its most common use was in the phrase *medium of exchange*, which means money or anything else that allows people to carry on trade. In recent times the plural form *media* has come to mean all the instruments of mass communication that serve society. The *media* include radio, television, newspapers, and magazines. A connotation of the word seems to be something ephemeral, something that does not remain important for long. Books are a medium of communication, but somehow they are usually excluded when we speak of the *media*.

Two objections may be raised against the word *media*: it is less specific and therefore less vivid than the words it replaces, and it is often misused by appearing with the singular form of a verb or pronoun. You should not say, "The media *is* responsible for much of the crime in America because *it* glorifies violence."

It seems far better to say something specific: "The story of how much he embezzled was spread all over the front page of the morning paper, and this evening it got five minutes on the television news."

Militate against/Mitigate

Mitigate means "to lessen," often for good reason. If you are charged in court with trespass for driving your power mower through your neighbor's prize-winning flower garden, your lawyer may claim the *mitigating circumstance* that you are allergic to roses and that your neighbor's profusion of roses makes your eyes water and your nose run and your head ache and your skin break out in hives. The judge may then *mitigate* the rigor of the law that applies in your case.

Militate is related to *military*, and anything that *militates against* a position offers a strong reason for not accepting it:

> My staff's unanimous opposition to the book *militates against* my using it in the program.

The common confusion of the two words comes about because people want a hard *g* sound to go with both words in the phrase *militate against*. So they use *mitigate against* when in fact that phrase makes no sense. Here is a rare instance in English where spoken rhythms, otherwise so desirable in speech and in writing, will lead the unwary reader astray.

Model/Replica

A *model* duplicates the appearance of something else but on a larger or smaller scale. A model railroad duplicates the appearance of a railroad but will fit on a table. A model of the DNA molecule is millions of times larger than the real thing and so will allow students to study it.

A *replica* must be like its original in every detail including size. The *replica* of the *Mayflower* in the harbor of Plymouth, Massachusetts, is exactly like the original ship. At least it is exactly like what we know of the original.

So the term *exact replica* is redundant. A replica is exact by definition.

More important/More importantly

It is incorrect to say, "The Yankees lost the pennant, but more importantly, they lost money." In constructions like this one, a clause is implied—*what is more important*. This elliptical clause (we call it *elliptical* because some of its words are omitted) works as a noun rather than an adverb. In this sentence, a *Time* writer uses the expression correctly:

> *More important*, he sat at Stengel's side, learning the game from one of its managerial geniuses.

You should also avoid saying *firstly, secondly, thirdly, fourthly,* and so on. The same rule applies. The elliptical clause is *what is first,* and if you have to write in numbers like this, you should say merely *first, second,* and so on.

Nauseous/Nauseated

When you are sick to your stomach and ready to vomit, you are *nauseated.* If you come on a dead horse and get sick at the sight, the horse is *nauseous:* it makes you vomit. Something *nauseous* will make you feel *nauseated.* So don't say, "I'm nauseous" unless you make people throw their hands over their mouths and run for the bathroom whenever you walk into a room.

Ongoing

A bureaucratic synonym for *continuing. Ongoing* is another of those flat, dull words that usually signal bad prose to follow.

-Oriented/Orientation

We live in a *goal-oriented* society.

He was *success-oriented* as a youth but *leisure-oriented* as an adult.

The suffix *-oriented* and the noun *orientation* turn up all over the place now. They are vague and colorless, keeping us and our readers from concrete thought. It is much better to say things like this: "We live in a society that demands that people set goals for themselves." And, "As a young man, MacDougal wanted success, but when he got older he wanted only to drink beer, play golf, watch television, and read trashy novels."

Parameters

This word has become a synonym for *limits,* a good, strong word that says everything most people mean by *parameters* and says it more clearly.

The only generally accepted meaning of *parameter* is as a variable in mathematics, including the applied mathematics of computer science. For example, you can set the parameters of a computer to give you sixty-six characters on a line and twenty-nine lines to a page, and the computer will paginate for you according to those numbers, no matter how many pages you write. If you are figuring compound interest at

18.5 percent per annum, your parameter is the figure 18.5, and if you compound interest monthly, that parameter will impose a shape on the sum that is being subjected to the interest.

Parameters may well be used on occasion in nonmathematical metaphors. We can say, "Grace and courtesy have always been parameters of social success," or, "Creativity is the intellectual parameter for all the great disciplines." But when *parameters* becomes only a glorified synonym for *limits*, the language becomes flatulent.

Posture

This has become a word much like *conditions* and *case* and the intensifiers *definitely, absolutely,* and *incredible.* It is popular—and says almost nothing that cannot be said more simply and more vigorously in other words. Instead of, "They adopted a waiting posture," why not say, "They decided to wait"?

Preplanning/Advanced planning

Both these terms are tautological. That is, they say the same thing twice. *Planning* must take place before the thing that is planned. You do not need to inflate the idea of planning by adding the prefix *pre-* or the modifier *advanced* as if some kinds of planning will go on after the occasion being planned for.

Presently/Currently/Now

The adverb *presently* most properly serves to denote something that is about to happen:

The actors will appear *presently.*

Recently the word *presently* has become a synonym for *now* or *currently* so that we get usages like this: "He is *presently* in a committee meeting." It seems better to hold to the older meaning of *presently* and to use either *now* or *currently* or let the present tense stand by itself to express something happening now: "He is in a committee meeting."

Principal/Principle

Principal always has the connotation of "first." It is most often an adjective meaning the first or the most important:

The *principal* reason I refused her invitation was that I am allergic to her cat.

It is sometimes used as a noun to designate a person of primary authority:

The *principal* of the grammar school taught his football team that sportsmanship was fine as long as it did not keep them from winning games.

The *principals* in the final drama of the Civil War were Ulysses S. Grant and Robert E. Lee.

Principle is always a noun meaning an ideal standard of conduct or an underlying system that helps explain some things we may see only in a superficial way until we think about them.

One man's *principle* is another's poison.

The *principle* of the thermometer is that liquids expand with heat and contract with cold.

Quotation/Quote

Quotation is a noun. *Quote* is a verb, although lately it has been more and more common as a noun. I still think it poor to write this sentence: "These quotes from Faulkner prove that he knew the Bible well." I like better the older usage: "These *quotations* from Faulkner prove he knew the Bible well."

Since *quote* is a verb, you can say:

He *quoted* a price that I found excessive.

Dickens continually *quoted* Shakespeare.

Relationship

Relationship seems to be here to stay. It says little that *relation* or *relations* does not say, and until fairly recently it was used only to denote blood kin. Then it became a synonym for relations that no one could precisely define, like those between men and women who lived together without getting married. It is now a regular substitute for concrete thought, since people who use it feel relieved of the obligation of saying exactly what it means.

Respective/Respectively

You should use these words only when some real confusion might result without them:

> The winners of first and second prizes were Jack Rowdy and Meg Loader, *respectively*.

Otherwise someone might suppose that Jack and Meg had somehow shared the two prizes. But unless there is such confusion, get rid of the word. It is probably better to write, "Jack Rowdy won first prize, and Meg Loader took second."

Simple/Simplistic

Something *simple* is uncomplicated. People, machines, novels, poems, and plans can be simple. Only ideas or utterances can be *simplistic*, and the connotation of *simplistic* is always bad.

A *simple* idea to raise enough money to repair the American highway system might be to impose an additional tax of ten cents a gallon on gasoline and diesel fuel. A *simplistic* idea might be to turn all the highways into toll roads. This idea would be simplistic since the person advancing it would not have thought of how much money it would cost to build and operate the toll booths, how many accidents they could cause, and how much they would increase fuel consumption by making cars stop and start again.

Societal/Social

What does *societal* say that *social* does not? No one has ever been able to explain the difference to me, and I suspect that *societal* is merely inflated language.

Supportive

Another new coinage seeming to carry some great weight although it is a bar to clear expression. Only a few years ago *supportive* was rarely used, and when it was, it meant that one physical thing supported another. An arch was supportive of a bridge; a beam was supportive of a roof. The word was rarely used because the verb *support* was and is stronger than the adjective *supportive*. It is much sharper to say, "The beam supported the roof." Now *supportive* is used in a vague way to express emotional support given by one person to another. We ought to get rid of that usage.

That

This excellent and useful word has lately been pressed into service as a synonym for the adverb *very*. *Very* is a weak adverb; *that* seems to be stronger. So we get sentences like this one: "The game wasn't that good." The usage is always in the negative, and the logical question is to ask what the referent of *that* might be. We can readily understand the word if it occurs in a sentence like this:

> I have been sunburned through a shirt, but my son's skin is not that sensitive.

The preceding statement about my sunburn gives some context to the statement that my son's skin is not *that* sensitive. But what of this sentence? "His skin was not *that* sensitive." How sensitive? We have no context to tell us.

Perhaps the original idiom was *all that good* or *all that bad*. By ellipsis it has been shortened to merely *that*. It was not a good idiom in the first place, and the shortening of it has made it worse.

This

Now and then you can get away with a vague *this* in your prose if your context is clear:

> Frederick Bazille and Claude Monet started painting in the open air; *this* was the real beginning of French Impressionist art.

The *this* in the sentence above refers to the act of painting in the open air described in the first independent clause, and we have no trouble understanding the reference. But the vague *this* often leads to confusion. In general it is better to have *this* refer to a noun or a noun substitute:

> Narcotics damage the brain and the rest of the body and harm not only the habitual user but also the society of which the user is a part. *This* social influence of drugs is the reason laws should regulate their sale and use.

Thrust

Another lazy word like *factor*, used by writers when they want to wobble and weasel. We hear of "the thrust of an article" or "the thrust of an argument." Writers telling us of the *thrust* are usually trying to tell us that they see many different issues but that they believe they have picked out the main line of discourse. They protect themselves from the accusation that they have missed the point, and they provide a clear space where they can turn around and run the other way if anyone challenges them.

When you are tempted to use *thrust,* try to make your statement more specific. Say something direct. Put your opinion on the line.

Tragedy/Calamity

Strictly speaking, *tragedy* is a drama played out in real life or on the stage in which a great human being is brought down to defeat by forces beyond his control either within himself or in the world around. Macbeth is tragic, and so is Othello. Macbeth cannot control his ambition, and Othello cannot control his jealousy. Tragedy has been part of the human experience for centuries, for it reveals the glory and depravity of the greatest of human beings and comforts us with the assurance that we are not alone in feeling both glory and depravity within ourselves.

But the rise of modern sensational journalism has confused *tragedy* with *calamity, misfortune,* and *accident.* In consequence, the tragic sense, having nearly vanished from our language, may be in danger of vanishing from our sensibilities. Now an airline crash is a *tragedy,* and so is a wreck on the highway that kills three people. *Tragedy* should be restored to its original high use, and other words should be used to describe accidents that do not involve high human characters so much as carelessness or mechanical failure.

Transpire/Occur

Transpire originally meant "to sweat," a meaning the French word *transpirer* maintains. From this meaning *transpire* took on the sense of "passing from the hidden to the open," a useful concept in sentences like these:

> It *transpired* that the killer was hidden in the attic all the while the police were searching the lower part of the house.

> It *transpired* after they had talked for a little while that they had both been in the same class at college thirty years before.

To use the word *transpire* as a synonym for *happen* or *occur* is portentous discourse, as in this sentence: "The game transpired on a golden autumn afternoon before 94,000 screaming fans."

Try and/Try to

The proper idiom is *try to,* although in speaking many people, especially in the Northeast, say *try and.*

I will *try to* attend the concert tonight.

Unique

Unique means "one of a kind," and it can be modified only by words like *nearly* or *almost.* You cannot logically say that something is *very unique* or *rather unique* or *the most unique* or *somewhat unique.* Something is either unique or it is not. If something is not unique, you can say that it is *rare, uncommon,* or *unusual,* or you can say that it is *almost* or *nearly unique.*

Varying/Various

The distinction between these two words gives unusual trouble. If you are discussing changes in the same thing from one time or place to another, the word is *varying.* If you are discussing different things with attention to the differences between them, your word is *various.* *Varying* is used before a singular noun, *various* before a plural. This sentence uses *varying* correctly:

> The cloud, he said, has spread out a bit since its first sighting here Jan. 27, and is now more than two miles long and of *varying* thickness.

We are talking about one cloud that is thicker in some places than it is in others. The following sentences use *various* correctly—with a plural noun:

> *Various* friends told her she was correct.
>
> The responses to my proposal were *various.*
>
> *Various* black musicians created jazz.

The following sentences use *varying* correctly:

> The ship moved at *varying* speed to avoid submarines.
>
> I feel most content in *varying* weather.

Viable options/Viable alternatives

Both are portentous discourse, inflated language designed to de-

ceive readers into believing that something important is being said. Are
nonviable options really options at all? If not, why should we bother
with speaking of *viable* options? The word *viable* should be reserved for
its proper meaning, as in the phrase *viable seeds*, meaning those seeds
that will germinate if we plant them.

Violent/Vehement

If you hit somebody with your fists or with a club, you are *violent*; if
you attack only with words, you are *vehement*. If you *violently* protest a
referee's call in a basketball game, you run out on the floor and hit him;
if you *vehemently* protest, you may yell at him or curse him or write
fiercely against him in the newspapers.

While/Although

Some writers use *while* as a synonym for *although*, with confusing
results: "While MacDougal was an athlete in college, he became as fat as
a keg when he stopped taking exercise." What does this sentence mean?
It could mean that although MacDougal was an athlete in college, he
stopped taking exercise after graduation and became as fat as a keg. But
some writers intend this sentence to mean that during the time Mac-
Dougal was an athlete in college, he stopped taking exercise and became as fat as a keg—but still remained an athlete. The example may be
extreme, although if MacDougal was a baseball pitcher, it is plausible.
While conveys a momentary confusion any time it is used as a synonym
for *although*, and good writers should protect readers from those momentary confusions whenever possible.

Who/Whom

This distinction provokes much acrimonious debate among writers
and grammarians. Some want to get rid of *whom* altogether or use it
only immediately after a preposition. So we would have sentences like
these:

> We did not care *who* he chose to represent us.

> She did not know to *whom* she spoke.

It may be true that *whom* is withering away. Richard A. Lanham,
U.C.L.A.'s distinguished authority on grammar, begins one chapter of a
good book with the title "Who's kicking who?" He says that "Who's kick-

ing whom" sounds stilted to him. It does not sound stilted to me, and most other conservative authorities would agree. But you must make up your own mind. Many people will object if you fail to use whom; no one will object if you use it in its traditional places.

If *whom* does sound stilted to you, try revising your sentence to get rid of it. *Who* and *whom* clauses are not frequent in some styles. You can read page after page of *Sports Illustrated*, *Time*, or *National Geographic* without encountering a clause introduced by *who* or *whom*. And many serious books also use such clauses rarely. Richard Ellmann's *James Joyce* can go for many pages without using a *who* or *whom* clause. It may be that good writers sense that such clauses introduce distracting elements in sentences. When you are tempted to use a *who* or *whom* clause, consider reducing it to a phrase or rewriting your thought to give the material in the clause its own sentence.

As in the great debate over *like* and *as*, some people want to preserve the distinction between *who* and *whom* but unfortunately do not know what the distinction is. The greatest problem with *whom* comes in the use of its associated pronoun *whomever*, although *whom* itself causes its proper share of grief. Some people, believing they are purists in language, will write a sentence like this: "He told his story to *whomever* would listen." But the proper way to write the sentence would be this: "He told his story to *whoever* would listen." The dependent clause *whoever would listen* is the object of the preposition *to*. But *whoever* is the subject of the clause and so must be in the nominative, or subjective, case.

But you might say, "She lent the horse to *whomever* she liked." Here *whomever* is the direct object of the subject *she* in the dependent clause. But then it would be far more graceful to say, "She lent the horse to anybody she liked."

Confusion also results from sentences like this: "Jack was the only person in the department who his boss thought could do the new job." You might be tempted to use *whom* in this sentence, but a little study shows that *who* is the subject of the verb *could do*. The clause *his boss thought* is parenthetical and does not act on *who*.

Whose/Of which

Some conservative authorities insist that the possessive *whose* can be used only when the antecedent is a person or a group of persons. They object to any use of *whose* to refer to an impersonal antecedent. But many writers have always used *whose* to refer to impersonal antecedents when the alternative would be unusual awkwardness. We do not say, "The aircraft the tail of which fell off on the approach to the airport landed safely." We say instead, "The aircraft whose tail fell off on the approach to the airport landed safely." We may rewrite the sentence to avoid the problem: "The aircraft lost its tail on the approach to the airport but landed safely." Often, though, such rewriting is neither feasible nor important.

-wise

Pricewise the German cars failed to compete with the Japanese cars, and *saleswise* the Japanese began taking over the market.

Sticking *-wise* onto the ends of nouns to turn them into adverbs has become a common practice. It is lazy language, and you should avoid it.

NINE

Making Arguments

Most writing is argument. Indeed it has been said frequently that all writing argues that we should believe something or do something. Some people dislike the word *argument*, but it is a civilized word; we make arguments rather than war. We persuade people rather than beat them into submission.

Many arguments are explicit. A lawyer making a case for a client accused of robbery argues either that the client is innocent or that mitigating circumstances require the judge and jury to consider this no ordinary robbery.

If your company sends you into the field to look at several possible sites for a new branch office, you must make an argument for the location you think best. If you want your university to sell its stock in companies doing business with South Africa, you must do more than carry signs and shout down opposing views; you must make an argument that divestiture (as getting rid of such stocks is called) will help bring progress to South Africa. We recognize such arguments at once for what they are. They call on us to do something, and they give us some sort of choice.

Other arguments are more subtle. If you take a long bike trip through Europe, you may write an article for *Bicycling Magazine*. The article would be a narrative, and you might not think of it as an argument. But you are arguing that your account is true and that it is interesting enough to make people read it. You are saying, "Believe me, and spend time with me."

You cannot argue well about things no one disputes. Few things bore a college teacher more than to read papers that take no risk, that argue only those positions that can scarcely be proved wrong: "Economics is important to society." "Shakespeare wrote some interesting plays." "Dickens often treated poverty in his novels." Few events delight teachers more than picking up a paper that makes an original and unexpected argument. "Some people may be allergic to exercise." "King Lear got what he deserved." "Macbeth failed because he was too moral to be a criminal."

College teachers are paid to read anything students write. Sometimes teachers become so tired from grading dozens and dozens of papers that they let themselves be bullied into giving a paper a good grade if the information in it is correct and the paper is written correctly. Such teachers often spend time and energy to encourage students to develop the habit of writing, and at a certain stage their sacrifice is both valuable and noble. But the reality every writer must face is that once out of college we find few readers as patient as composition teachers, and we waste the time we put into writing and lose all the reward we might get from our work if we produce something so dull that nobody will read it.

USING EVIDENCE

Most arguments begin with a process noted early in this book and worth repeating here. We look for patterns in what we observe, ideas that seem to unite seemingly unrelated parts of what we are studying. Paul Fussell, in his remarkable book *The Great War and Modern Memory*, shows that there was a pattern in how soldiers in World War I observed the dawn, sunset, and the sky, and he shows us that the writers who came out of the horrible experience of fighting in the trenches reacted vigorously to their vision of the sky. Fussell relates some of those reactions and makes them into a powerful argument for how soldiers in that war perceived some things. You can read Fussell's arguments for yourself. My point is that he perceived a connection, a synthesizing idea, and that connection allowed him to discern a pattern that he conveys as an argument.

Here your writer's notebook will help you, for as you jot down notes about what you observe and as you read those notes over again, you will see patterns forming that you can develop into a good paper. Part of the trick is to keep asking yourself questions that drive your mind to see things more clearly.

Here the writer of a paper on English literature makes arguments in much the same way as the scientific theorist. Each gathers information by careful observation; each feels that she sees something that others have not noticed; or each feels that others have not put the information together in just the way it belongs. And if the writer and the scientific theorist work hard at assembling their data—and perhaps if they have a little luck—they come to a creative moment, an instant of illumination or insight when they perceive some new way of joining the information.

Professor Fussell probably read dozens (and perhaps hundreds) of poems, novels, memoirs, diaries, letters, and other literary products of World War I and the recurring way in which diverse writers referred to dawn, sunset, and the sky would have suddenly struck him as important. He would have compared what these literary relics told him with similar relics from World War II where, astonishingly enough, British writers, at least, avoided large descriptions of these phenomena. And so he was onto an argument.

Legions of writers small and great have had a similar experience. Charles Darwin observed small differences between the beaks of birds on the Galapagos Islands and their cousins on the distant South American mainland, and he puzzled mightily over how these differences might have come about. The birds' beaks were by no means the only biological problem he found on those blackened volcanic islands, but they loomed large in his mind, and they helped him dramatically in the formulation of his theory of biological evolution. He made a great many careful observations, he made connections between them, and he arrived at a brilliant insight. Anyone reading *The Origin of Species* today must be impressed still by the enormous amount of data he compiled and by the way he orders his data by means of his theory.

How did the insight come? No one can give a precise answer to such a question. "The light dawned" is a common cliché to describe the feelings we have when an insight comes to us. Always the light dawns after a period of hard work — observing, assembling data, thinking, worrying about it, arranging it in various patterns. The investigative reporters who wrote about the Watergate burglary of June 17, 1972, put together details until they had a theory that accounted for most of those details: they thought that the burglary had been planned by high White House staff members and that Richard Nixon knew about it either beforehand or soon afterward and had tried to cover up the involvement of his associates. Their case was so plausible that others began pecking away at Nixon's defenses. Had these reporters spun out their theory without the long, difficult, and perhaps dangerous work of gathering data, or evidence, no one would have paid any attention to them.

The great literary scholars have followed much the same process in studying and writing about poets, playwrights, and other writers in our tradition. These scholars first read the text — not just once but again and again and again. They make notes. They ask questions. They make comparisons. They write out their thoughts. And they arrive at that moment of great pleasure and excitement when they can say, "I've got it." Cleanth Brooks, studying the Faulkner novel *Absalom, Absalom!* early in the 1960s, realized that it is a mystery story and that Faulkner does not tell us exactly what brought about the doom of his character Thomas Sutpen. Two college boys, Quentin and Shreve, sitting in a cold dormitory room hundreds of miles from Mississippi, fit the story together and try to arrive at a solution, but Brooks pointed out that we do not know if their solution is the right one.

Most of us reading *Absalom, Absalom!* for the first time probably overlook the significance of the way the story is told and so overlook the significance of the novel beyond mere storytelling. Brooks studied the text with great care, hit on a different way of seeing it, and gave that way to us in a brilliant critical essay in the Spring 1962 issue of the *Sewanee Review.*

A good argument always produces evidence. In this book my evidence is the collection of quotations from other writers to prove that my analysis of what writers do is correct. You must present evidence to support *your* arguments. Otherwise you will be reduced to making naked assertions. If you have a reputation as a great authority in the field where you write, your assertions may be worth something, but most of us lack the authority to convince people merely by declaring our opinions. We convince them only with evidence.

Aristotle was the first enduring writer to sort out different ways of making arguments from evidence. His classifications are not airtight, and they often overlap. Still, most people since Aristotle who have written about argument depend on his categories either directly or indirectly. These classifications allow us to see what we do more clearly and, I hope, to use those arguments more effectively.

PERSUADING AN AUDIENCE

Early in his *Art of Rhetoric,* Aristotle gives us a long discussion of human nature. He defines various passions, including indignation, anger, envy, and so on. He knew that no orator (he addressed himself to speakers, not writers) could persuade without some understanding of human nature. Both speakers and writers must know something of the fears, the longings, the ambitions, the sensibilities of the audiences they address. As I have mentioned earlier in this book, a critical error of inexperienced writers is their belief that their only audience is the teacher who will grade their papers. And they often assume that the teacher will see their efforts in the best possible light. In fact, you will never write persuasively unless you develop some mature concept of your readers and seek to appeal to your best estimate of who they are.

When you argue, you must begin with something that shows your readers that you and they share some qualities. You are not exalted and overwhelming; neither are you inferior and weak. You should show your audience that you and they have a common nature or a common interest or a common purpose.

Many speakers show commonality with their audiences by beginning with a joke. A room filled with people laughing together immediately gives the impression that audience and speaker are bonded together. Writers seldom begin with jokes, but as I showed in the chapter on the essay, they often begin with stories, quotations, and statements of intention that make readers say, "This person and I share something; we are alike; I want to go on with this."

When you begin well, your argument is half won; when you begin badly, you can seldom redeem your argument. And if at any time in your writing you break the bond between yourself and your audience by making some offensive remark, you run the risk of losing readers unless your evidence and your arguments are so compelling that readers must keep going. Not many arguments have that power. James Watt, Ronald Reagan's first secretary of the interior, had an astonishing ability to offend audiences with remarks that made them suddenly think he supposed they were not serious about many of the great social movements of our time. He claimed that he intended no such thing, but the impression he gave was devastating, and he finally had to resign because he had alienated so many Americans. The consequence of alienating an audience is that you lose your ability to persuade. And writers should always think about the sensibilities of their audiences as part of argument.

DEFINITION AND DESCRIPTION IN ARGUMENTS

We can always describe something or define it. We can say that our subject belongs to a class of similar things and then show how it is different from the other things in its class. The ninth edition of the Merriam-Webster *New Collegiate Dictionary* defines *lemon* as "an acid fruit that is botanically a many-seeded pale yellow oblong berry and is produced by a stout thorny tree." So a *lemon* belongs to a class of similar things called fruits. It differs from other members of that class by its acidity, its pale yellow coloration, its being produced by a stout thorny tree, and its being botanically a berry. It is usually fairly easy to place a word to be defined within a general class; it is more difficult to distinguish it from other members of that class.

Definitions rarely make whole essays, though they may do so. They usually make beginning statements on which an essay may be built. And they are always useful in clarifying ideas in our own minds.

In universities the study of literature is divided by both periods and genres. What is the difference between a work of the Renaissance and a work of the Enlightenment? Before we can properly answer that question, we must define both Renaissance and Enlightenment, and we must make some classifications that include works written in each period. Students often err by assuming that we are all agreed on a definition. So they write sentences like this one: "Machiavelli's *The Prince* is a typical example of political thought and action in the Renaissance." They do not realize that before we can accept such a sweeping generalization, we must know what the writer means by the word *Renaissance*. It happens to be a word that has been defined so many different ways that any writer takes a huge risk in assuming that there is agreement on a single definition. The careful writer would revise our example to make a much less sweeping and more concrete statement: "Machiavelli's *The Prince* held that rulers are judged finally more by their success or failure than they are by their morality." Often when writers realize they cannot use a term like "Renaissance" in a way that provokes general agreement, they are forced to rethink their ideas and use more acceptable terms.

When we consider them carefully, the problems of some definitions create a general and healthful reluctance to use some big words thoughtlessly. Professor Gilbert Allardyce introduces his article "What Fascism Is Not: Thoughts on the Deflation of a Concept" with some ruminations about a definition:

> "Perhaps the word fascism should be banned, at least temporarily, from our political vocabulary," S. J. Woolf wrote in 1968. Historians who have confronted the problem of defining this mulish concept may sympathize with this modest proposal. Unfortunately the word "fascism" is here to stay; only its meaning seems to be banned. Nevertheless, the German philosopher-historian Ernst Nolte is probably correct in stressing that historians do not have the responsibility to invent new terms simply because the existing ones seem inadequate. But they do have the responsibility to confess how truly inadequate the term fascism has become: put simply, we have agreed to use the term without agreeing on how to define it. This article is concerned with the reason for this unfortunate state of affairs.[1]

The same problems that Allardyce notes with the word *fascism* can be found in many other words in common usage — *humanism, romanti-*

[1] Gilbert Allardyce, "What Fascism Is Not: Thoughts on the Deflation of a Concept," *American Historical Review*, April 1979.

cism, enlightenment, socialism, country, music, jazz, narcissism, and many others. Grand words like these originate as ways of describing qualities shared by several things or people — works of art, essays, novels, political views, rulers of states, or whatever. Soon the large term assumes a life of its own, a kind of phantom existence that provokes writers to imagine that they have said something important if they apply these words to anything they choose.

Many of us recall the 1960s, when many people hurled the term *fascist* at any opponent, whether a university dean, a scholar, a police officer, or a parent. Everybody was a fascist who believed in the exercise of authority. Others, often calling themselves conservatives, used the word *radical* to describe anyone who opposed American involvement in the Vietnam War, and suddenly some people were called radical merely because they believed in the freedom of speech granted by the American Constitution. A few decades earlier the words *red* and *Communist* were used as a devastating weapon against people who were devoted to liberal and humanitarian causes. Words like *Communist, red, fellow traveler, un-American,* and others developed a strange power just because no one bothered to define them.

So the need for sharp definition is always with us. Especially when words take on a life of their own, writers should subject them to special scrutiny. Do enough individuals within a group share enough qualities to allow the use of any general word to describe them? Before you start using any sweeping collectives like *socialism, democracy, romantic,* and many others, you should ask yourself exactly what you mean by them and write out definitions so that you and your readers may begin with some common assumptions.

Your definitions should always be fair. If some people disagree with them, you should take that disagreement into account. You do not have to discard your definition merely because others disagree with it, but you help yourself and your readers if you describe the disagreement and then give your own view forthrightly. In that way your readers can begin by knowing how you are going to use the word in your essay.

Remember that if you define a word unfairly or in sharp disagreement with its common usage, you may lose your audience.

COMPARISON IN ARGUMENTS

Papers that compare things or people turn up frequently. Teachers love them. They guarantee that students will study two things instead of one. "Compare *Hamlet* with *Macbeth.*" To write the paper, the student must read both plays. "Compare Hitler with Mussolini." The student must know something about both men. The demand for comparison enlarges the scope of knowledge, and it also gives writers some help in observing. How are two things alike? How are they different? (The question is often posed like this: "Compare and contrast the beginning of World War I with the beginning of World War II." But the *contrast* is redundant; no one can compare any two things well without showing the differences as well as the similarities.)

Comparisons have obvious values, but they can be overdone. Any two things can be compared. You can compare a novel to a freight train: each has a beginning that pulls a line behind it. The train pulls cars; the novel pulls scenes. The cars on the train have content, as do the scenes in the novel. And both the train and the novel have an end. The absurdity of such a comparison becomes evident as we go on with it. We read along a little while and then ask ourselves, "Who cares?"

You should ask the same question of any of the comparisons you make for a college paper. The mere reporting of similarities and differences may be tedious and bewildering. A comparison paper must show that something is to be gained by the comparison. Not long ago one of our students compared the articles in the 1890 *Scientific American* with those in a recent issue of the same publication. The only conclusion he made was that the articles in 1890 were practical and the recent articles were theoretical. His comparison involved bare reporting, valuable perhaps in certain circumstances, but producing a paper not especially interesting.

We told him that his paper could have been much more interesting if he had drawn inferences from his evidence. It seemed possible to suggest, for example, that the definition of science itself had changed between 1890 and the present: then science had been almost synonymous with technology because in the nineteenth century people thought of science primarily as a way to make practical improvements in human life; now the selection of articles seems to suggest that science and technology have become distinct and that science is a highly theoretical discipline pursued by scientists in search of pure knowledge rather than practical application.

I am not sure that these inferences are true. But if our student had made them, he might have posed for himself some questions that could have led him to some interesting answers, and he would have interested his readers much more than he did with his bare chronicle of differences. I would not waste my time reading an involved and perhaps cute comparison between a freight train and a novel; neither would I care to read a naked comparison between *Macbeth* and *Hamlet* unless the writer made me believe that I was learning something important about both plays and perhaps something about Shakespeare's evolution as a dramatist.

Comparison works best when it enlarges our vision and helps us see more clearly the object of our study. One of the best scholarly papers I ever heard was delivered by the historian David Donald at a commemoration of the one-hundredth anniversary of the Gettysburg Address. Professor Donald compared the Gettysburg Address with Lincoln's previous utterances about the Civil War and pointed out that whereas before, Lincoln had spoken continually about preserving the *Union*, the major word in the Gettysburg Address was *Nation*. Professor Donald suggested that as the horrible war continued, Lincoln had come to see the conflict as the forging of a united people rather than as a united collection of political entities. He argued his point quietly and persuasively. Everyone I spoke to afterward felt that we had been made to see a familiar document in a new and revealing light.

The *a Fortiori* Argument

Comparison is not in itself an argument, but in making comparisons you can move on to a couple of forms of argumentation frequently used and sometimes abused throughout the history of writing and speaking. The first is what the Romans called *a fortiori*, "to the stronger," the argument that proceeds from this question: "If we know that A is true, we may infer with all the more certainty that B is true, too." The argument gains power if what we state in the first proposition seems improbable. In his *Canterbury Tales*, Chaucer praised the "poor parson of a town" for his virtue and made this metaphor: "If the gold rust, what shall iron do?" He counted the priests as the gold in English society, the lay people as the iron. Priests had to be pure to keep the people pure. It is not probable that gold should rust, but if it does, how much more likely is it that iron should do the same?

We use the *a fortiori* argument in many inferences. We know, for example, that statistics show that cigarette smokers' risk of lung cancer is much higher than that of nonsmokers. Since cigars give off a much stronger smoke than cigarettes, the argument from comparison lets us suppose that if cigar smokers inhaled, their risk of lung cancer would be much higher than that of cigarette smokers. Most cigar smokers do not inhale, and such a study of the inhalation of cigar smoke has not been made — at least to my knowledge — but to make this inference, we argue *a fortiori*.

The *a fortiori* argument is used frequently by lawyers, especially in establishing the credibility of witnesses. If a lawyer can prove that a witness has lied in making one statement, it is much easier to make a jury infer that the witness has lied in other statements as well. "We have proved that the accused lied when he said he was not having an affair with the victim's wife; isn't it likely that he also lied when he testified that he did not kill the victim?"

The argument is also used in advertising. Back in the days of the Volkswagen Beetle, the company advertised the improvements made year by year in new models of the little car. The implied argument was something like this: If Volkswagen has always been a good buy, it is now an even better bargain.

Only a few years ago, the *a fortiori* argument influenced the course of the Vietnam War. Some Air Force generals argued that American air power could be used to bomb the North Vietnamese into submission. Foes of the view pointed to the failure of heavy British and American bombing to break the will of the Germans in World War II or even to halt German war production. Many studies concluded that the bombing of German cities had only increased the German will to resist; therefore, they argued, it was unlikely that bombing could reduce the will of the North Vietnamese.

Relying as it does on inference, the *a fortiori* argument is essential to the writing of history. The evidence historians rely on is always fragmented and maddeningly incomplete, and history itself is a process of assembling a puzzle made up of broken and missing pieces. Historians must always fill in the blanks of their picture by making intelligent speculations drawn on inference. They can know some things with a fair degree of certainty: South Carolinians subdued Fort Sumter with artillery in April 1861. Other things remain forever uncertain. Did Lincoln deliberately provoke the South Carolinians into becoming aggressors?

Historians assemble all the evidence they can and try to frame it into a plausible, coherent picture that puts the pieces of the puzzle together. Barbara Tuchman describes this process of historical inference in her own research:

> If the historian will submit himself *to* his material instead of trying to impose himself *on* his material, then the material will ultimately speak to him and supply the answers. It has happened to me more than once. In somebody's memoirs I found that the Grand Duke Nicholas wept when he was named Russian Commander-in-Chief in 1914, because, said the

memoirist, he felt inadequate to the job. That sounded to me like one of those bits of malice one has to watch out for in contemporary observers; it did not ring true. The Grand Duke was said to be the only "man" in the royal family; he was known for his exceedingly tough manners, was admired by the common soldier, and feared at court. I did not believe he felt inadequate, but then why should he weep? I could have left out this bit of information, but I did not want to. I wanted to find the explanation that would make it fit. (Leaving things out because they do not fit is writing fiction, not history.) I carried the note about the Grand Duke around with me for days, worrying about it. Then I remembered other tears. I went through my notes and found an account of Churchill weeping and also Messimy, the French War Minister. All at once I understood that it was not the individuals but the *times* that were the stuff for tears. My next sentence almost wrote itself: "There was an aura about 1914 that caused those who sensed it to shiver for mankind." Afterward I realized that this sentence expressed why I had wanted to write the book in the first place. The "why," you see, had emerged all by itself.[2]

Aside from being a splendid account of the role of inference in the writing of history, this paragraph gives us the *a fortiori* argument: If we know that these other men wept, may we not assume that the Grand Duke Nicholas wept, too? If we know that all these men wept at the outbreak of World War I, may we not assume that they realized how disastrous for all humankind this war was to be?

The *a fortiori* argument can go wrong—as all arguments can. No baseball fan would make this argument: Since Carl Yastrzemski hit a meaningless home run in a game that the Red Sox were winning ten-zero at the end of the season, was he not more likely to hit a home run in the World Series? Courts generally rule out this argument in rape trials: Since we know that this woman willingly had sexual intercourse with several men before the alleged rape, may we not assume that she consented on this occasion, too?

The Argument of Similitude

The use of comparison can also go wrong when writers claim that because two things or two people are alike in some things, they must be alike in all things. This is the argument of similitude, and it can be misleading and immoral.

When Richard Nixon, a skilled rhetorician, ran his first campaign for the U.S. Senate in 1950, he faced Helen Gahagan Douglas, a

[2] Barbara Tuchman, *Practicing History* (New York: Alfred A. Knopf, 1981), 23. Copyright © 1981 by Alma Tuchman, Lucie T. Eisenberg, and Jessica Tuchman Matthews. Reprinted by permission of Alfred A. Knopf, Inc.

member of the U.S. House of Representatives from California. Nixon was eager to paint Douglas red at a time when the tirades of Senator Joseph McCarthy, the Korean War, and the terror of Stalinism in Russia made Americans fear anything that smacked of communism. Nixon compared the voting record of Douglas in the House with that of Vito Marcantonio, a truly radical congressman from New York. Marcantonio had supported the Soviet Union foreign policy. In domestic policy he had supported price controls, public housing, civil rights, and health insurance. But most people knew him only for his hysterical speeches in support of the Soviet Union.

Nixon's associates tabulated 353 votes in which Douglas and Marcantonio had been on the same side. These votes had nothing to do with the Soviet Union, but Nixon went doggedly from the indisputable fact of these 353 votes to a fallacious conclusion: If Helen Gahagan Douglas had voted with Marcantonio on so many occasions, she must agree with him in everything else.

Frank Mankiewicz, a Douglas campaign worker, pointed out that Nixon himself had voted with Marcantonio 112 times in four years. Even the most vigorous anti-Communist might, on reflection, doubt Nixon's implication that 353 bills introduced into the U.S. House of Representatives were Communist-inspired. But few people reflected on this because the times were mad, and Nixon won the election.

Yet the argument of similitude can have an honored place in rhetoric. Common sense—not to mention justice and fair play—tells us that the important caution is to be sure always that the basis for a comparison is genuine. The argument for similitude usually works better for groups than for individuals, and it is frequently used in polls. It is indispensable for some research in the social sciences.

For example, a study a few years ago showed that Volkswagen owners were likely to be further to the left politically than were owners of Fords and Chevrolets. The same study showed that the owners of Saabs and Volvos were likely to be the furthest to the left on the American political spectrum. The study did not claim that every Volvo owner was a political radical; it made its conclusions about groups rather than individuals. No one argued that *because* someone bought a Volvo she would be to the far left in politics; that argument would be absurd. If the study had any validity, it was only to show that a willingness to break with long-established American custom might express itself in both car buying and politics.

Some life insurance companies will offer you lower rates if you do not smoke. Nonsmokers live longer as a group than smokers. But no one would argue that every nonsmoker will live longer than every smoker. A few nonsmokers die every year from lung cancer, and a few people smoke two packs of Camel straights every day and die at age eighty-five when they are run over by a truck while jogging. Comparisons that classify people by groups offer only probability to the individuals within each group; they do not rigorously predict what will happen to each individual.

So the major value of the argument of similitude in human affairs is that it enables us to make some fairly accurate predictions about groups. It can help us predict how an election will go or how the public will respond to a new model car or how good or bad health will be in a group that shares a pattern of nutrition. Every election year some pollsters work their way through the so-called model precincts in the United States, precincts that have nearly always voted for the winners in national elections. The argument of the pollsters—borne out by much experience—is that if they measure the attitude of voters in those precincts, they can predict the outcome of the election.

In the same way a manufacturer may market a new washing machine in regions that seem to represent a cross section of American taste. The theory is that if people here buy the new product, people everywhere will buy it, too.

The argument from comparison may stir our research. We may read a novel by Dickens and see that he always gives us an economic report on his characters. We can infer from reading a couple of his novels that he may have this interest in all of them, but we do not have to leave that notion to inference alone; we can read the novels and check on it.

A concern for what comparison may prove acts as a restraint against those tedious papers described in the beginning of this section. If you have a point to make in a comparison, you may write an excellent paper. If you report only on the similarities and differences and don't try to see any significance in what you observe, you will probably be dull.

CAUSE-AND-EFFECT ARGUMENTS

The argument from cause to effect or from effect back to cause is one of the most common in human discourse; it is also one of the most useful and one of the most dangerous. We want to know why things happened—why war was declared, why cancer struck, why the economic recovery came, why a novel was popular, why crime increased, why the president was elected.

On the surface the argument from cause to effect appears simple, but the supposed simplicity is often misleading. Why do black players dominate professional basketball? One school of thought holds that blacks have a muscle mass that enables them to jump higher and with greater agility than most whites. The argument—which to some seems racist—is supported by some respectable researchers. Another school of thought holds that basketball is the only sport open to the poor urban child and that black children start playing it early and play it often while white suburban children are doing other things. With more black children devoting more time to basketball, more of them grow up to be professional basketball players.

This particular debate illustrates the difficulty of cause-and-effect reasoning: the causal relation between two events is often almost impossible to establish beyond any doubt. When the argument is emotionally charged—as any argument about race may be—the difficulties are all the greater.

Some causes can produce more than one effect; it is misleading to isolate only one cause and pin all the effects on it. No historian would dare argue that World War I was caused only by the assassination of the heir to the throne of the Austro-Hungarian Empire in 1914 or that the Civil War in the United States was caused only by the election of Abraham Lincoln in 1860. We may say that the assassination and the election were precipitating causes, the immediate causes that made people act decisively. Good historians know that the great crises in history build up like gas escaping slowly and steadily into a house. Then some accident provides a spark, and an explosion results. Without the accumulated gas, the spark would remain just a spark.

To make effective arguments from cause and effect, you must assemble data carefully and make your argument measured. Avoid sweeping generalizations that claim much more than your evidence suggests. Support what you do claim by continual reference to the data that support your views.

The most common fallacy in cause-and-effect reasoning is to claim too much for one cause. In our own world we may fall into this fallacy because we try to give to our reasoning about history or other disciplines in the humanities the same certainty that we know in some areas of science. For example, in the last century Louis Pasteur discovered that by heating milk to a temperature slightly less than the boiling point, most harmful germs would be killed. Here was a clear relation of cause and effect: pasteurization caused safer milk.

We would like that certainty in everything, but human events offer much less of it, and informed readers with some sense of how things happen in the world become annoyed when they believe that a writer is claiming much more for a cause than seems plausible. Nearly everyone who has taught the history of Western civilization has had a student who believes that the Roman Empire fell because the Romans used lead improperly and poisoned themselves. To some people such simple explanations seem to offer comfort because they make the great mysteries of human existence more manageable and less subject to chance. But simple explanations are almost always false, and readers know they are false and scorn writers who make them.

Another great fallacy in the argument of cause and effect is called *post hoc, ergo propter hoc,* a Latin phrase meaning that because one thing happens after another, the first is the cause of the second. Not long ago I read in a newspaper a passionate letter to the editor arguing that sex education in the public schools had caused the increase in violent sex crimes that we have all noted with foreboding in recent years. The letter argued that before sex education was instituted, sex crimes were less frequent and therefore sex education had caused these crimes. Someone quickly replied with another letter saying that this kind of argument could prove that the demise of the TV program "Leave It to Beaver" was the real culprit; it could be demonstrated, this writer said, that sex crimes dramatically increased after that program went off the air.

It is easy to spot fallacies like these since the relation between cause and effect is so nebulous. But many arguments are much more complicated and subtle, and many people—even the writers who use them—may be deceived. Honest writers will always examine the evidence with care to see if it proves what they want to prove. If the evidence does not support the case, good writers will say so; if the evidence may be interpreted several different ways, honest writers will say that, too. We may yearn for simple answers, but truth is always best served when we see how complicated some events are, how difficult they are to explain, and how mysterious they often remain even when we have done our best to understand them.

Yet for all its obvious dangers, the argument from cause to effect or from effect back to cause is indispensable in every field of thought. Strange indeed would be the essay that did not have at least one paragraph devoted to this kind of argument.

In writing such essays well, you often must use inference—a process we examined in discussing argument from comparison. You observe something carefully, you compare it with your other experiences, and you try to think out a pattern of cause and effect that explains the observation.

One of my favorite writing assignments early in a course is to have students look at the popular advertising of clothing in newspapers and magazines at various times in recent history and then ask them to speculate on the role of men and women as implied by the ads. For example, what did people think of women and their place in the world in a day when the fashion ads showed female models so laden with clothing that we wonder how they had strength to walk? The assignment is an exercise in cause and effect. The effect of the advertising is obvious — the fashionable clothing would be sold. But what was the cause? To answer this question, one must use inference imaginatively.

Once I had students in a writing class visit a funeral of their own choosing and write an essay on the event, making some inferences about the social function of the various practices they observed. What is the social function of a eulogy? Why do we usually pray at funerals? What scriptural texts are read, and why are those texts chosen? What does a funeral tell about the people to whom it is addressed or at least about the view of the person in charge? The questions are endless, and most of them involve some speculative use of the cause-and-effect argument, inferences that will lead from the obvious to the less obvious.

Inferences may not be provable. Good writers always advance arguments drawn from inference in a spirit that is confident without being arrogant. What seems to be a perfectly plausible cause-and-effect relation to one person may seem implausible to another. When you are making an inference that you cannot prove, you must be careful. And you must trust your readers. If your inference is sound, thoughtful readers are likely to accept it. If it is not sound, your readers may tell you why they do not accept it. Then you may reconsider the cause-and-effect relation you have argued and revise it.

It is probably worth repeating something I said earlier: you make the cause-and-effect argument best when you pile up evidence to support the case you are making. The argument from cause to effect or from effect back to cause works best when you present it one step at a time, making your statements, explaining them, and giving examples to support them. Avoid sweeping generalizations. Avoid simplistic assertions. Advance confidently but not arrogantly; infer carefully; and always keep in mind the skeptical readers, the good man and the good woman who must be convinced if they are to believe that your reading of cause and effect is correct.

ARGUMENTS OF NECESSITY

The argument from necessity holds that no choice exists in a matter that requires an audience to act. The writer or speaker says, in effect, something like this: "Things are as I say they are, and you cannot do anything other than what I say you must do." It is an argument intended to make people do something without second thoughts and without holding back. It is almost always the argument of those who lead nations to war.

On Monday morning, December 8, 1941, President Franklin D. Roosevelt made a great speech to Congress asking for a declaration of war against Japan. He began by presenting an undeniable fact in an unforgettable way:

> Yesterday, December 7, 1941 — a date which will live in infamy — the United States of America was suddenly and deliberately attacked by naval and air forces of the Empire of Japan.

He moved from this statement of fact to the argument that the United States now had no choice but to declare war on Japan. The Congress and the American people believed him.

In the Vietnam War, the same argument was used by those advocating an all-out American effort to win. They said that since 30,000 or 40,000 or 50,000 young Americans had died already in the war, the conflict must be pursued to victory to ensure that so many had not died in vain. Others said that since South Vietnam was an ally of the United States, our national honor required that we defend that nation from North Vietnam's attacks. Congress and most of the American people were not convinced by these arguments because they did not believe that the facts presented necessitated the action called for.

The argument from necessity is always vulnerable and seldom worthwhile. An opponent can always say, "But the facts are not as you present them," or, "Even if your statements are true, your conclusion about what is to be done is false." Always the point is that a choice is assumed; yet the argument is that no choice exists. It is a paradox: I am asked to choose war and am told at the same time that I have no choice but war; I am asked to vote for a candidate who promises a balanced federal budget, and I am told that if I do not want the country to fall into ruin, I have no choice but to vote for such a candidate. The argument works only if the audience believes that the necessity does exist and assumes that people must do willingly what they are compelled to do anyway. The argument can often backfire and damage both the credibility and the moral reputation of those who use it wrongly.

ARGUMENTS FROM AUTHORITY AND TESTIMONY

The Argument from Authority

Aristotle called the argument from authority the ethical argument. He did not mean that the good ethical argument was more moral than the bad ethical argument; he meant *ethical* in the Greek sense, meaning "character, what we think of the person who communicates with us."

We believe some people because they exude an aura of authority. We believe them not merely for the logic of their discourse but for the force of their personalities and for their reputation. We trust them. So the argument from authority may be the least logical of all arguments in rhetoric; but it also may be the most believable.

When you begin an essay or a speech by making your audience believe that you share some of its good qualities, you are using the ethical argument. You are saying, "I am like you in some important particulars; you are good people, and I am a good person like you. So believe me."

We use the argument from authority all the time. Every time we make a statement, we use our authority, and people believe us in so far as they think we are to be trusted. When we write and make statements not immediately substantiated by evidence, we are using the argument from authority. It is a staple of discourse.

Academics are especially prone to use authority. I once heard T. S. Eliot say in a lecture that Hawthorne was the greatest American writer of prose. He did not make an argument for Hawthorne's greatness; he merely asserted that Hawthorne was great. The packed assembly listening to Eliot in Wolsey Hall at Yale University believed him—at least for that moment—because we knew Eliot's reputation and supposed that if he made a literary judgment, it must be true.

To make the argument from authority, you must satisfy several requirements. You must have had sufficient experience in the subject to be taken seriously. If you have bicycled across America, you may write a good book about the experience, and readers will take your word for routes, equipment, and tactics because your experience on a bike for more than three thousand miles validates your statements. You don't have to prove your judgments; you can state them and be believed.

You must speak in a tone that makes your readers think you are judicious and unprejudiced. If you use hysterical language to advocate an argument, readers will suppose that you have some special benefit to be gained from your argument or that you are insecure and afraid. If you talk down to your audience and use arrogant language to advocate your point of view, your readers will be angry with you and will do their best to refute what you say. If you sound too humble, readers will believe that you are inferior and weak, and they will delight in proving that you don't know what you are talking about. You do best if you write with confidence, gentleness, and calm certainty. Make people respect you by the tone you use and by the credentials you bring forward, and they will believe you.

We find belief in authority wherever we turn. If my doctor tells me to cut down on coffee so I will sleep better at night, I do not ask him for a long proof of his advice. Perhaps I should; doctors can be wrong. But the likelihood is that I will cut down on my coffee. He is an authority; I believe him.

If your English professor tells you that *Great Expectations* is a greater novel than *David Copperfield*, you will likely read *Great Expectations* with some expectations of your own. You may not agree with your professor in the end. But her authority makes you observe the two books in a different light and makes you reluctant to disagree with her overtly.

The Argument from Testimony

Above all, you should try to be an authority yourself. Nothing is quite so stultifying as to read prose whose author has been so uncertain about making conclusions that no firm word of his own comes through anywhere. To repeat a point I made earlier in this book: you should not assert your opinions as if you were blowing a trumpet and making it seem that no one else's opinions mattered; but you should know enough about your topic to make assertions quietly and confidently and to give your readers the impression that they are in good hands.

The argument from testimony brings in the authority of people other than the writer, and it often has a powerful effect. When you write a literary essay about a novel, you can help your cause immensely if you find an article by a well-known critic who agrees with you. If you argue that Castro's government in Cuba has nearly destroyed the civil liberties of the Cuban population, you can strengthen your case immensely by quoting the authority of a writer who spent years in one of Castro's jails. If you believe that the United States should not give military aid to El Salvador, you can submit the testimony of people who have suffered at the hands of the government we support there. The opportunities for testimony are nearly limitless, and good testimony can help your case immensely. You must work hard to dig out supporting testimony, and you must be sure that your witnesses are fair and truthful. But once you have done that work, you will find that it is all worthwhile because of the strength it adds to your own writing.

The Confident Statement

In any paper you will use several modes of argument. Sometimes you will make simple statements of fact; these statements are one form of the argument from authority. But the most important form of the argument from authority is your modest, confident statement that the facts mean something that your careful study has revealed to you. Anyone can know the facts merely by studying them. But what do the facts mean? Your careful interpretation may be new and exciting. If you have gathered a lot of evidence, if you have used it carefully, and if you demonstrate that you have thought much about what you have learned, you can easily be accepted as an authority by your readers. If you have not gathered evidence, if you have not thought about all sides to the questions you address, and if you present your opinions as demands to be believed without any reason, you will not be an authority.

LOGICAL FALLACIES AND THEIR USES

No discussion about argument can be complete without a few words about logical fallacies. An honest writer will avoid fallacious reasoning; a good reader will recognize bad logic when she sees it used by others.

Straw Men

A "straw man" is an argument one claims one's opponents are making when in fact they are not making that argument at all. One attacks that argument instead of facing the real issue. The setting up of straw men that can easily be burned or otherwise disposed of is an affliction of current political discourse. It is one of the curses of our times. Someone opposes prayer in the public schools, and advocates of school prayer accuse him of being against religion. Someone opposes book censorship by school boards, and someone else accuses her of loving pornography.

Someone opposes abortion, and someone else accuses him of wanting to keep women in a subservient position. A college president points out the hazards and the difficulties of divesting university-held stocks in corporations doing business in South Africa, and students accuse her of racism.

In serious writing, the setting up of straw men is an immoral act, and readers with their wits about them will rightly disdain the cowardly practice by writers who cannot or will not face an opposing argument at its strongest point. Examples of straw men could be almost endlessly multiplied. Notice it in the writing of others; avoid it in your own writing.

The *ad Hominem* Argument

The words *ad hominem* are Latin for "against the man," and the fallacy called by this name is an attack on a person rather than a serious effort to deal with his arguments. The attack assumes that a bad person cannot produce a good program or a worthwhile thought. As in the straw-man fallacy, the *ad hominem* argument is all too common in public discourse, especially in political campaigns.

Fortunately the American people have proved themselves surprisingly impervious to the *ad hominem* argument and, if anything, have tended to react in the opposite way to what the argument's users intended. Jimmy Carter probably did himself much more harm than good by his attacks on Ronald Reagan in the 1980 presidential campaign. Reagan seemed like a nice guy, and in making his furious attacks—especially since they were phrased in a clumsy style of speaking and wooden rhetoric—Carter appeared vindictive and angry. Americans do not like vindictive, angry presidents.

On a lower level the *ad hominem* argument is painfully common and sometimes effective:

> My opponent is a homosexual; therefore nothing she says about national politics can be trusted. I, on the other hand, consort only with members of the opposite sex; therefore my sentiments about national policy are almost infallible.

> People who buy Japanese cars are unpatriotic; but since I drive a Chevrolet, I love my country.

> My opponent was expelled from school for cheating when he was twenty years old; therefore none of his opinions about law enforcement

are worth anything. But no one has ever caught me cheating; therefore, all my opinions are true.

Reduced to these terms, the *ad hominem* argument can seem ridiculous, but in practice it is not ridiculous at all. People long for goodness as well as for truth, and they have trouble believing that the people they think are wicked can have good opinions. Attacking the character of one's opponent can turn the weight of an argument from issues that should be debated to personalities that have little or nothing to do with the wisdom or foolishness of a policy. Senator Joseph McCarthy poisoned the air of American politics for several years during the 1950s by assaulting the persons of his opponents.

On occasion it is worth pointing out that one's opponent has been involved in perfidy. But anyone writing about public policy should first define the issues and debate them without regard to the personalities of those on the other side.

The Bandwagon Argument

According to the bandwagon argument, since everybody is doing something, we should do it, too. It is another argument that courses through American discourse during political campaigns. Candidates use public-opinion polls to show that their victory is assured and in so doing try to win the votes of people who have not yet decided to cast their vote for that supposedly assured victor.

The strength of the bandwagon argument lies in our human propensity to seek out the company of our own kind and to be social beings. We do not like to be isolated. Most of us hate to speak against strong public opinion. If everybody is doing something, our social nature tells us that we ought to be doing it, too. The bandwagon mentality makes some people hesitate to express an opinion until they know what others are thinking. A group of college students discussing a movie will often wait cautiously for someone to express an opinion; then they will all agree with that opinion, no matter what they really think. Their professors will often hesitate to express their dislike for one of the great literary classics because they are afraid of being thrown off the bandwagon of academe.

I am always startled at the enthusiasm with which an academic group will greet a colleague's brave pronouncement that he does not like *Moby Dick*. Common academic opinion holds that we must like *Moby Dick* or else lose our credentials as card-carrying professors. When somebody says, "That book bores me to death," the relief in the group is often explosive.

The Impressionist painters in late nineteenth-century France had a hard time winning acceptance because traditional art was on the bandwagon, and few critics were brave enough to admit in public that they liked the new, bright style of the Impressionists.

Yet the bandwagon argument is often fallacious. Although public opinion supports a war or a political candidate or a social program or a piece of legislation relating to some moral issue, public opinion may be wrong. It may be that some brave writer or speaker must get off the bandwagon and try to wave it to a stop before it goes to disaster. The strength of the American Constitution and our democracy rests on the freedom to stand alone, and the mere statement of near unanimity of views does not necessarily argue that those views are correct.

Like the other fallacies in argument, the bandwagon argument has some proper uses although it is often used improperly. If, for example, all the authorities in a discipline are fairly well agreed about something, you may say so if you are arguing for a position those authorities support. A student of mine recently wrote a paper advocating a constitutional amendment that would give the president a single six-year term. He supported his argument brilliantly by showing that the last four presidents of the United States had advocated a similar idea. In a sense he was calling on his readers to get on the bandwagon, to join the authorities who knew most about the situation, the men who had actually held the presidential office.

Not long ago some nonmedical people became convinced that a compound called laetrile could cure cancer. The nearly unanimous response of cancer specialists was that this claim was nonsense. Here the argument of testimony from specialists should be taken seriously, and so it has been. In a sense, we get on the medical bandwagon when we agree with the people who have studied the matter most carefully.

The general connotation of the bandwagon argument is that people emotionally take up a position merely because others have done so whether they know anything about the argument or not. It is often associated with the *ad hominem* argument because people who preach the bandwagon frequently pass on to the declaration that their opponents are foolish and even despicable beings. It is worth remembering that bandwagons may turn into stampedes and that stampedes rarely do anybody any good.

CONCLUDING REMARKS ON ARGUMENT

Argument is essential to democracy. From the smallest meetings in our communities to the greatest debates in the Congress of the United States, argument helps us see our way, make choices, and abide by them. It is a high mark of civilization, and when people lose the ability to argue well or to follow the arguments of others, all our democratic institutions are threatened. Never be afraid to argue; but always be prepared to argue well.

TEN

Avoiding Wordiness

As E. D. Hirsch, Jr., has said (and as I have repeated early in this book), writing must be efficient. That is, you should not use more words than are necessary for the information you wish to convey and the tone you wish to produce. You should always be as brief as possible given your intention.

Shakespeare tells us that brevity is the soul of wit; he does not tell us how difficult brevity is to achieve. Ernest Hemingway worked as hard as anyone ever has to create a lean style. He rarely wrote more than four hours a day; in those four hours he tried to produce about four pages. He went over his prose again and again, seeing what words he could cut. His sentences are short. He rarely used the passive voice, and he used few adjectives. Dozens of writers—perhaps thousands—have tried to imitate him. Few have succeeded in creating the same effects. I doubt that many have worked so hard at trimming off the fat in their sentences.

No book can simplify the road to brevity or efficiency. You must convince yourself that efficiency is a goal. Then you must work over your sentences until you have squeezed out every unnecessary word. If you follow the advice in this book, your first drafts will be rambling and wordy. In them you should try to get all your thoughts down on paper. In your second drafts you should give those thoughts a design. Shape them into an essay. Until you have written a second draft, you probably will not have a clear idea of exactly what thesis you want to develop. Once you have decided on the design, you can start cutting out unnecessary words, rewriting sentences to make them sharper and briefer, and choosing words that most clearly express your meaning.

Make writing a habit; that is the first step in being a good writer. Make revising a habit, too. See your sentences as puzzles. The object of the puzzle is to make every sentence as efficient as you can. When you have developed the habit of revision, you will review sentences like this one, typical of a first draft:

> It was evident from his smile as he got off the plane that the young marine was happy to be home at last from Lebanon.

And you will turn it into something like this:

> The marine got off the plane smiling, happy to be home from Lebanon.

What thoughts went into this revision? If something was evident, you don't need to say *It was evident*. Smiles are usually happy; only if they are not happy do they require an adjective. *Young* is unnecessary because marines are almost always young, and the phrase *at last* is also unnecessary. So you think a bit, and you revise, and the revision is more efficient.

Many clauses can be shortened to phrases, especially adjectival clauses that begin with *who, whom, which,* and *that*. You don't have to say, "Ralph, who was my best friend, advised me to publish the book." You can say this instead: "Ralph, my best friend, advised me to publish the book." You don't have to say, "The car that is in the driveway is mine." You can say this instead: "The car in the driveway is mine."

The passive voice creates wordiness. Don't say, "It must be recognized." Say instead, "We must recognize." Don't say, "It is not to be thought." Say, "We should not think." Don't say, "The car was repaired by my neighbor." Say, "My neighbor repaired the car." Don't say, "You will be reminded by this letter that your bill is three months overdue." Say, "Your bill is three months overdue."

Try to be as natural as you can. People who strain for effects usually become wordy. We find an unnatural style in many institutional publications. Professor Richard Lanham of U.C.L.A. calls this wordiness "the official style." Here is an example of the official style taken from a university job listing:

> Network Engineer. Office for Information Technology. Responsible for the planning, design and implementation of communications networks carrying data, video and voice signals throughout the University. Evaluates the relative technical merits of alternative technologies and design approaches. Prepares initial system specifications and designs for proposed networks or subnetworks.

The author of this document intended to avoid ambiguity about the job but fell hard into the cumbersome official style. Note words like *implementation* and *alternative* and nouns like *information* and *design* used as adjectives. Professional writers don't *implement* things; they *do* them or *perform* them. They don't talk about *alternative* technologies; they speak of *various* technologies. Could the listing be translated into something like this?

> Network engineer wanted to design and install various communications lines throughout the University. Should know modern technology and design.

Must a network engineer be told that she should be qualified to design and install various systems of communication? Such abilities seem to go with the profession. But suppose we keep all the elaborate qualifications of the original. We could still have a simpler, less wordy announcement:

> Network engineer. Responsible for designing and installing communications networks for data, video, and voice signals throughout the University. Evaluates the technical merits of various technologies and designs. Prepares specifications for systems and designs for networks.

This cumbersome, fearful style seems to be everywhere. It tries to explain everything, to qualify everything, to leave no possible room for misunderstanding. You should always explain what requires explanation, but you should never explain too much. And you should not qualify too much. Look at how the following paragraph from a good scholarly article tumbles headlong into the official style:

> Both Paul the Deacon and Liudprand of Cremona belonged to Lombard society, separated by little over a century and a half. Both lived in turbulent times and witnessed the overthrow of native kings by transalpine invaders; moreover, both participated in the intellectual and administrative life of north Italy before and after invasions from the north. Paul and Liudprand wrote of the events which in their minds formed their respective contemporary worlds. Their interests in human history provide modern historians with significant records both of the Lombards and of north Italy on the eve of two crucial turning points.[1]

Could the writer have said this?

> Paul the Deacon and Liudprand of Cremona lived in Lombardy about a century and half apart, but both witnessed the overthrow of native kings

[1] Jon N. Sutherland, "The Idea of Revenge in Lombard Society in the Eighth and Tenth Centuries: The Cases of Paul the Deacon and Liudprand of Cremona," *Speculum*, July 1975, 391.

by transalpine invaders, and both shared in the intellectual and adminis-
trative life of north Italy before and after invasions from the north. They
wrote about the events of their times, providing records both of the Lom-
bards and of north Italy on the eve of two great turning points in the Middle Ages.

The first version of this paragraph — the one published in a scholarly journal — offers no impossible barrier to understanding. But similar
paragraphs, plodding one after another, dull the effect of a good article.
Anyone can get away with writing an occasional ponderous sentence.
But a line of ponderous sentences, tramping like ancient elephants
across a memo or a scholarly journal or a book, makes readers nod and
doze and finally turn away unless they are already so interested in the
topic that they cannot put the piece down.

People fall into this "official" style because they fear they will not
be taken seriously if they write clearly. They do not wish to communicate so much as they wish to shield themselves or make their ideas
seem more important than they are. So they become not only wordy but
also opaque. And their work is a horror to read. As I have said so often in
this book, good writing comes out of confidence. If you are confident
that you have something worth saying, you can be brave enough to say
it as simply and as efficiently as you can.

Shortening your own prose will prove to be immensely satisfying.
You feel in control of what you write. You see writing as a process of
thought much like the carving of an object out of a piece of wood.
Writing becomes a craft, and you become the person who can make a
thing good no matter how rough it looks at first.

Different writing tasks require different sorts of brevity. If you
must summarize a complicated document so that people in your office
can get the gist of it in a page, you may have to go over the document
repeatedly to separate the essential from the nonessential. Writing summaries provides excellent discipline for all writing tasks and for thinking.
But summaries are different from essays. The summary may give the
conclusions and leave out the supporting evidence, and it is almost
always written in a less textured style. Nevertheless, good summarizers
contribute to the efficiency of their own work as well as to the clarity of
their thinking and writing, and people love to have them around.

In longer pieces your aims are different. You present fully
developed arguments, including evidence. You quote from others. You
often use adjectives and adverbs that you would eliminate from a summary. Even in these longer pieces, though, your prose should be as effi-

cient as you can make it. You should not use one more word than necessary to convey the information you want to convey and to create the tone you want to create.

There are no easy shortcuts to a brief style, and no one idea about brevity can suit everyone. You will pick up the habit of brevity if you study your drafts carefully. Here I must repeat some advice. The best thing a writer can do to improve her writing is also the simplest thing: she should read everything she writes several times before letting it go. I have mentioned that my style of revising used to be to type the same page again and again until it seemed to be right. Typing it all over again made every word come through my fingers and my brain in a way that made me see everything anew. You may choose to read with a pencil in hand, marking changes you wish to make. Nowadays you may use a computer with a word-processing program and scroll your entire paper across the screen, adding here, deleting there, until you are ready to print out. Whatever you do, read your work again once you have finished it. Read slowly. Give yourself enough time to think through every sentence, every word.

Cut out the fancy words, the verbose phrases, the unnecessary modifiers. Combine sentences whenever possible. Examine some stock phrases to see if they can be shortened.

Stock phrases can often be eliminated. In a first draft, you may write the following sentence:

> In the final analysis, the Japanese victory at Pearl Harbor was really a disaster for Japan.

We find the stock phrase *In the final analysis.* And we find the common word *really.* You can eliminate them both:

> The Japanese victory at Pearl Harbor was a disaster for Japan.

You can follow this sentence with some evidence to support your opinion.

Remember that you should be wordy in your first draft. Then you are trying to arrive at what you want to say. You are using your hands to help your mind generate thoughts and call up memories that will give substance to your opinions. You are making the first shaping of your essay. After that first draft, think of ways to become more efficient.

COMMON PROBLEMS OF WORDINESS

No chapter, indeed no book, can help you solve all the problems of wordiness. But in the following pages I address some common problems, and I hope that as you study them, you will develop more sensitivity to your own style. When you see that some things can be changed, you will think of others.

When you eliminate some wordy expressions, you must often rearrange the whole sentence. At times you cannot revise merely by cutting out the unnecessary word or phrase.

Area/Region

Don't say, "The weather in the area of the Southwest is often hot and dry." Say this instead: "The weather in the Southwest is often hot and dry."

Aspect

Reconsider when you are tempted to use this word. Don't say, "Another aspect of the problem that should be considered is the feasibility of the project." Say this instead: "We should also consider whether the project can be done."

At the present time/At this point in time/ At that point in time

Eliminate these expressions. Say *now* or *then*, or let the present or past tense give the time you want.

Case/Cases

You can often revise phrases including these words. Don't say, "In this case we see Faulkner's use of an old woman as oracle." Say this instead: "Here we see Faulkner's use of an old woman as oracle." Don't say, "In some cases exercise can kill." Say this instead: "Sometimes exercise can kill."

Certainly/Assuredly/Surely/Obviously

These words can often be eliminated. Paradoxically enough, we use them only when we realize that a statement may not be obvious to someone else. If we are drawing an inference that may not be shared by our readers, we tag our inference with one of these words. Someone may write this: "He refused to let the police enter his house without a search warrant; obviously he had something to hide." The writer cannot prove that the person had something to hide; the writer merely makes an inference and tags it with the word *obviously*. But it is not obvious at all.

Character/Manner/Nature/Color/Stature

You can often eliminate these words. Don't say, "The love affair was of a complex nature." Say this instead: "The love affair was complex." Don't say, "Mr. Dawson had an ingratiating manner." Say this instead: "Mr. Dawson was ingratiating."

Close proximity

Use *near* instead. Don't say, "The barn was in close proximity to the house." Say: "The barn was near the house."

Consensus of opinion

The word *consensus* implies opinion. Don't say, "The consensus of opinion in the group was that boxing is barbaric." Say this instead: "The consensus in the group was that boxing is barbaric."

Considering the fact that

Use *although* or *because* instead. Don't say, "Considering the fact that she had been sick, she ran the marathon in good time." Say this instead: "Although she had been sick, she ran the marathon in good time."

Despite the fact that

Use *although* instead. Don't say, "Despite the fact that he loved to ski, he refused to take the time." Say this instead: "Although he loved to ski, he refused to take the time."

Doubled phrases

English has a special liking for doubled phrases, such as *null and void*, *cease and desist*, and *advise and consent*. They come from our legal tradition, and they sound like judges making their opinions unmistakable. In ordinary writing such doubling is usually unnecessary. Don't say *pick and choose*. Say *choose* instead. Don't say *each and every*.

Say *each* instead. Don't say *first and foremost*. Say either *first* or *foremost*. Don't say, "For all intents and purposes the Red Sox were out of the running by June." Be bold. Say: "The Red Sox were out of the running by June."

Due to the fact that

Replace with *because*.

Each individual

Don't use these two as adjectives to modify a noun. Don't say, "Each individual member of the team has her own talents." Say this instead: "Each member of the team has her own talents."

End result

Say *result* instead.

Final outcome

Eliminate *final*.

Free gift

Eliminate *free*. We assume that gifts are free.

Full and complete

A doubled phrase. Say *full* or *complete* but not both.

Future plans

Plans are always for the future. Don't say, "Her future plans include a bike trip across the nation." Say this instead: "She plans to bike across the nation."

If and when

A doubled phrase. Use either *if* or *when* but not both.

In a sense

Often unnecessary.

In effect

Usually omit.

In other words

Usually omit.

Instrumental

Often wordy. Don't say, "She was instrumental in establishing the poetry group." Say instead: "She helped establish the poetry group."

Intensifiers

In informal speech we often try to convey strong feelings by using intensifiers that may be wordy in writing. Usually eliminate intensifers such as *absolutely, basically, certainly, definitely, fabulously, incredibly, intensely, perfectly, positively, utterly, really, quite, rather, simply,* and *very.*

In terms of

Almost always wordy. Don't say, "In terms of weather, it was rainy." Say instead: "It rained a lot."

In the event that

Replace with *if.*

In the final analysis

Either say *finally,* or make your final point without announcing that it is final.

In the realm of

Omit or use a shorter word. Don't say, "It is in the realm of possibility that he will come." Say instead: "He may come."

Is in a position to

Say *can* instead. Don't say, "She is in a position to help him." Say instead: "She can help him."

It is possible that

Say *can* or *may* instead. Don't say, "It is possible that we may have a nuclear war." Say: "We may have a nuclear war."

Observed fact

Usually omit. Don't say, "It is an observed fact that people can read magazines more easily than they can read their tax returns." Say this instead: "People can read magazines more easily than they can read their tax returns."

One of the things that

Usually omit. Don't say, "One of the things that you ought to practice is revision." Say this instead: "Revise your work."

On the occasion of

Use *when* instead. Don't say, "On the occasion of her arrival, we shall all proceed into the open to offer our greetings." Say this instead: "We will all go out to meet her when she comes."

Positive effects

Revise to eliminate. Don't say, "The rehabilitation program has had some positive effects." Say this instead: "The rehabilitation program has done some good."

Prior to

Replace with *before*. Don't say, "Prior to the game we had a picnic." Say: "Before the game we had a picnic."

Prove conclusively

Something is either proved or not proved. Omit *conclusively*.

Situation

A vague word that often leads to wordiness and confusion. A good Boston sportswriter recently produced this almost incomprehensible sentence:

Fisk and Lynn have been allowed to leave Boston in the last few years, and the Red Sox management is on the edge of the players' perception as becoming another Calvin Griffith situation.[2]

He meant something like this:

> The Red Sox lost Carlton Fisk and Fred Lynn became the owners would not pay them enough money. The remaining players are on the verge of seeing the Red Sox as the Boston version of the Minnesota Twins, where owner Calvin Griffith sells good players rather than pay them high salaries.

I have lengthened my version for readers unacquainted with baseball. The writer could have said this:

> The Red Sox lost Fisk and Lynn, and the remaining players are beginning to think Boston's management is like Calvin Griffith's.

The killer word is *situation*. It is so vague that both writers and readers lose track of the thought it is supposed to convey.

Take into account

Use *consider* instead. Don't say, "We must take the weather into account when we make our plans." Say this instead: "We must consider the weather when we make our plans."

The question of whether

A common padding phrase. You can trim it. Don't say, "We must consider the question of whether subways are efficient means of mass transport." Say this instead: "We must ask whether subways are efficient means of mass transport."

To some extent

A phrase that can often be shortened to *some*. Don't say, "To some extent living in the suburbs has advantages." Say this instead: "Living in the suburbs has some advantages."

Veritable

Almost always unnecessary. Don't say, "He was a veritable wonder." Say: "He was a wonder."

---

[2] Peter Gammons, *The Boston Globe*.

Voiced the opinion

Use *said.*

With a view toward

Revise to eliminate. Don't say, "She bought the boat with a view toward fishing." Say this instead: "She bought the boat so she could fish."

With regard to

Revise to eliminate. Don't say, "With regard to letter writing, she was slow." Say this instead: "She was slow to write letters."

CONCLUDING REMARKS ON WORDINESS

This list is not exhaustive. No list could be. Nor is it enough to memorize a set of taboo words and phrases. You must use the list to make your own perceptions about wordiness more acute. Once you have the perceptions, you can take a lifetime to use them.

ELEVEN

Grammar and Mechanics

Most Americans, given half a chance, will moan loudly about their ignorance of English grammar, sometimes in tones that smack suspiciously of pride, as if knowing grammar were almost as embarrassing as knowing the names of the stars on the old "Lawrence Welk Show." To some, grammar seems almost effete, a collection of perplexing rules that ought to be ignored by hearty men and women.

Others take an opposite view. They believe that grammar is the soul of writing, and they delight in shooting down things they read by attempting to find faults in the grammar. Too many high school teachers believe that teaching grammar is the same thing as teaching writing and so lead many students to suppose that if they write correctly they are also writing well.

In both views of grammar there is a piece of the truth. The most important quality of a writer is having something to say, and high school students would profit much more from developing the habit of writing than from doing unending drills in the parts of speech and from filling in the blanks in tedious grammatical exercises. Writing should come first; grammar, later on. Yet writers destroy the effectiveness of what they say when they make mistakes in grammar. Their readers lose respect for them, and the piece of writing may be confusing.

Most of us do know grammar better than we may admit. We start learning grammar as we learn to talk. When grammar works, children communicate with their families. When they communicate, they get what they want. As they succeed, they remember the speech patterns that gave them success, and they use those patterns again to satisfy their next desire.

Most of us continue to use the grammar we picked up as children by trial and error. We often cannot recall the technical terms. Not many educated people can name the eight parts of speech off the top of their heads, but they use those parts of speech well enough. Few can make a lightning distinction between a conjunctive adverb and a conjunction, but they use both conjunctive adverbs such as *moreover* and conjunctions such as *and* without any trouble.

Since about 1890 the grammar of literary English has been remarkably stable. It works in print and on radio and television and in our daily utterances. We can understand Australian movies and English newspapers. A few differences crop up now and then. The English usually write this: "If one persists on betting on the horses, one will lose one's shirt." An American will usually write this: "If one persists on betting on the horses, he will lose his shirt." The English use plural verbs with many collective nouns. They say this: "The committee are undecided." Americans usually say this: "The committee is undecided." Apart from these slight variations, we use the same grammar.

Grammar cannot be a science; it is the collection of proved conventions or patterns that allow communication to go on. Despite the best efforts of scholars in linguistics, we do not know just why these patterns developed. Why have we rejected *ain't* as a contraction for *am not* or *is not*? Why is "he *don't*" wrong and "he *doesn't*" right? Why can't we write this: "Thomas Jefferson and Karl Marx was both heirs to John Locke"? The only worthwhile answer is that the "erroneous" sentences are contrary to the conventions developed over the centuries.

These conventions used to be much looser than they are now. The coming of mass literacy and the development of publications that nourish mass literacy have created a much more inflexible grammar than that which Shakespeare or Chaucer used. Mass production of anything works best by standardization. Standard forms are easier to teach and easier to learn and also easier to recognize. When only a few people could read and when readers read aloud—as they did in the Middle Ages—grammar could be much more flexible. But when readers rapidly scan print in silence, irregularities trip them up and often force them to read something again before they can get the point of it. A standard grammar—like standard tools of all kinds—helps a mass society work. The few people who claim that any attention to grammar smacks of elitism have badly misread history and dangerously misconstrued how large, literate societies hold together.

Since television and other mass media make for communication across society, most of us learn the standard grammar of communication without giving it much thought. In my native South, among the rural people where I grew up, the word *ain't* is disappearing. People my age still use it; their children use it much less. I have often discussed this fading of a once-popular word; I am not the only one to have noticed it. Why is it going? I suspect that it is passing away because people are not hearing it on television, and the thousands and thousands of hours spent before the tube affects language as much as all the English teachers in America combined.

SOME PROBLEMS IN GRAMMAR

Writing is harder than speaking—as this book has repeatedly pointed out. A few problems in grammar vex most good writers from time to time, and mechanical problems in punctuation abound in most student papers. (We cannot learn how to use commas and semicolons by hearing people speak on television or in person.) In the following pages I have included a brief review of problems that afflict many papers I see. The list is not intended to be exhaustive, and for a complete review of grammar you should consult a good handbook.

1. Make the subject and verb agree in number.

Check clauses and phrases—even short ones—placed between a subject and a verb. When you put a phrase or a clause between the subject and the verb, you may make careless errors in agreement. Don't confuse the object of a preposition with the grammatical subject of your sentence. Don't say this: "The list of available computers and their software packages were posted yesterday." This sentence confuses the words *computers* and *packages* with the grammatical subject *list*. *Computers* and *packages* are objects of the preposition *of*. The sentence should read like this:

> The list of available computers and their software packages *was* posted yesterday.

Long clauses between subject and verb may be especially troubling. Don't write this: "The solitary automobile which has been parked in the grove of trees in the field beyond the houses have been reported stolen." Write this instead:

> The solitary automobile parked in the grove in the field beyond the houses *has* been reported stolen.

Now and then a compound subject considered as a unit takes a singular verb:

> Cops and robbers is an old American children's game.

But don't assume that readers will always see the unity you may see in a compound subject. You may write, "The gathering and classifying of data goes on relentlessly in all the sciences." In your mind *gathering* and *classifying* may be a single act, and you may use the singular verb *goes*. But many readers will assume that they are two acts, and you will confuse them with a singular verb. Except in a few idiomatic expressions, use the plural verb with a compound subject.

Revise to eliminate constructions that make readers do a double take. Some people accept these sentences: "A number of movies produced last year were boring." "A majority of the class were absent with the flu."

2. *When used as the subject of a sentence,* anybody, everybody, anyone, everyone, each, either, neither, nobody, *and* someone *require a singular verb.*

Everybody in the audience *is* applauding.

Someone is coming.

Nobody knows what happened to the Johnsons.

Either of the choices *is* possible; *neither is* probable.

When these words are used as the antecedent of another pronoun, the pronoun should be singular:

Each was aware that *her* choice would decide how *she* would spend the rest of *her* life.

Someone in the far distance lifted *his* voice in song.

3. *When a singular noun subject of a sentence is joined by* or *or* nor, *the verb should be in the singular.*

Neither economics *nor* history *is* an exact science.

A tub *or* a shower *is* located in every room.

4. *When a plural noun in a compound subject is joined by* or *or* nor *to a singular noun, the verb agrees with the nearest noun.*

Neither the singer nor her *managers are* happy.

Neither her managers nor the *singer is* happy.

Sentences like these should usually be revised to eliminate the unpleasant awkwardness of the constructions: "The singer and her managers are unhappy."

> 5. *Use the subjective case for a pronoun when it is the subject of a dependent clause, even if a dependent clause itself serves as an object.*

Don't say this: "He was prepared for whomever might ask a question." Say this instead:

He was prepared for *whoever* might ask a question.

Don't be confused by parenthetical clauses within dependent clauses. A parenthetical clause has no grammatical effect on the subject of the dependent clause of which it is a part:

The woman *who* he believed was drunk was in a coma.

His aunt, *who* he said had known Virginia Woolf, kept a diary.

The parenthetical clauses beginning with *he believed* and *he said* have no effect on the subjects of the dependent clauses in which they are embedded. The verb *was* in the first dependent clause and the verb *had known* in the second each take the pronoun *who* as their subject.

Now complications enter. When you write a pronoun that is the subject of an infinitive, the pronoun is always in the objective case:

She supposed *him* to be a friend.

We imagined *her* to be wise and good.

And the pronoun is in the objective case even if the infinitive is understood rather than written:

He thought *him* ugly.

The subject of an infinitive acts as the agent of the action that the infinitive describes. Any subject of an infinitive always follows a transitive verb, a verb that takes a direct object. Infinitives themselves are nonfinite verbs; we sometimes call them *verbals*. A nonfinite verb cannot express past or present or future time by itself. To express time, a verbal must be joined to a finite verb: "He wanted to be famous." The past tense of the verb *wanted* adds time to the infinitive *to be*, which has no time of its own. We could just as easily say, "He wants to be famous," or, "He will want to be famous."

If the infinitive has a subject, the subject becomes part of an infinitive phrase and serves as the direct object of the preceding transitive verb. A pronoun as the subject of an infinitive:

They told *us* to be careful.

6. *Use the objective case for a pronoun that serves as a direct object, an indirect object, or the object of a preposition. Do not use the objective case for a pronoun that serves as a subject.*

Don't say, "Just between you and I, his poetry is terrible." Say this instead:

Just between you and *me*, I stop my ears when he reads.

Don't say, "He laughed at Clara and I." Say this instead:

He laughed at Clara and *me*.

Don't say, "*Her* and *me* decided to make the trip." Say this instead:

She and *I* decided to go by bike.

Don't say, "Richard and *myself* invite you to our holiday party." Say this instead:

Richard and *I* invite you to our party.

7. *Form the possessive case of a common noun in the singular by adding 's even if the noun ends in* s.

It was *Jane's* typewriter.

It was *Erasmus's* first book.

That is *Burriss's* house.

This rule is not observed in some traditional phrases:

For goodness sake!

in Jesus' name

8. *Use the correct verb form after the adverb* there. *In a sentence that begins with* there *and a linking verb, the verb must agree with the subject, which usually comes immediately after the verb.*

Don't say, "There is singing and laughter upstairs tonight." Say this instead:

There are singing and laughter upstairs tonight.

Better still, when you have a plural form after *there*, revise the sentence "The people upstairs are singing and laughing tonight."

9. *Use the correct verb tense.*
Tense *is the time of a verb. English has six tenses:*

present: I play.

past: I played.

future: I will play.

present perfect: I have played.

past perfect: I had played.

future perfect: I will have played.

Each tense has a *progressive* form that expresses continuing, or progressive, action within the time noted by the tense:

present progressive: I am playing.

past progressive (imperfect): I was playing.

future progressive: I will be playing.

present perfect progressive: I have been playing.

future perfect progressive: I will have been playing.

The present tense may do three things. First, it reports habitual action

Birds migrate every year.

The sun rises every morning.

Wars are caused by stupidity.

Habitual action extends to verbs that describe the action in literature since the written word is assumed to be always speaking:

> David Copperfield *is* not as interesting as the other characters in the book.
>
> Socrates *teaches* that the way to wisdom begins with the command, "Know thyself."

Second, the present tense, in the form of the present progressive, describes a specific action. It is the most idiomatic way we have of speaking of something happening right now:

> She *is coming* down the street.
>
> They *are repaving* the highway between Boston and Lynn.

The present progressive can become a future tense by adding an adverb of future time:

> She is coming *tomorrow*.
>
> They are playing softball *next Sunday*.

Third, adding *do* or *does* to the present tense shows emphasis. The present emphatic is used in negations:

> I *do not* like snakes.
>
> She *does not* like people who do not like snakes.

It is also used to affirm something that someone else has denied. For example, someone has said that you do not try to stay out of debt, and you answer:

> I *do try* to stay out of debt.

The present tense creates confusion for writers who get carried away with the sense of action conveyed by the present. These writers often use the present tense to describe past action, especially when they are writing about history or an exciting story:

> Franklin Roosevelt is elected because he promises to do something about the Depression, and Hoover keeps on saying that the Depression is almost over. Roosevelt takes over in March 1933, and in his inaugural address he promises bold action and tells the American people that the only thing they have to fear is fear itself.

Narration in the present tense has been used successfully by some novelists and journalists. But in general it should be avoided in writing about the past. Use the past tense for history. The present will likely confuse both your readers and you.

The simple past is usually formed by adding *-ed* as a suffix to the present stem of the verb: "I play" becomes "I *played.*" But English is complicated by having about three hundred irregular verbs in common use. These verbs are irregular because they form the past tense or the past participle in special ways:

I draw.   I drew.   I have drawn.

You see.   You saw.   You have seen.

I run.   I ran.   I have run.

Usually we learn irregular verbs as we learn to talk and hear others using them. In some regions of the country these verbs differ from those of the literary tradition. In the rural neighborhood where I grew up, people said, "I seen him when he done it," and, "He drawed me a plan for the house." They were intelligent, sensible people, and such people in other regions of the country today may use verbs in ways that are not standard in the literary tradition. When you are in doubt, consult a dictionary. Any good dictionary always lists the various standard forms of irregular verbs.

The simple future tense is formed with *shall* and *will.* Strict grammarians used to insist that *shall* should be used with the first person and *will* with the second and third persons. American writers generally ignore this distinction. We nearly always say, "He will be fifty on his next birthday," and, "We will be happy to see you at the party." We sometimes use *shall* for emphasis: "They shall not pass."

All the tenses use a progressive form made from the present participle (the verb form ending in *-ing*) to show action that continues. The past progressive, or imperfect, is probably the most common form of the progressive. Use it to show action going on while something else is happening:

I *was traveling* west during June.

The sentence means that while June was going by, I was traveling west.

He *was sleeping* when the robbery occurred.

The tense is imperfect, or progressive, because the end of the action is not described; that is, the action of sleeping continued as long as the robbery occurred, but we are not told how long that was.

The progressive tenses will give you little trouble as long as you think of the time they are supposed to represent and of how we talk and write about the relations that join moments in time.

10. Avoid illogical mixing of verb tenses.

The simple verb tenses offer little trouble because we combine them fairly logically. We would never think of saying, "I was there when you will come." We do say, "I am arriving when you will be there," because we understand that the present progressive verb phrase *am arriving* becomes a future tense because of the adverbial clause that follows it. Sometimes we see problems in joining the past tense with the present, as in sentences like these:

> Plato believed that the soul is immortal.
>
> Thomas More thought that death is not the worst fate.
>
> John Maynard Keynes taught that governments should use deficit financing during depressions.

This combination of past and present tense is appropriate in each example because the present tense expresses a habitual truth, one valid not only for the time these people expressed it but, according to their thought at least, valid for all time.

Normally the past tense in a first clause will demand a past tense in a second clause, and we usually join such clauses without difficulty:

> He played baseball because he loved the game, not because he was paid a high salary.
>
> She grew up in a neighborhood that was close and friendly.

Problems with mixing tenses usually arise when the perfect tenses are used. The present perfect always conveys a sense of action that started in the past and carries forward somehow to the present, where either the action itself or its effects continue. The present perfect tense is formed by using the present tense of the verb *to have* with the past participle of the main verb in the construction:

> We *have worked* since yesterday afternoon.

The work started in the past and continues to the present. It is not complete at the time reported by this sentence.

> He *has been* a great baseball player.

This sentence says that the beginning of his great baseball playing was in the past and continues to the present.

The present perfect tense can easily be used in combination with the present tense:

> He *has been* a great baseball player, but his great days *are* behind him, and he *is retiring* at the end of this season.
>
> She *has been grinding* rust off the car all afternoon with the electric sander, and now she *is tired.*

The present perfect can also be used with the future, since both tenses join at the time when the statement about future action is made:

> They *have been traveling* all night, and they *will travel* all day today and tomorrow.

The past perfect tense uses the past tense of the verb *to have* with the past participle of the main verb in the construction. It always implies that an action ended before or just as another action began:

> They *had been waiting* an hour when the train *arrived.*

In this sentence the waiting ended at the moment the train arrived, and both actions took place in the past.

The past perfect cannot be used before the present perfect; we cannot say, "Country music had been popular and has remained so." A reader wants to know, "It had been popular before what?" The past perfect sets up the expectation of an end point, and if you do not have an end point, you must either provide one or change the sentence:

> Country music *had been* popular before 1950, but in that year it *became* a national interest.

Here the prepositional phrase *before 1950* provides the end point that the past perfect causes us to expect, and the later clauses go on from that point to make another statement.

Sometimes we imply the end point, especially in oral English. We may speak of a friend who came to an early-morning history class in a tuxedo. Someone says, "Did you know that John came to class this morning dressed in a tuxedo?" You ask why, and your friend says, "He *had been* at a party all night long." From the last sentence spoken by your friend, you infer an end point already mentioned in an earlier sentence. The implied thought is this: "John had been at a party all night long and came to class in the morning in his tuxedo." The end point of the action *had been* is his arrival in class.

You also cannot properly use the past perfect with the present tense. You should not say, "He had to learn to walk before he learns to run." You should not use the past perfect as a substitute for the simple past. That is, don't say, "Henry VIII had been born in 1491" unless you intend to follow that sentence with another related to it by the simple past. It is better to say, "Henry VIII was born in 1491."

You may use the past perfect in a paragraph whose sentences lack a dependent clause only if the end point of the past perfect is clearly stated in another sentence:

> Henry VIII came to the throne in 1509. He *had not been meant* to be king. He *had been born* the second son of Henry VII. His older brother Arthur *had been* heir to the throne, but Arthur died. A persistent legend holds that young Henry *had been destined* to become a priest, but Arthur's death changed that destiny and the destiny of England as well.

Here we have several sentences in the past perfect, all moving toward the end point, which is stated in the first sentence.

The past perfect tense is often used too much, especially in the writing of history. Use the simple past unless the past perfect is clearly needed.

The future perfect tense describes a future act that must be concluded before or just as another future act begins:

> We *will have been* here a week before you arrive.

> The apples *will have been picked* by then.

As in all perfect tenses, the future perfect makes you think of the time when one action ends and another begins. The action in the future perfect tense must end before some future moment or just as some future action begins.

Always recall that perfect tenses imply a time considered as the end point of an action, a time when the action of the sentence is complete from the point of view of the sentence. You may say, "I have been waiting for an hour," using the present perfect tense. You may go on waiting for another hour, but that other hour is not the concern of this sentence. This sentence is concerned with the action that has gone on for an hour, and that hour is complete by the time that sentence is written or spoken.

> *11. Use the subjunctive form of the verb in dependent clauses that make a statement contrary to fact.*

I wish I *were* in the Bahamas.

I am not in the Bahamas; hence the subjunctive *were*.

If he *were* more tactful, he would have more friends.

He is not more tactful, so he does not have more friends.

Use the indicative form in dependent clauses that make simple statements about what may or may not be true:

If what she said *was* true, he was guilty.

You don't know whether what she said was true or not true. You merely make the statement that if it was true, he was guilty. So use the verb *was* in this dependent clause.

> *12. Use a comma between independent clauses — clauses that can stand alone grammatically as sentences — when those clauses are joined by the coordinate conjunctions* and, but, nor, or, *and* for.

I like baseball, *but* I am not addicted to it.

They would live in peace, *or* they would die.

> *13. Use a comma after a long introductory clause or phrase that precedes the subject of an independent clause.*

Because the temperature on the highway was 115 degrees, the air conditioning in the diner nearly knocked me flat.

Backed up against Antwerp, the Belgian army furiously counterattacked the Germans in September 1914.

14. *Use commas to set off parenthetical clauses and phrases that add descriptive material not essential to the principal assertion of the sentence.*

A parenthetical phrase set off with commas:

The motorcycle, *a gift from his father,* carried him three thousand miles across the country to Los Angeles.

That the motorcycle was a gift from his father is not essential to the main assertion of the sentence. The detail adds interest, and the writer may choose to develop something from that detail in sentences to come; but the main assertion of this sentence is that the motorcycle carried someone three thousand miles across the country to Los Angeles. The assertion would remain the same without the phrase, and so the phrase is set off by commas.

A parenthetical clause set off with commas:

The personal computer, *which was unknown only a decade ago,* now dominates advertising on the business pages and finds a place in hundreds of thousands of American homes.

The parenthetical clause adds an interesting detail, but it is not necessary to the assertion that the personal computer dominates advertising on the business pages and finds a place in hundreds of thousands of American homes.

Do not set off clauses and phrases that are indispensable to the main assertion. An essential clause not set off with commas:

The reporter who spent ten days in jail on a phony drunkenness charge wrote a great story about his experience behind bars.

You are not talking about just any reporter. You are talking about the one who spent ten days in jail on a phony drunkenness charge. If you leave out the clause *who spent ten days in jail on a phony drunkenness charge,* you leave out the definition that gives meaning to the rest of the sentence. You do not set off such a clause with commas.

You can change the meaning of a sentence by setting off a clause or phrase with commas or by not doing so. Suppose you say this:

> Faculty members who are slipshod and lazy rob their students.

Since you do not set off the *who* clause with commas, it is an essential part of your statement. You are saying that only those faculty members who are slipshod and lazy rob their students. But suppose you say this:

> Faculty members, who are slipshod and lazy, rob their students.

Now you are telling your readers that they can lift out the *who* clause without damaging your main assertion. So you can have a sentence like this: "Faculty members rob their students." Your addition of the nonessential clause announces that all faculty members are slipshod and lazy. You are delivering a double insult. You condemn the teaching profession for robbing students, and you announce that all members of that profession are slipshod and lazy.

Some writers want to set off all appositives with commas, but this habit may lead to confusion. Suppose you write this sentence:

> In his novel, *For Whom the Bell Tolls*, Ernest Hemingway made a tragedy of the Spanish Civil War.

The commas make the title parenthetical, something that could be removed without damaging the central meaning of the sentence. They say to your readers that your main assertion is this: "In his novel Ernest Hemingway made a tragedy of the Spanish Civil War." You imply that Hemingway wrote only one novel and that it was called *For Whom the Bell Tolls*. In fact he wrote many novels. So in the sentence above, you must not set off the title of the book with commas.

15. Use ellipsis marks correctly.

Ellipsis marks consist of three typed dots with a space before and a space after each. Ellipsis marks are not made without space between them (...). They are spaced (. . .) to show that you have left some words out of a direct quotation.

Here are some sentences from Paul Fussell's book *The Great War and Modern Memory*:

> Recourse to the pastoral is an English mode of both fully gauging the calamities of the Great War and imaginatively protecting oneself against them. Pastoral reference, whether to literature or to actual rural localities and objects, is a way of invoking a code to hint by antithesis at the inde-

scribable; at the same time, it is a comfort in itself, like rum, a deep dug-out, or a woolly vest.[1]

Here is part of a paper that quotes from this text, using ellipses to indicate some omitted words:

Fussell shows that English troops in World War I used the pastoral tradition as an anodyne against the horrors they met in the trenches. He says, "Pastoral reference . . . is a way of invoking a code to hint by antithesis at the indescribable; at the same time, it is a comfort in itself."

Notice that the ellipsis marks show that words have been omitted between *reference* and *is*. You can see what those words are by looking at the original. Notice that there is a space between *reference* and the first dot and a space after each of the dots, including the space between the last one and the word *is*.

Notice, too, that ellipsis marks are not used at the end of the quotation although the word *itself* is not the last word in Fussell's original sentence. The quotation marks are sufficient to show readers that here you stop quoting. They naturally assume that Fussell's text goes on, and they do not need ellipsis marks to show them that you are not quoting all of it.

Remember that the major function of ellipsis marks is to show that you are leaving something out between your first quotation marks and your last. The quotation marks themselves set off what you are quoting from what you choose not to quote in your source.

Sometimes you may leave out a whole sentence, several whole sentences, or an entire paragraph from a long quotation. Then you will have to punctuate the last sentence before the ellipsis marks:

In 1930, W. E. B. DuBois reviewed his controversy with Booker T. Washington. "These were the opposing arguments. . . . They were set forth by earnest men, white and black, philanthropist and teacher, statesman and seer."

The writer is quoting DuBois, and the ellipsis marks show that words have been omitted after the sentence ending with the word *arguments*. That sentence is punctuated with a period. Then there are three spaced dots to show that words have been omitted.

[1] Paul Fussell, *The Great War and Modern Memory* (New York: Oxford University Press, 1975), 235.

If your quotation ends before the sentence you are quoting ends and you continue to quote afterward, again use a period (or a question mark or exclamation mark if that is used in the original) and then the three ellipsis marks:

> Fussell said that the pastoral ideal became "a comfort in itself, like rum. . . . The Golden Age posited by Classical and Renaissance literary pastoral now finds its counterpart in ideas of 'home' and 'the summer of 1914.'"

Here the first dot is the period, and the ellipsis marks indicate that words have been left off the end of the quoted sentence. After the ellipsis marks, the next sentence takes up.

16. *Make a dash by typing two hyphens on the typewriter (--), and don't put spaces around the dash, separating it from the words to each side.*

The dash offers the opportunity of using punctuation to achieve strong emphasis. When we see a phrase or a clause set off with dashes, we look at it sharply, but the effect is ruined if we cannot tell whether or not we are looking at a dash. One hyphen is a hyphen, not a dash. We read this sentence without trouble:

> The temperature on Christmas morning was twelve below zero—cold enough to make the trees crack and all of us stay indoors by the fire.

When we replace the dash with a hyphen, we have trouble:

> The temperature on Christmas morning was twelve below zero-cold enough to make the trees crack and all of us stay indoors by the fire.

A rapid reader will probably see *zero-cold* as a hyphenated word and will have to read the sentence twice to discover that the hyphen is supposed to be a dash.

17. *Use double quotation marks to set off direct quotations. If material you are quoting includes material in quotation marks, use single quotation marks (the apostrophe key on the typewriter) to set off those words that are within quotation marks in the original.*

According to Irving Howe, "a combination of local bosses dividing the spoils could also become a fellowship of allies ('All there is in life,' said Boss Croker, 'is loyalty to one's family and friends')."

18. Do not use quotation marks to set off slang, clichés, or other words that you wish to apologize for.

Only inexperienced writers use apologetic quotation marks that seem to say, "I know this is a cliché or some other lazy language, but at least I have put it in quotation marks to let you know that I know I'm being lazy." When you are tempted to put quotation marks around a cliché, you should think of some better expression that will make your language lively.

Don't do this:

> He did not want to "count his chickens before they hatched," but he didn't want to be "left at the starting gate" either.

19. Use quotation marks to indicate a usage by others that you do not share.

> In a "people's democracy" the people have a chance to be democratic about anything except the oppression they all feel from the state.

20. Do not put quotation marks around block quotations.

When you quote more than three or four lines from a source, you should put the material in a block that is indented five spaces from your left margin. That indentation in itself is sign enough that you are quoting. You should not add quotation marks, for then readers will suppose that you are quoting a quotation.

Remember that block quotations are often necessary, but it is usually much better to paraphrase your source or to quote parts of it than it is to present large blocks of quoted material.

21. Use colons to set off lists and some quotations.

> She wanted these things: a good job, respect, and a future.

Notice that the colon comes at the end of an independent clause. A colon should not break into an independent clause. You should not say this: "She wanted: a good job, respect, and a future."

As you can see from this book, colons frequently set off block quotations that are set off by indentation from the main body of a text.

22. *Semicolons rather than colons usually join independent clauses.*

The sky shone; the fields smelled of spring.

Colons can join independent clauses when the second clause is clearly meant to be a consequence or a clarification of the first:

Jackson was furious: someone had given him a monkey for Christmas, and he hated pets.

Nuclear war may make all life on earth extinct: so much dust would be hurled into the atmosphere that it would block the sun and create a hundred years of freezing temperatures at the equator.

Sexist Language

For centuries ordinary English seemed to imply that only men were important. We have now progressed to a different perception, and the consequences for writing have been confusing. This discussion will, alas, not clear up all the confusions, but some of its advice may be helpful. At the very least it will show some places where the confusion is most troublesome, and it will show some other places where it may be clarified.

The most troublesome problem in sexist language is this: What do we do with the standard English custom of using *he, his,* or *him* when we use a pronoun to refer to an indefinite singular noun, a noun that in reality may include either a male or a female? In common English we have for years written this: "What do we want our reader to think about us? We want him to believe that we know what we are talking about, that we respect his point of view, and that we hope he will seriously consider ours." We know that "our reader" may be male or female. What do we do now, with the different consciousness of this age?

With the preceding example the solution is easy. We turn the singular into the plural, and we say this: "What do we want our readers to think about us? We want them to believe that we know what we are talking about, that we respect their points of view, and that we hope they will seriously consider ours."

At times we must use the singular in a sentence, as in a sentence like this: "The thief entered the house by breaking a pane of glass in the back door, cutting himself in the process, and left a trail of blood through the kitchen. The wound must not have been serious since he not only stole my typewriter but came back and stole five reams of paper as well." Now what are we to do? In some sentences we might write both the feminine and the masculine pronoun, but in this sentence the effect, to me at least, seems clumsy: "The thief entered the house by breaking a pane of glass in the back door, cutting himself or herself in the process, and left a trail of blood through the kitchen.

The wound must not have been serious since he or she not only stole my typewriter but came back and stole five reams of paper as well."

We may get away with using the masculine and feminine pronouns now and then when repetition is unnecessary. We can say easily enough, "The company promised to give the first-prize winner a week's stay in any hotel in the country that he or she may choose." But we get into trouble when we start saying this: "The company promised to give the first-prize winner a week's stay in any hotel in Hawaii that he or she may choose and promised also that he or she might take along a friend and that he or she would also be given free use of a rental car for the week and free meals in the restaurant of his or her choice."

Here again we may revise to eliminate the difficulty: "The company offered a first prize of a week's stay in a hotel of choice in Hawaii for the winner and a friend, free use of a rental car for a week, and free meals in any restaurant on the island."

Occasionally we can use the pronoun *one* as a substitute for *he* or *she*: "Anyone who works on the night shift for twenty years will discover that one's view of life changes with such an experience in ways incomprehensible to one's neighbors." But to many, such usage is uncomfortable.

Increasingly I hear well-educated people saying things like this: "Anybody who thinks such a silly thing should have their heads examined." The plural pronoun *their* offers a nonsexist solution to the problem of *he or she*. But that solution offends me and most others who have for good or for ill been steeped in the customs of standard grammar, and I don't expect it to be adopted soon by most editors and professional writers, though who can tell? I see it occasionally in advertising and even in the slick-paper magazines.

My own solution, used in this book, is to vary the pronoun, to say *he* sometimes and *she* sometimes. A few people I know say that male writers should use the pronoun *he* and that female writers should use *she*. To many, either solution seems awkward, and women writers as diverse as Barbara Tuchman and the late Mina Shaughnessy have used the traditional *he* without feeling that they betray the cause of women. I must admit that *he* comes to me much more naturally, and I must admit, too, that I don't believe that this particular pronoun has much effect on the fate of women's rights. In countries such as France or Hungary where the languages allow a neuter singular pronoun, women are traditionally subservient and discriminated against in law and custom.

I find myself torn at times. I don't want to do anything to offend an audience unnecessarily. I have offended audiences by writing too stridently or too certainly, and I have always regretted it because an offended audience rejects out of hand the argument that the author wants readers to believe. Just now hardly anything offends people more than the issue of sexist language. The problem for writers is that some men and women are going to be offended no matter what we do. If we sound clumsy in our efforts to avoid sexist language, we are going to offend traditionalists of whom there are many. If we refuse to take note of the problem and go on using *he* and *him* as if everyone on earth worthy of respect had been born male, we are going to offend the large and rapidly growing number of people who believe that clumsiness of language is a small price to pay for sexual equality.

Aside from the difficulties with pronouns, we can fairly easily avoid some of the traditional offenses of sexist language. You don't have to say *policeman*; you can say *police officer*. I have no special problem in writing *chairperson* instead of the traditional *chairman*. Some journals now use the word *chair*, a word that seems to be taking hold. *Freshperson* seems unbearably clumsy to me as a substitute for *freshman*, but we can always say *first-year student* instead.

Where once we spoke of *mankind*, we can now say *humankind*; where we once wrote *man*, we can usually find a substitute. Instead of saying, "The average man," we can say, "The average person." Instead of saying, "Man is the highest form of life," we can say, "The human species is the highest form of life." Whenever you are tempted to use a word that seems to show superiority of men over women, pause to think of another, sex-neutral word.

Some words should be used with extreme caution or not at all. *Poetess* for a woman poet now seems degrading. Women should never be referred to as "the fair sex" or "the distaff side," and a wife should not be called a man's "better half" or any of the other humorously demeaning terms so long in vogue at male clubs. The word *lady* often has a negative connotation these days, and the word *woman* is nearly always better.

Above all, readers should not be addressed as though the only important people among them were men. You should not identify women by telling who their husbands are unless that information has some special importance. It would be thoroughly improper to write this sentence as a lead in a newspaper story:

Mrs. Calberta Carmichael, wife of Jack Carmichael of 401 Pleasant Street, has won the Pulitzer Prize for fiction.

Mrs. Carmichael's husband may be an illiterate boob, and he has no business poking his nose into a story about her accomplishments.

The proper titles for women also offer some difficulty. The term *Ms.* is now common, and I would address letters to "Ms. Calberta Carmichael." But some women object to the title and prefer the more traditional *Mrs.* or *Miss.* Courtesy requires that you call people what they want to be called, and an occasional editor may prevent you from calling women by titles that both you and they may prefer; as of this writing, the *New York Times* still does not consider *Ms.* fit to print.

All these matters are difficult. They require a willingness to change and broad-mindedness about language, and we are a long way from resolving all the questions about sexist language that arise. But we must do what we can to make ourselves more sensitive to an issue that is both real and important.

Clichés

abreast of the times
acid test
across a wide spectrum
across the spectrum
add insult to injury
against the current
agony of suspense
all work and no play
avoid like the plague

(the) ball's in his court
beat a hasty retreat
be that as it may
better late than never
beyond a shadow of doubt
(the) birds and the bees
bite the dust
bitter end
bloody but unbowed
blue as the sky
bolt from the blue
bottom line
bottom of the barrel
bottom of the deck
brave as a lion
bright as a new penny
broad array
broad daylight
brown as a nut
brutal murder
burn the midnight oil
bustling cities
by the same token

calm, cool, and collected
center around
chip off the old block
cold as ice
cold, hard facts
cold light of day
come to grips with
consensus of opinion
cool as a cucumber
crack of dawn
crisis of confidence
cut and dried

dead as a doornail
deaf as a post
deep, dark secret
diabolical skill
(the) distaff side
doomed to disappointment
do or die
down and out
down but not out
down the primrose path
dyed in the wool

each and every
every dog has its day
every tub on its own
    bottom

face the music
factor
facts of life

(the) fact that
fatal flaw
few and far between
first and foremost
fit as a fiddle
fleecy clouds
fond memories
fond recollections
fresh as a daisy
frozen north

gone but not forgotten
go over like a lead ballon
go over with a fine-tooth
 comb
green with envy

hands-on
happy medium
hard row
head up
heave a sigh of relief
highest priority
hit the nail on the head
hotter than hell
hustle and bustle

in a nutshell
in a very real sense
in back of
innocent as a newborn
 babe
in some cases
in terms of
in the final analysis
in this day and age
it goes without saying
it is incumbent upon
it is interesting to note

ladder of success
larger than life
last but not least
last straw
learning experience

light as a feather
like father, like son
little lady
little, tiny
live and learn
live from hand to mouth

make a shambles of
man about town
meaningful experience
meaningful relationship
method in her madness
mind like a steel trap
mitigate against
more sinned against than
 sinning
more than meets the eye
murmur of approval

neat as a pin
needle in a haystack
never, ever
nip in the bud
nose to the grindstone
no sooner said than done
nothing ventured, nothing
 gained

off his rocker
off of
off the beaten track
off the track
one rotten apple spoils the
 barrel
ongoing
on the fast track
other side of the coin
out of the blue

painfully obvious
paint the town red
paramount importance
pass the buck
pave the way
pebble on the beach
pencil thin

people who live in glass
   houses shouldn't throw
     stones
pertinent facts
pick and choose
pivotal figure
plain as the nose on your
   face
plain Jane
pleased as punch
poor but honest
precondition
preplanning
pride and joy
primrose path
prioritize
proof is in the pudding
proud possessor
put your foot in it

quick as a flash
quick as a wink
quick as lightning

raise its ugly head
rank and file
rather unique
raving lunatic
rear its ugly head
rude awakening

sadder but wiser
scarce as hens' teeth
sell like hot cakes
sharp as a tack
short and sweet
short end of the stick
shot in the arm
shoulder to the wheel
sigh of relief
sink or swim
skeleton in the closet
slow but sure

smelling like a rose
sneaking suspicion
sober as a judge
soft place in my heart
sound as a dollar
spread like wildfire
stick out like a sore thumb
stock in trade
straight and narrow
strike while the iron is hot
sunny south

tangled skein
tangled web
tempest in a teapot
tender mercies
thin as a rail
thusly
tiny, little
tired but happy
to all intents and purposes
tried and true
truth is stranger than fiction
twinkling of an eye

undercurrent of excitement
up in arms

viable alternative
vicious circle
vicious cycle

walk a chalk line
walk the line
walk the straight and
   narrow
wet blanket
when the going gets tough,
   the tough get going
white as snow
work like a dog
work like a horse
wreak havoc

Glossary of Terms

absolute

A phrase beginning with a noun followed by a present or past participle and modifying the entire clause rather than any single element within the clause:

The guys hung out on the corner, *their motorcycles parked in a row on the street.*

She sat for hours, *her eyes looking off into space.*

Sometimes the participle in an absolute is understood. In the following example, the participle *being* is understood after the noun *heart*:

He reflected on life, *his heart full.*

adjective

A part of speech that adds some descriptive thought to, or *modifies*, nouns and pronouns:

The streets were *glossy* with rain.

Rotting ice floated in the *thawing* river.

Heavy people run a *larger* risk of heart disease.

Adjectives answer the questions "What kind?" "Which one?" "How large?" "What color?"

adverb

A part of speech that adds descriptive information to verbs, adverbs, and other adverbs. An adverb may modify an entire clause.

The plane rose *swiftly.*

In a moment it was *nearly* invisible.

Her departure left us in *very* deep sadness.

Adverbs answer the questions "How?" "Why?" "When?" "Where?"

case

The form of a noun or pronoun that indicates its use in a sentence. Nouns change their form only to make the possessive case, which shows ownership or some special relation.

The possessive case of singular nouns is formed by adding an apostrophe and an *s* even to words that end in *s*:

Dickens's novels
Melville's works

The possessive case of plural nouns is formed by adding an apostrophe to nouns whose plurals end in *s* and an apostrophe and an *s* to those whose plurals end in some other letter:

The Raiders' passing game
The children's books

The case of definite pronouns is usually indicated by their form. The subjective case includes the following:

I, you, he, she, it, we, they

The possessive case includes the following:

my, your, yours, his, hers, its, our, ours, theirs

The objective case includes the following:

me, him, her, us, them

Indefinite pronouns do not change their form except in the possessive case, which they form according to the same rules that govern the possessive of nouns.

conjunction

A part of speech used to join words, phrases, or clauses.

Coordinating conjunctions include *and, but, or, nor,* and *for.* Some writers use *so* and *yet* as coordinating conjunctions.

Subordinating conjunctions include such words as *although, because, if, though, unless, whether,* and *when.*

The parts of a sentence joined by a *coordinating* conjunction should have equal grammatical importance. Coordinating conjunctions may join independent clauses:

She loved cars, *but* he did not.

They may join words in a series:

McDonald said she would take bread, crackers, *or* biscuits.

Subordinating conjunctions most often join dependent clauses to other clauses:

The fire was already out of control *when* the neighbors saw it.

dependent clause

A clause that serves as a noun, an adjective, or an adverb.

The following *noun clause* (in italics) acts as the direct object of the verb *said*:

He said *that he would arrive tomorrow.*

The following *adjective clause* (in italics) acts as an adjective modifying the noun *house*:

The house *that he painted* was the wrong one.

The following *adverbial clause* (in italics) modifies the verb *began* in the independent clause:

> *When the sun went down,* the birds in the cactus began to sing.

finite verb

A verb that can be used as the main verb in a clause. Finite verbs express time — present, past, future, present perfect, past perfect, future perfect.

free modifier

A participle or a participial phrase that occurs at the end of a clause, set off by a comma and modifying the subject of the clause:

> She leaped into space, *tumbling wildly, laughing, waiting for her parachute to open.*

gerund

A verbal used as a noun in a sentence. Gerunds almost always take the form of the present participle:

> *Walking* delighted her.

independent clause

Sometimes called a *main clause.* A clause that can usually stand by itself as a complete sentence. A more technical definition is that an independent clause does not serve as a noun, adjective, or adverb for a part of speech in another clause. The independent clauses in the following sentences are in italics:

> *Charles Darwin arrived at the idea of biological evolution* after he had thought for years about the reasons for different species of plant and animal life.

> *Darwin's ideas frightened many people* because he seemed to leave no place for God or morality.

> *Many people always fear new ideas,* but *new ideas are inevitable.*

infinitive

A nonfinite form of a verb made by placing the infinitive marker *to* before the present stem. (A nonfinite form of the verb has no tense.) The infinitive of *make* is *to make*; the infinitive of *sit* is *to sit*.

Occasionally you may see or use a past infinitive, which is made with the verb *have* and the past participle of the infinitive verb:

> *To have sat* so long was a great tribulation.

Infinitives may work as nouns, adjectives, or adverbs:

> *To win* was his only ambition. [noun]

> Her desire *to succeed* ruled her life. [adjective]

> She stood up *to read.* [adverb]

A *split infinitive* occurs when a word, usually an adverb, is placed between the infinitive marker *to* and the verb:

to speedily go
to gracefully move

interjection

A part of speech that denotes sudden emotion. Interjections include words like *ouch, wow,* and many common obscenities and profane words.

non-restrictive clause

A clause that adds information to a sentence without being essential to the main statement that the sentence makes. Non-restrictive clauses are set off with commas:

Jesse Owens, who did brilliantly at the Olympic games in Berlin in 1936, died of lung cancer.

noun

A part of speech that denotes substantives capable of being described. Nouns may be persons, places, things, actions, thoughts, or anything else capable of having an adjective used to describe it. The articles *a, an,* and *the* always signal a noun to follow soon.

object

All objects in a sentence must be nouns or pronouns, or they must be clauses or phrases that serve as nouns or pronouns.

Direct objects take the action of a transitive verb:

Kant taught *philosophy.*
Oakland won the *Superbowl.*
Lightning hit the *barn.*

Indirect objects do not receive action, but they show the purpose of an action. (You can often discover an indirect object by mentally placing a *to* or a *for* before it.)

My father and mother bought *me* a computer.
Lincoln told *Americans* the truth about slavery.

The *object of a preposition* completes a prepositional phrase.

The Trojans brought the wooden horse into their *city.*
High cholesterol in a *diet* may cause heart attacks.

participle

The form of a verb that may be used either in a verb phrase or as an adjective. Present participles end in *-ing;* past participles usually end in *-ed,* but English has about three hundred irregular verbs that form the past participle in unpredictable ways.

The past tense of *dance* is *danced,* and the past participle is *danced.* But the past tense of *sing* is *sang,* and the past participle is *sung.*

preposition
A part of speech that never changes its form. Prepositions serve to introduce phrases that include a noun or a pronoun. The prepositional phrase allows the noun or the pronoun to be used in an adverbial or adjectival sense in the sentence.

The book *on the table* is mine. [adjective]

He ran *for help*. [adverb]

pronoun
A part of speech used as a substitute for nouns and noun phrases.

Definite pronouns are such words as *I, she, it, we, they, him, her, them, our.*

Indefinite pronouns are such words as *anybody, everybody*, and *everyone.*

Reflexive pronouns are such words as *itself, themselves*, and *myself.*

The *relative pronouns* are *which* and *that.*

The *demonstrative pronouns* are *this, that, these*, and *those.*

restrictive clause
A clause that is essential to the basic statement made in a sentence. Restrictive clauses are not set off with commas:

We loved the snow *that fell on Christmas Eve.*

Socrates lived in an Athens *that had just endured a humiliating military defeat.*

That *which is impossible to do* is immoral to command.

verb
A part of speech that reports action or condition. Verbs tell what happens or what exists.

verbal
A nonfinite form of a verb—that is, a verb form that has in itself no sense of time. Verbals include *participles, infinitives*, and *gerunds.* They may be used as nouns or adjectives and sometimes as adverbs.

Index

ABOUT THE AUTHOR

Richard Marius is director of the expository writing program at Harvard University. He received his M.A. and Ph.D. from Yale University in Reformation Studies, and has taught at Gettysburg College and the University of Tennessee. He was one of the first five graduates of the University of Tennessee School of Journalism, and for five years worked on a small newspaper in Tennessee. A frequent contributor to numerous journals, he has had two novels published by Alfred A. Knopf, *The Coming of Rain* and *Bound for the Promised Land*. He has written biographies of Martin Luther (1974) and Thomas More (1984), and is working on another novel.

A NOTE ON THE TYPE

The text of this book was set on the Editwriter 7500 in a typeface called Elante, a version of Electra. Electra is a Linotype face designed by W. A. Dwiggins (1880–1956). It cannot be classified as either modern or old-style. Electra is not based on any historical model, nor does it echo a particular period or style. It avoids the extreme contrast between thick and thin elements that marks most modern faces and attempts to give a feeling of fluidity, power, and speed.

Printed and bound by R.R. Donnelly & Sons Company, Harrisonburg, Virginia.